OUR HISTORY, THEIR HISTORY

OUR HISTORY, THEIR HISTORY

The Contrasting Historical Narratives of East and West

G.S. CHEEMA

MANOHAR
2025

First published 2011
Reprinted 2019, 2020, 2021, 2023, 2024, 2025

ISBN 978-81-7304-920-0

Published by
Ajay Kumar Jain *for*
Manohar Publishers & Distributors
4753/23 Ansari Road, Daryaganj
New Delhi 110 002

Printed at
Replika Press Pvt. Ltd.

Contents

Introduction

Human nature is the same everywhere and in a given situation, people will behave in a similar manner wherever they may be. For instance, most people in positions of power tend to become overbearing and arbitrary and exploit their position to acquire riches. Yet there are striking differences in the way states have evolved in India and Europe. If one was to take a more global view one would notice that most of our observations regarding India would also be applicable to much of Asia, particularly Islamic West Asia and Central Asia. In Europe there is the traditional divide between East and West, and Eastern Europe is, in many ways, a transition between Asia and Western Europe. That is not surprising since much of East Europe, for many centuries, had been ruled by people from the East, known variously as Turks, Mongols or Tartars—a fact which is often forgotten, obsessed as many of us still are with the imperialism of the last two centuries. Since the latter part of the eighteenth century the imperialists were almost invariably 'Western' but this has not always been the case.

Politically and culturally, the term Western Europe would also include Canada and the United States, and the latter has been the undisputed leader of Western Christendom (the term given by Toynbee to the civilization of the West) for the past sixty years—and arguably since the beginning of the twentieth century. Australia and New Zealand, which were also colonized by the British and share the Anglo-Saxon ethos, can be described as lonely outposts of Western civilization. Until recently Latin America was dominated by right-wing dictators. With a history of unstable governments and frequent military coups the region seemed an exception to the general rule, but the Castilian temperament has always been quite different from the Gallic, Anglo-Saxon, German or Italian. There is little regard for human rights and a wealthy oligarchy comprising big landowners and mining interests has dominated most Latin American countries for most of their history. But then Spain and Portugal, which were the former colonizers of Latin America, have never been able to develop strong representative institutions at home either.

The Castilian temperament, in particular, was averse to democracy. Even the poorest *hidalgo* preferred the glamour of the sword to the labour of the plough, and the thousands of tons of gold and silver yielded by the mines of Mexico and Peru only served to inflate prices in Spain and Europe; they contributed little to the Iberian economies. But then Iberia too has been ruled by Arabs and Moors for more than 700 years of its history—longer than the Turkish rule in the Balkans. After the decline of the Moorish kingdoms which began in the twelfth century, Spanish society resembled that of India insofar as it was divided into different castes with the Christians assuming the character of the ruling kshatriya caste, with trade, agriculture and the artisanal crafts left to the defeated Jews and Arabs. The expulsion of the latter two (including those Jews and Moors who had adopted Christianity) in the sixteenth and seventeenth centuries led to disastrous economic consequences.[1]

The first thing that strikes the casual reader is the relative fragility of Indian and Asiatic states. The political structures of the European kingdoms were incomparably stronger. Europe had relatively small kingdoms, but they were apparently eternal. In India great empires rose and fell with surprising rapidity; the smaller kingdoms which arose out of the wreckage had no permanence. In most cases they were accidental creations and disappeared after a few decades. Europe too has had its imperial obsession but no Holy Roman Emperor or Napoleon was ever able to destroy any of the ancient kingdoms of Europe, all of which were founded between the ninth and the tenth centuries.

What is so special about Western Europe that Asia, and particularly India, missed? Why is the history of India so different from that of Western Europe? It isn't that Europeans were better or superior to us. European history is as violent, and probably much more sanguinary than that of India. Weapons of mass destruction were after all developed by Europeans, and Indians are a much more tolerant people than the Europeans. There has never been systematic religious persecution in India; even Islamic West Asia has been much more tolerant than Christian Europe. The poor peasantry of Western Europe was no better off than the Indian peasant. In fact, even today, landlordism flourishes in the West. There are still people owning thousands of acres as individuals, and they don't feel the need to be apologetic about it.

This study is an attempt to identify the factors which are responsible for the different courses our histories have taken. What makes Indian history so particularly different from the European? Why are we the way we are and they what they are?

NOTE

1. Americo Castro, *The Spaniards: An Introduction to Their History*, Berkeley & Los Angeles: University of California Press, 1971, pp. 81-5, 151, 236-52, 319-20.

CHAPTER 1

The Puzzle

I always used to wonder, even as a child, why our country's history was so different from that of the West. In those days history was a full-fledged subject in the school curriculum and not just a section of 'Social Studies'. We studied Indian History *and* British History, which later broadened into European or World History (there being little difference between the two, at least as far as we were concerned). In the 1950s our education was, quite understandably, Euro-centric, and we still studied Shakespeare in school. It was but natural. The Second World War had just been fought, and Japan, the one Asian power that had dared to challenge the old world order, had been vanquished. Britain had indeed granted independence to India, her former colony, but the composition of the Security Council of the new-born United Nations left no one in any doubt as to who controlled the levers of power in the post-War world. China had been admitted to that body by virtue of being on the winning side but its civil war had just concluded, and with Mao about to launch his revolution it was clear that it would be a long time before China would count for anything in the counsels of the world.

It was therefore understandable that our generation—like that of our parents before us—was much more conscious of history than those that would come thereafter. The freedom struggle and the two world wars, not to mention the ongoing Cold War, used to be the subject of casual table conversations. Some people's parents or uncles might even have fought in the war, for notwithstanding the freedom movement, several million Indians had participated in the two world wars and sacrificed their life for a King-Emperor they had never even seen. There was even a monumental arch erected in New Delhi to commemorate the dead of the First World War and the Third Afghan War. Everyone had heard of someone or the other who had fought in North Africa or Italy, or had been taken prisoner by the Japanese in Burma or Singapore. Even women had enlisted in the Women's Auxilliary Army Corps for clerical jobs. Some had indeed gone over to the other side and joined the Indian National Army or the Indian Legion which were raised by Subhas Chandra Bose in Japanese-occupied Malaya and Germany. Their numbers were not very impressive considering the numbers the Japanese held as POWs but the very fact that a few thousand did volunteer was an indication that the King-Emperor could no longer take the loyalty of his Indian subjects for granted.

All this is just to stress that our generation was acutely conscious of past history and the events that were still shaping the world. We were therefore constantly comparing the history of our country with that of Britain and Europe. We were aware that our country had had a glorious past, but somehow the historical narrative suffered in comparison with that of Europe. For one it was tedious and boring. Maybe the textbooks which we read were not well written, certainly the illustrations were unexciting, but there was also something qualitatively different between the two narratives. This work is an attempt to identify these points of difference, and to understand how they came about. It ultimately boils down to discovering what sets us apart from the English and other Westerners, beyond the obvious superficialities of race and colour.

This will involve a comparative study of the civilization of the 'West' and that of India, with occasional references to other Asian civilizations like those of Iran, Turkey and China. The term West, as used here, is interchangeable with Toynbee's Western Christendom and includes the USA, and wherever the word Europe, or Western Europe, is used, it is within that context. The march of events in the past two decades has shown that the cultural divide between Western and Eastern Europe, that is, between Western Christendom and the Eastern Orthodox civilization is real, and even though Belarus,

Ukraine, Romania, Bulgaria, Serbia and Montenegro are undoubtedly European, they belong to the Eastern Orthodox world rather than Western Christendom. Race is not as important as we once thought. The Poles, for instance, are Slavs, as indeed are the Croats, but they are Catholic rather than Orthodox, and that explains partly why the former could never be reconciled to the Russians or the latter to the Serbs.

Of course, there are other factors too. Most of the East European countries were former members of the Warsaw Pact, and used to be subordinate satellites of the erstwhile Soviet Union during the Cold War, a situation which they resented. Unfortunately, this relationship had no compensatory economic advantage either. Although most were economically better off than the USSR, and enjoyed higher per capita incomes, they were far worse off than their neighbours on the western side of the Iron Curtain. So once the border fence was torn down and the USSR itself folded up, these states clamoured for admission to the European Union and NATO. Some of them have indeed already been admitted but only time will show whether these crossings of the cultural fault-line will last.

Similarly, Turkey's historic enmity with Russia, and the American eagerness to ring the USSR with military bases happily coincided, but there is no such coincidence in Turkey's desire to join the EU and the latter's desire to expand. As far as the EU is concerned the Turks are Muslims, *ergo*, they can never be Europeans. They had trouble enough reconciling themselves with an independent, largely Muslim Bosnia, and Albania—the other largely Muslim state—was a pariah, and remains a pariah. In Italy and Greece the Albanians have the same kind of reputation as the Chechens have in Russia. It was far easier for the Europeans to overlook Croatia's Fascist past as a collaborationist puppet state during the Second World War. There is something weird about Europe's inability to accept pluralist multi-religious states—of which I will have more to say later—but for the present, being European means being Christian, and that's that. It is only recently, in the last fifty years, that even Britain has permitted the construction of mosques and temples of Asian religions. But we shall come to that later.

'A COUNTRY OF BLOODSHED AND MISERY'

It was customary in the old days to compare the stability of European states with India's apparently chronic instability. European states were well-run and orderly, while large parts of India, somewhere or the other, seemed to be in a state of perpetual disorder with insurgency and armed rebels keeping the countryside, and sometimes cities as well, in a state of turmoil. My late father was fond of recalling the words of one of his professors in pre-Partition Lahore in this connection. The gentleman (who of course was British) liked to begin his lecture with the rhetorical question–and he would write it on the blackboard–'What was India before the British?' After a brief but pregnant pause, as if to give time for the question to sink into the brutish minds of the young 'natives' who would be sitting in respectful silence on the benches before him, he would himself supply the appropriate response. He would write it down too. It ran thus: 'A country of bloodshed and misery.' It would remain there throughout the lecture, a provocative template, impressing the students with its rather obvious message: 'You will be nothing without us. You were nothing before we came. We are good for you!'

This was in the early 1930s when independence was only a distant and rather improbable dream. But the question with its provocative rejoinder and vaguely insulting sub-text had had its effect; my father could still recall it after the passage of nearly half a century. I, of course, listening to him in the 1960s was not so impressed. After all, the Khalji sultans and Mughal *padishahs* had also conquered and unified pretty much the whole of India, and the latter certainly had reigned longer than the British. Further, India was a subcontinent and its population much greater than that of Europe. Trying to compare it with small, compact 'nation states' like Britain and France was like comparing chalk with cheese. Arnold

Toynbee had completed his monumental work *A Study of History* by then, but its ripples had not yet touched the schoolrooms of India that is Bharat, and we were still being taught the same old stuff. England, we were told, had been 'one' from the time of King Alfred the Great, which was more than a thousand years ago, and the French had found their totems in Clovis and Charlemagne. The Germans of course were a little different in this respect—they would not achieve unity until 1870—but then those Germans, for all their militarism, our Anglo-Indian teachers would declare, were incompetent. You know how badly they messed up the two world wars!

THE PERMANENCE OF EUROPEAN STATE BOUNDARIES

Now even though Europe—even today—has only achieved a very imperfect unity, the one truly remarkable thing about it is the permanence of its internal boundaries. In spite of its history of sanguinary conflicts, the basic political units appear to be indestructible. State boundaries may have shifted a little here and there (in the case of France and Germany by about 200 km) but nearly all the European states that we know today have been in existence for a very long time, some for as much as a thousand years. The three kingdoms of the British Isles, the Scandinavian states, France, Germany, Poland, Lithuania, Austria and Italy—they have all been around since the thirteenth century. The Scandinavian states have united at various times in different combinations—Finland was at one time part of Russia as well—but neither of them has ever lost its individual identity. The union between England, Scotland and Ireland has taken various forms. Ireland (save for Ulster) is independent today, and the Scottish parliament, abolished since the Act of Union of 1707, has recently been revived.

Germany and Italy are indeed special cases, but there has been a nominal kingdom of Germany since the time of Henry the Fowler (AD 919-36), and there were kings of Italy long before Victor Emmanuel, starting with Theodoric the Goth (AD 493-526). Spain emerged as a united country towards the end of the fifteenth century with the marriage of King Ferdinand of Aragon with Queen Isabella of Castile. At first the union of the two kingdoms was a personal one, but eventually it was transformed into a perpetual union. The Swiss Confederation had its beginnings towards the end of the thirteenth century.

The name of the Netherlands, or the Low Countries, is applied to what were originally a clutch of counties, duchies, bishoprics and lordships, the most famous of which were Flanders, Hainault, Brabant, Liege, Holland and Zeeland. They were originally part of the German kingdom and the Holy Roman Empire, and were brought together (barring the bishoprics) for the first time by the Duke of Burgundy, scion of a cadet line of the Valois kings of France. But after the last duke, Charles the Bold, was killed fighting the Swiss in 1477, his daughter (and heir), Mary, married Archduke Maximilian, King of the Romans and future Emperor, and her possessions (barring the territories–like the duchy of Burgundy–which were held as fiefs of the French Crown) passed to the Habsburgs. Mary's son Philip the Fair, in turn married Joanna, the heiress of Aragon and Castile, and in the family partition that followed in the later years of the reign of Emperor Charles V, the Netherlands went to the Spanish branch of the Habsburgs.

During the Reformation, Calvinism gained ground in the northern provinces (mainly Holland and Zeeland) which were already chafing under the heavy taxation necessitated by the wars of Charles V. They at length revolted to establish the Republic of the United Provinces. Eighty years of intermittent war followed but ultimately the independence of the United Provinces was recognized by the Empire in the general peace of Westphalia (1648). The southern provinces, predominantly Catholic, remained with the Habsburgs, but after many vicissitudes emerged finally as the kingdom of Belgium in 1831, which is thus the youngest of the major European states. But even if the Kingdom of the Belgians is young, its components, Flanders, Hainault, Liege and Brabant go back to the dawn of the Middle Ages. With minor changes, Belgium's boundaries are those of the Spanish Netherlands.

What I consider truly remarkable is that all the major states that were in existence in the fifteenth and sixteenth centuries are still around today. A few (*very* few) may have been added since then (like the aforesaid Belgium), but none whatever have been destroyed conclusively. Of course, this does not apply to the principalities below the regal rank, of which there were several hundred at the start of the seventeenth century in Germany. Although by the terms of the Peace of Westphalia they were recognized as sovereign (their numbers were considerably reduced by the time the war came to an end) they were technically part of the medieval kingdom of Germany, and indistinguishable from other feudal fiefs. Some of them like Brandenburg-Prussia, Saxony and Bavaria were even given the rank of kingdoms, but they were never truly independent since they remained part of the Empire and the subsequent Confederation, which replaced it in 1815. Some of them survive today as states of the Federal Republic.

As mentioned earlier, once upon a time there used to be a medieval kingdom of Italy also, and the medieval emperors used to be crowned kings of Italy as well, but this kingdom never embraced the whole of Italy and Emperor Charles V was the last to be actually crowned as such in Pavia. The title, however, continued to be used till 1648. Naples and Sicily, however, were also kingdoms and therefore never, even notionally, part of the Italian kingdom. After the Congress of Vienna (1815) Lombardy and Venezia came under direct Austrian rule, while the rest of Italy came under the sway of foreign princes, usually Habsburgs or Bourbons. The Pope was also a territorial prince (though by no means popular) and the Papal States straddled the Appenines in Central Italy. So when the House of Savoy took up the cause of Italian unification the local dynasts were swept away like chaff, and their subjects showed no regrets at their passing. They had tasted liberty during the Napoleonic period under the mild rule of Prince Eugene, viceroy of the kingdom of North Italy (whose king was Napoleon himself), and in the south under King Joachim Murat of Naples. The reinstatement of the *ancien regime* under the likes of King Ferdinand of the

Two Sicilies, or Habsburg archdukes in Tuscany or Modena was hardly likely to be popular. The difficult part was driving the Austrians out of Lombardy and Venezia, and here Victor Emmanuel had the military support of Napoleon III.

Victor Emmanuel, the first king of a united Italy was, however, no Napoleonic upstart. His family, the House of Savoy, was one of the oldest in Europe and could be traced as far back as the year 1000 to one Humbert 'Whitehands', the first Count of Savoy. In 1946, when the last king, Victor Emmanuel III, fatally compromised by his close association with Fascism, was forced to abdicate, it was, arguably, the oldest ruling house in the world.

There is nothing comparable in India. There were, indeed, a number of states—mainly that clutch of erstwhile kingdoms or *rajwaras* that make up Rajasthan—that can claim *nearly* (but not quite) comparable antiquity, but except for a relatively brief period they are only a sideshow of Indian history. Their early history is so foggy; often all we have is a string of names. There are no accounts of what they did, and whom they married, the names of their consorts and of the younger sons have long been forgotten. Only the *bhats* their traditional minstrels, preserved fragments of their annals which were passed down orally from father to son, each generation probably adding its own embellishments.

The modern states of the Indian Union are entirely artificial constructs. In Mughal days modern Uttar Pradesh (UP) was split into the *subas* of Awadh, Agra and Allahabad. Much of western UP was included in the *suba* of Delhi. The Punjab comprised two *subas*, Lahore and Multan, while Sirhind or the Cis-Sutlej territory was included in Delhi. The present states are linguistic states; in most cases they are artificial constructs with no history behind them. They certainly cannot be compared to Flanders, Burgundy, Bavaria or Hesse.

THE STABILITY OF SOCIETY

Like the state system, European society seems to have a similar permanence, a continuity going back to medieval times which no wars or revolutions have been able to seriously disrupt. The kingdom of Poland may have gone under 200 years ago, but a Princess Radziwill still featured on the society pages of the print media not so very long ago. No doubt this 'princess' was only an American adventuress,[1] but there was an actual Prince Radziwill from whom she derived her courtesy title. A few years back, in 2002, Princess Gloria von Thurn und Taxi auctioned off the contents of her deceased husband's ancestral *schloss* in Regensberg. It was the highlight of the auctions that year. More sales would follow in the years to come–art, antiques, companies, even the family bank. In this case the widow was *not* American. She was German, of impoverished noble stock,[2] who had lived much of her earlier life in Africa, and even worked as a waitress before her marriage. The interesting thing is that Germany and Austria became republics as long ago as 1918 and all titles have been abolished, but this does not seem to have made the slightest difference. They are still flaunted in society and nobody finds them the least bit ridiculous. Barons, counts, grafs, margraves, dukes, princes and their female counterparts still haunt the drawing rooms of Europe's upper crust. A wing of the magnificent Palais Schwarzenberg, abutting the Place Schwarzenberg (where an equestrian statue of a Schwarzenberg is the dominating landmark) in Vienna is still a family residence (the rest of it is a luxury hotel). The present chief, His Serene Highness Prince Karl Johannes Nepomuk, is a citizen of Switzerland and the Czech Republic. Curiously enough, he has been active in Czech politics and was appointed foreign minister in 2007, although he left Czechoslovakia in 1948 (when the Communists seized power), and had been living thereafter in Austria. However, after the collapse of Communism in the 1990s he returned to Czechoslovakia and was able to recover some of the family property, including the ancestral castle of Orlik. About a dozen castles and tens of thousands of hectares of land (mostly forest) have been returned to former aristocrats by way of restitution over the past fifteen years. One would have thought that the Czechs would regard all former German noblemen with the same hatred which the Irish Catholics reserved for the Ascendancy families who traced their roots to England,[3] but nostalgia for the old days, and the anti-Communist reaction have enabled many of the old Austrian aristocrats to stage a comeback.

In France a gentleman named Henry calls himself the Count of Paris and claims to be the rightful heir to the throne of France.

The Prince of Liechtenstein is also fighting for the restitution of old estates in Slovakia in the International Court of Justice. The lost family holdings in Moravia and Slovakia totalling about 600 sq km, far exceed the area of their sovereign principality—which is only 142 sq km.

On the other hand, one has never heard of a Khalji or Tughluq pretender to the throne of India. Nor do we have any Mughal claimants to the Red Fort of Delhi. There are indeed descendants of the Mughal emperors still living (even in Delhi) but barring a few, their condition is so pathetic that they would prefer to remain in obscurity. Nor have I heard of any family—apart from the Nizam of Hyderabad and his kinsmen—that claims descent from any of the great noblemen or *umara* of the old Mughal empire. Doubtless they must exist, but they too prefer a discreet obscurity. The descendants of Wajid Ali Shah and Tipu Sultan also reside in Kolkata but nobody knows them outside a very narrow circle of faded gentry.

Even our *haute bourgeoisie* is modern. Barring a few, scarcely any of the great Marwari, Chettiar or Parsi families of today were notable in the mid-nineteenth century. I am told that the descendants of the once famous 'Juggut Seth' of Bengal still inhabit a crumbling palace in North Kolkata but they certainly don't feature in the society columns of the print media. We just do not have the Indian equivalents of families like the Rothschilds of Europe. Coutts Bank of London goes back to the closing years of the seventeenth century. Lloyd's of London also dates back to the same period.

INDIAN AND EUROPEAN WARS

Indian wars are also quite different from European wars. Most European conflicts had a definite cause. Princes did not just set out to conquer. They usually had a claim of some kind to some territory or a throne which may have fallen vacant. But in medieval Indian history one usually searches in vain for plausible reasons. Whenever reasons are offered they are usually improbable and scarcely credible. For instance, we are assured, the reason for the umpteen invasions of Sultan Mahmud of Ghazni was a vow, made on the occasion of receiving the letters patent and *khillats* of his investiture as Yamin ul-Daulah from the Caliph of Baghdad, to devote the rest of his life to waging a perpetual *jihad* against the *kafirs* of Hind. Then we have stories of sultans who were infatuated with queens they had never seen. Sometimes they received letters from disenchanted queens, inviting them to attack and take over their husbands' kingdoms. Sometimes it all sounds as improbable as a tale from the *Dastaan-i-Amir Hamza.*

Muhammad Ghori and the sultans or *padishahs* who followed him apparently waged war merely for the sake of conquest, to recover provinces that had broken away and to punish governors who had, for some reason, decided to revolt. No principles of international law seemed to apply in India. It was truly, quite literally *dar ul-harb*, or the land of war. Even when the great Akbar decided to embark on the conquest of the Deccan, he first sent his minister Fyzee on an embassy to the Deccan sultans to persuade them to acknowledge him as their overlord. When the latter, quite understandably, declined, Akbar set his armies in motion and the war began.

At the same time, one observes, the triumphs of these great conquerors appear to be strangely superficial. Every fort, every province, is required to be conquered again and again. One is reminded of Ravana or the hydra-headed monster which immediately sprouts a fresh head as the first is cut-off. Ranthambhor, situated a mere 350 km from Delhi, was besieged at least eight times during the first hundred years of the sultanate. Sultan after sultan had to send punitive expeditions for the pacification of Mewat, situated a mere stone's throw from the imperial capital. Bengal revolted at least six times in the first two hundred years of Turkish rule and was independent for long stretches of its history. Seven dynasties of independent rulers reigned in Bengal during this period!

European wars and conquests, on the other hand, were of an entirely different character. Once the cycle of wars sparked off by Fredrick II's seizure of Silesia ended with the Peace of Paris in 1763. Silesia remained Prussian, and would probably have remained so, but for the Second World War which radically changed the Polish-German frontier. France acquired Alsace in 1648, and Lorraine in 1737, and but for a break of 49 years (from 1870 to 1919) both provinces remain French to this day.

It has rarely happened like that in Indian history. Nothing was permanent in the Indian world. It is almost as if the European states were built with bricks and mortar, while Indian kingdoms were a house of cards.

In spite of its fearful wars the West presented a picture of stability and continuity. The same families continued to rule without interruption for hundreds of years, while the most exclusive circles of the social upper crust remained the preserve of ancient landed families bearing aristocratic titles—even though the state might have become a republic. No wars or revolutions have been able to shake their social pre-eminence.

India, on the other hand, is like a kaleidoscope; its patterns fluid, ever changing, and in constant flux. No doubt there are some constants here as well, like the caste system, but they are very different from the familiar salients of European history. Even the Indian caste system has probably changed much more than the class divisions of Western society. On closer examination, the old cliché of the 'unchanging and timeless East' is completely fallacious; it may perhaps be more accurate to speak of the unchanging West.

NOTES

1. Caroline Lee Bouvier was the younger sister of Jacqueline Kennedy. She married Stanislas Albrecht Radziwill in 1959. It was her second marriage (for Stanislas it was the third). She divorced her 'prince' in 1974 and went on to marry two other men thereafter. Stanislas was the son of a Polish nobleman who had served as

a minister in Pilsudski's government, and later suffered imprisonment under Stalin. The son (Stanislas) became a British citizen. The Radziwills had been wealthy landed magnates of Lithuanian origin but all their property was confiscated when the Communists took over Poland.

2. Born Countess Maria Gloria von Schonburg-Glauchau, she was dubbed the 'Punk Princess' and 'Princess TNT' by the media because of her Bohemian lifestyle. Her husband, thirty years her senior, and the scion of an ancient fourteenth-century noble family, was seriously rich, still owning large estates and wide-ranging banking and business interests. His lifestyle too was Bohemian and he left behind debts to the extent of $350,000,000.

4. Just as most Ascendency families traced their origins to the 'plantations' of Tudor times, the Protectorate of Cromwell or the Battle of the Boyne (1689), most of the great German magnates of Bohemia and Moravia, like the Schwarzenbergs, date their estates back to the Battle of the White Mountain in 1620, at the start of the Thirty Years War.

CHAPTER 2

European Kingdoms–Indian Empires

We like to believe that India is an ancient civilization while Western or European civilization is young and relatively unsophisticated. This assumption is only partly correct. While it is correct that in the first-century Germany and the country eastward was indeed largely forest, inhabited by relatively primitive tribes, it must be remembered that large tracts of India were also under forest (at least until recently) and the inhabitants of those tracts were (and are) regarded as tribals and thought to be so unsophisticated that their rights had to be protected by special legislation. Even today this special legislation is considered indispensable. Whether it has succeeded or not is open to question, but we have no comparable tribes anywhere in Europe. The Sami or Laplanders of the far north in Scandinavia are possibly the only exception, but even they cannot be compared to our Bhils, Gonds or Santhals.

The Mediterranean basin was the real cradle of Western civilization, and some sites are as old as any in India. The Mycenaean period is dated between 1600 and 1100 BC, and the cyclopean ruins of its acropolis with its Lion Gate are certainly more impressive than Mohenjo-Daro. The former is built in stone while the latter is constructed with burnt bricks. The Minoan civilization of Crete is even older, going back to 2400 BC. That would make it nearly as old as the Indus Valley Civilization, the oldest layers of which go back to 3000 BC and the latest are dated around 1500 BC. Of course, the Egyptian and Mesopotamian civilizations are even older, with the former going back to 4000 BC.

There is, however, one very important difference which distinguishes the Indus Valley Civilization from the others—we know practically nothing about it. Of course, the ruins are there before our eyes, the reports on the excavations have been published, the potsherds, sealings, bronzes and terracotta toys and statuettes have all been drawn, photographed, classified and catalogued. But that is all. The curious symbols on the seals have not yet been definitively deciphered, and we really have no idea as to who were the people who built those cities, and what happened to them. There are no traditions or legends associated with the mounds under which these cities lay buried. On the other hand, Mycenae is associated with Homer's *Iliad.* It is supposed to have been the seat of King Menelaus. Likewise the Minoan ruins at Knossos are associated with the legends of King Minos and the monstrous bull called the Minotaur. But there are no comparable legends associated with the remains of the ancient cities of the Indus basin. Mohenjo-Daro simply means 'the mound of the dead'. And the dead here tell no tales. Nobody has ever tried to connect them with the *Ramayana* or the *Mahabharata.*

In contrast, the amount of information we have on Egypt is almost embarrassing. In the 'dynastic period' which starts from *c.* 3100 BC we have the names of approximately 240 kings belonging to 31 dynasties. The list is not exhaustive; for instance, the Fourteenth Dynasty (*c.* 1720-1665 BC) is supposed to have 'perhaps as many as 76 kings', but the name of only one is known. Similarly the Sixteenth Dynasty is said to have 'about seventeen kings' but we have the names of only seven. The Thirteenth Dynasty (*c.* 1786-1668 BC) is supposed to have 'at least sixty-five kings' but we have the names of about forty.[1]

Similarly, the earliest dynasty of ancient Mesopotamia is the First Dynasty of Ur (*c.* 2563-2387 BC). The number of known kings of Ur, Assyria, Babylon and the Hittites runs into nearly three hundred. All the scripts of Egypt—hieroglyphic, hieratic and demotic—have been deciphered and all the epigraphs and papyri read. Mesopotamian cuneiform holds no mysteries; whole archives of clay tablets have been discovered and scholars have studied them.

In comparison, so poor is the knowledge of ancient Indian history that John E. Morby, the compiler of the *Wordsworth Handbook of Kings and Queens* threw up his hands in despair and listed only two pre-Islamic dynasties, the Mauryan (321-180 BC) and the Gupta (AD 275-550) 'because of a lack of reliable data'. After including the Islamic dynasties we have 101 names. China's history is far better known, Morby has listed 232 rulers from 221 BC to AD 1912. India is truly unique among the great nations and civilizations of the world, embarrassingly unique, one may say.

But as Toynbee has pointed out, the present Western civilization does not begin with ancient Greece or Rome. It is undoubtedly affiliated to the preceding Romano-Hellenic civilization, but it was born in the barbarian invasions that overwhelmed the enfeebled Roman Empire of the West towards the end of the fifth century AD. Likewise the present Indian civilization (Toynbee calls it the Hindu Civilization to distinguish it from the preceding, dominantly Buddhist, 'Indic Civilization') was born in the barbarian invasions that followed the death of Harsha in AD 640.

In that sense both civilizations are of approximately the same age. Of course, civilizations develop over time and it is impossible to pinpoint the exact date of birth. New currents enter the stream, and the flavour changes. Homer and Virgil are gradually forgotten and the *Chanson de Roland* and the *Nibelungen Lied* and the *Volsunga Saga* take over. In India Mahayana Buddhism gives way to the Vedanta of Shankaracharya, the *Ramayana* and the *Mahabharata*. Some memories and traditions of the preceding civilizations will survive, or be rediscovered with time, but there is a break somewhere. Somewhere along the line a new world has been born, with a new way of looking at things.

We must also bear in mind that 'barbarian' is not the same as 'savage'. The Germans of Tacitus are not an unattractive people. They may 'never live in cities' and wear only a 'cloak fastened with a brooch or a thorn', often without undergarments, but their marriage code was strict and their women virtuous, and they lived 'uncorrupted by the temptations of public shows or the excitements of banquets'.[2] They practised agriculture and were acquainted with the use of iron.

Come to think of it, the lives of most rural Indians were not very different as late as fifty or sixty years ago. The differences were minor; the Indians, for instance, wore garments of handspun cotton instead of wool or animal skin. Etymologically, the word barbarian merely meant a foreigner, one who was neither Greek nor Roman. And of course, throughout history, everywhere, people have always been condescending, if not downright hostile to foreigners.

Tacitus wrote his *Germania* towards the end of the first century AD. By the fifth century when the Western Empire was expiring the world had changed immensely. By this time the Roman armies were composed mainly of barbarians. Often the generals, the consuls and *magisters militum* were 'barbarians' of German stock. In fact, the last emperor of the West, Romulus Augustulus[3] was scarcely Roman. Most authorities agree that he was not quite a barbarian, and that his father was a Roman provincial, a native of Pannonia, which is today's Slovenia. Probably a hundred years earlier the Pannonians would have been regarded as barbarians. At the time that district had been ceded to Attila the Hun, and Romulus's father, Orestes, had actually held a position on the staff of that undoubted barbarian![4] The Emperor Maximinus, known as 'the Thracian' who reigned 200 years earlier (235-8) has also been described as a barbarian, being the son of a Gothic father and Alanic mother.

The history of India during this period is unfortunately not very well recorded. But about the same time that Attila was ravaging the provinces of the Western Empire, another branch of the Huns, commanded by Toramana, was ravaging the north-western provinces of the declining Gupta Empire. The last of the Guptas was Vishnugupta and after his death in AD 550 north India split into a number of petty kingdoms. In the next century there was an apparent rally when Harshavardhana of Thanesar conquered a number of petty states and established his capital at Kanauj in the year 606. Harsha exchanged embassies with the T'ang emperor of China, and during his reign the celebrated traveller Hsuan Tsang visited India on a pilgrimage to the various places associated with the Buddha. Thanks to this visitor we have a good description of northern India around this time. Harsha died in 647 without leaving any heirs, so his state disintegrated again.

What happened thereafter is uncertain. The history of the next three centuries, particularly in north India, is obscure. While in south India and the western Deccan we have strong dynastic kingdoms, viz., those of the Chalukyas, Rashtrakutas, Pallavas and Pandyas, in the north the picture is confused. The Pratiharas were the only significant state with imperial pretensions. Their origins lay in the Marwar region of Rajasthan in the sixth century, and by the eighth century their rule extended up to Malwa and Gujarat, and by the end of the ninth century they had taken Kanauj and Magadha. But within a hundred years they had again shrunk to a small kingdom around Kanauj.

The Rathors were originally their feudatories but by the eleventh century they had supplanted the Pratiharas. They were still there in Kanauj when Shihab ul-Din Muhammad bin Sam, more commonly known as Muhammad Ghori, invaded India in 1175. But soon after the second battle of Tarain in 1206 in which Prithvi Raj Chauhan was defeated and Delhi fell to the Turks, the days of the Rathors too were numbered. The Turkish cavalry spread eastward along the Gangetic plain and the Rathors of Kanauj were soon dispersed, their kingdom destroyed.

These centuries have been described as the Dark Ages of European history. But when we compare them to the corresponding period in Indian history they appear to be positively bathed in light. Unlike India the Hellenic world had a rich tradition of historiography. The republic and the first three centuries of the Roman Empire have been well recorded by Livy, Plutarch, Tacitus, Suetonius, and Ammanus Marcellinus. Even the mighty Julius Caesar took time off to write an account of the Gallic wars. And even in these supposedly Dark Ages we have the history of Jordanes, and the accounts of Priscus of Panium and Procopius. In India, on the other hand, we have only lists of rulers; the details have to be fleshed out with the aid of archaeology, by collating numismatic evidence with scattered epigraphs, the accounts of foreign pilgrims (in this case Chinese), copper plate title-deeds, and chance references in literary compositions.

It is very rare to come across a work like Banabhatt's *Harsha-charita.* Thus while we have a fair account of the European campaign of Attila, we have no written accounts of the corresponding campaigns of Toramana and Mihirakula. While we have comprehensive accounts of the early barbarian kingdoms of the Vandals, Ostrogoths and Visigoths, and know exactly how the Frankish kingdom came up, and how the Franks and Lombards fought each other in Italy, we have very little knowledge of how the Pratiharas and the Rajput kingdoms that followed them arose, and what exactly happened after the death of Harsha. Here we are truly groping in the dark, making supposedly 'intelligent' guesses from scraps of archaeological evidence.

What we do know, however, is that by the time of the Turkish invasions north India was dominated by a number of Rajput states. These Rajputs identified with the ancient kshatriyas or the warrior caste, but this is probably a later rationalization. The general view is that they are in fact a new people of mixed race, viz., the Huns intermixed with earlier foreigners like the Indo-Scythians, Indo-Parthians, Kushans, and others. The Gurjars and Jats are also supposed to have arisen about the same time. Probably all these so-called 'royal tribes' came from the same melting pot, and the different names signify only a class distinction, for nearly all Jat clans claim Rajput origins. The Rajput population is, compared to the others, thinly spread, and they are never found in such concentrations as the Jats and Gurjars in their respective areas. Whatever the truth, they are comparable to the barbarian kingdoms of the West in that they are of foreign stock (i.e. non-Roman in the European context), and have no affiliations with the preceding states in that geographical area.

They also share another characteristic. They are tribal states rather than simple territorial agglomerations. In Europe we have a Visigothic kingdom in Spain and Southern France, the Ostrogothic kingdom of Theodoric in Italy, a Frankish kingdom in northern France and Germany, and a Vandal kingdom in North Africa. Likewise, in India we have a Chauhan kingdom centred in Ajmer, a

Rathor kingdom based at Kanauj and later Banaras (still later they would move to Marwar), a Sisodiya or Gehlot kingdom in Mewar, and a Tomar kingdom at Delhi.

There is, however, a difference between the tribal kingdoms or chieftaincies of Europe and India. In Europe the barbarians appear to have swamped the original Roman citizens. The character of the population changed. After a couple of centuries everyone who was somebody was identifying himself with the Goths or the Franks— or any other German tribe. It has been suggested that the Roman population was in decline. Some ascribe it to lead poisoning arising from the use of lead plumbing, others to plague and other virulent pestilences. The old Mediterranean people had decayed and lost the will or ability to procreate; their fertility too was in decline while the younger, more vigorous barbarians were much more fecund.

The arguments may be fallacious. The Indian caste system may have something to do with the apparent disparity in numbers. In Europe there were no castes; people were either free or slave. The free men were divided into patricians and plebians, and while anyone could be raised to the rank of a patrician, the term had lost all meaning by the third century, and was reduced to a mere honorific, routinely awarded to generals and governors. It never became a caste with all the attendant rules and restrictions with respect to marriage and social intercourse so familiar to us Indians. India, however, already had a complex caste system, but the ruling or dominant elements among the new barbarian bands had been readily accommodated in the existing caste hierarchy by the brahmins as honorary kshatriyas and given the distinctive appellations of Rajput, Thakur or Rana. Once placed in a privileged position it was in their interest to keep the numbers of the elite limited, so the old tribal democracy gave way to the stratification of a caste-ridden society. This process never ceased; Rajputization was still going on in the twentieth century in the tribal areas of Orissa, Chhota Nagpur and Bastar.[5]

The net result was that the European tribal states were stronger, while the Indian states were far more fragile. So when new invaders came, the Frankish and other Germanic kingdoms proved much more resilient as compared to their Indian counterparts. They were able to survive the onslaughts of Scandinavian Vikings, and the Moors from Spain, while the Rajput states of the Indo-Gangetic plain were swept away like a puff of powder. It was only in the relatively inhospitable regions of Rajasthan and Central India that they were able to survive.

A tribal state by its very nature is limited in its aspirations. Once all the members of the tribe inhabiting a compact area have been brought under one chief it ceases to grow. The Pratiharas were the only dynasty that established a state of any size, but within 200 years they were in steep decline. Thereafter, no other Rajput kingdom seems to have aspired to dominate the northern plains, leave alone India. Even the great Maharana Sangram Singh of Mewar, who is supposed to have presented the most serious challenge to Babur after Ibrahim Lodi, led only a confederacy of chiefs to battle at Khanwa. His own kingdom was Mewar; whatever influence he enjoyed beyond its borders was entirely due to his own personality, his reputation of being 'the bravest of the brave' and the exalted regard in which the Gehlots and Sisodiyas were held by all other clans.

When the Mughal state declined during the long reign of Muhammad Shah there was no attempt by any combination of Rajput princes to establish their hegemony, even though they were admirably placed to do so. At one time Maharaja Ajit Singh of Marwar held both Gujarat and Rajasthan, and his son Abhai Singh would, in turn, be *subedar* of Gujarat as well. Maharaja Jai Singh II of Amber was thrice *subedar* of Malwa but he practically handed over that vital province to the Marathas. The latter were the scourge of the Deccan and raided far afield, to the east and the north. Though upstarts in comparison with the over-romanticized Rajputs they did have a vision of sorts. On two separate occasions it appeared that they might supplant the effete *padishahs* of the house of Timur, much as Pepin disposed of the Merovingians. But on the first occasion they were checkmated at Panipat by the Afghans led by Ahmad

Shah Durrani. The second opportunity arose when Mahadji Scindia was appointed the emperor's *Vakil-i-Mutlaq*, that is, his keeper and regent, exercising plenipotentiary powers. The revolt of Ghulam Qadir which occurred during his regency had left the emperor blind and helpless, but now the 'Great Maratha' was checkmated by the intrigues of the court of Poona. There would be no subsequent opportunities; his successor Daulat Rao and the later *peshwas* were incompetent; the English advancing from Bengal would very soon overtake them.

The facility with which empires (or Universal States, as Toynbee would call them) rose in India constitutes the most striking contrast between the current civilization of India and that of the West. Muhammad Ghori and his immediate successors, Aibak and Iltutmish, were able to effect the conquest of north India in the short span of three decades. Then followed a pause; the threat of a Mongol invasion was real; the sultanates of Central Asia and the Great Seljuks of Iran collapsed before the *furor Mongolicus*, but soon, within fifty years Ala ul-Din Khalji had set-off on his Deccan adventure. He reigned for only twenty years, but in that short span the south was conquered. The conquest was superficial; Ghiyas ul-Din Tughluq who ascended the throne a mere four years after his death had to virtually reconquer the Deccan. The southern provinces of the empire again disintegrated during the reign of the brilliant but unstable Muhammad; his successor Firoz was left with only the north. But after a gap of one hundred and seventy years, under Akbar the Great, the third *padishah*, the empire would be revived. This Universal State would prove more substantial, but within one hundred and fifty years, it was evident that the Mughal Empire too was falling apart. Then arrived the British. In fifty years—by the year 1803—they were in a commanding position and the *fainéant* emperor was now their ward. But within one hundred and fifty years they too had furled their tents and left.

Within 750 years India witnessed three attempts at building a Universal State. The first—that of the Khaljis and Tughluqs—proved transient and can be called a failure, but the other two achieved substantial results. None were as successful, or as long-lived, as the old Roman Empire, but the facility with which they were achieved presents a striking contrast to Europe. True, a little over 300 years after the deposition of Romulus Augustulus the Empire had been resuscitated in the person of Charlemagne who was crowned by Pope Leo III as the Holy Roman Emperor. But this empire fragmented as a result of family partitions soon after his death. While it lasted it embraced pretty much the whole of Western Christendom with the exception of the British Isles. Scandinavia and Eastern Germany were still outside the Christian-fold while the Iberian peninsula had passed under the control of the Moors and Arabs. In 962 Otto the Great again attempted to restore it, but his empire never extended beyond Germany and Italy. The Germany of those times was much more bloated than that of today, and the Italian south remained outside imperial control. Sicily too had passed under Arab (or 'Saracen') rule.

But even in Germany imperial authority remained weak. Medieval states were organized on feudal lines which were not conducive to the rise of strong, centralized empires. In the twelfth century the Hohenstauffen emperors made a brave attempt to give substance to the empire, but they failed. Imperial and papal interests clashed in Italy, and ultimately it was the papacy that triumphed. Thereafter the empire remained a phantom. The Habsburgs who held the (nominally elective) imperial crown from 1438 onwards, practically without a break, concentrated more on enlarging and consolidating their hereditary family possessions.

It was not until the French Revolution and the accession of Napoleon that a serious attempt was made to convert Europe's contending kingdoms into a United States of Europe under the hegemony of France. Napoleon sent a brusque note which was read out on 1 August 1806 by his emissary in the Imperial Diet. In effect, the note declared, the Emperor (of the French) no longer recognized the German Constitution which had become unworkable and that some of the princes had resolved to form a confederation to protect themselves against future emergencies. Further, the Emperor had agreed to be the *Protector* of this *Confederation of the Rhine.* Five days later the *other* emperor, Francis II (his future father-in-law), 'convinced of the utter impossibility' of fulfilling the duties of his imperial office 'relinquished the Imperial Government' and the 800-year-old Holy Roman Empire came to an end.[6] The alternate arrangements which the emperor of the French had made also collapsed in 1815. The Napoleonic Universal State did not last even ten years.

In the twentieth century instead of France we had Germany. Kaiser Wilhelm II was the latest *enfant terrible.* The world war that he and the Austrian Kaiser had provoked, bled Europe white; four empires lay in ruins at the end of it, while revolution and counter-revolution swept through the ravaged lands of central and eastern Europe. Economic collapse, hyper-inflation, starvation, and the influenza pandemic—which killed more people than the actual fighting—wrought further misery. After a truce of twenty years the struggle for the mastery of Europe was resumed—with even more disastrous results. It was only in the 1960s that an exhausted Europe—now purged of all delusions of world dominion—took the first steps towards a Common Market. Militarily, western Europe was dominated by the United States through NATO, just as the Communist east was dominated by the Soviet Union through the Warsaw Pact.

There were only two world powers in reality after 1945, the United States and the Soviet Union. The United States was in fact the greatest economic power even as early as 1900, and just as Britain had financed the various coalitions against Revolutionary and Napoleonic France, it was the USA that would bankroll the struggle against the Central Powers in the First World War, and against the Axis Powers in the Second. But in 1900 it had not yet realized its strength; the crowned heads of Europe, with their brilliant courts and ancient aristocracies still intimidated the Americans, and American heiresses vied with each other to grab titled husbands—just as younger sons of British peers and impoverished continental aristocrats hoped to restore their family fortunes by hitching up with the daughters of American millionaires.

Thus Indian history—and of the Orient generally—is dominated by the rise and fall of empires, while the history of Western Christendom is the history of regional powers or nation states. These were much smaller than the empires but they were much more stable, and notwithstanding the savagery of European warfare, give the impression of permanence.

A quick survey of the history of the European states would be enlightening. Before we do that, however, I would like to make a few observations on the concept of the nation.

With the rise of the European Union the nation state has lost much of its old appeal. Formerly, particularly during the latter part of the nineteenth century, the nation had acquired a certain cult status. It was considered noble and fitting to die for one's country—and it was considered particularly praiseworthy in case one's country was a nation. Some states, admittedly, were not nations—such as Luxemburg and Liechtenstein.

The former was created as late as 1815 as an autonomous grand duchy linked with the kingdom of the Netherlands in a personal union (the king was also the grand duke). Luxemburg was not even an ancient possession of the house of Orange-Nassau, the royal house of the Netherlands. The earliest lord of Luxemburg was one Siegfried, Count of Ardennes, who built a castle on the rock of Luxemburg in 963. In 1126 after the extinction of the Ardennes line it was given (by the emperor) to the counts of Namur. From the house of Namur it passed to the house of Limburg, whose sons were the first to style themselves Counts of Luxemburg. This family also acquired the kingdom of Bohemia, and produced four emperors. Thereafter the county (now raised to a duchy) passed to the dukes of Burgundy, who represented a younger branch of the Valois kings of France. After the death of the last duke, Charles the Bold, it passed to the Habsburgs through Philip's daughter Mary who married the Archduke Maximilian, the future emperor. Thereafter it remained with the Habsburgs until the Revolutionary and Napoleonic wars when the whole of Europe was turned upside down. The house of Orange-Nassau is no doubt ancient but in 1815 they were brand new in Luxemburg.

When the southern provinces broke away to form the kingdom of Belgium in 1830, the western francophone districts of Luxemburg were ceded to the new kingdom. But in 1890 there was another crisis when the male line of the house of Nassau died out. King William III of the Netherlands had no son, but while his daughter Wilhelmina could succeed to the throne of the Netherlands, the Salic law debarred her from succeeding to the grand duchy. According to an old Family Compact of the Nassau house, only males could succeed to the German possessions of the family. Now Luxemburg, unfortunately, inadvertently or otherwise, had been left in the German Confederation at the time of the general settlement arrived at the Congress of Vienna in 1815. So the personal union between the two states came to an end and the grand ducal crown passed to a male cousin.

The story of the principality of Liechtenstein is even stranger. Oddly enough the principality takes its name from the family, rather than the other way round which is much more usual. The counts of Liechtenstein are an old Austrian family, distinguished for their services to the Habsburg emperors. The original Schloss Liechtenstein is located in Lower Austria which the family possessed from the twelfth century to the fourteenth, and then from 1807 onwards. In the course of their services to the emperors they acquired great estates in Styria, Moravia and Silesia, but unfortunately none of them were held directly from the emperor, and that alone could have entitled them to a seat in the Chamber of Princes in the Imperial Diet and the coveted rank of a Prince of the Holy Roman Empire. After a diligent search they managed to negotiate the purchase of the minuscule lordship (*Herrschaft*) of Schellenberg and the adjoining county of Vaduz from the counts of Hohenems in 1699 and 1712, respectively. The Emperor Charles VI then united the two to constitute the principality (*Furstentum*) of Liechtenstein 'in honour of his true servant Anton Florian of Liechtenstein'. This happened in 1719. But the acquisition was valued only for the political benefits which went with it. Several decades would pass before the first prince actually set foot in his mountainous principality.

Even today their Serene Highnesses are only occasional visitors to their hill-top castle, Vienna being the preferred residence. The famed art collection of the princes is also located in Vienna, rather than in Liechtenstein itself. The very insignificance of the principality has been the key to its survival. In the political upheavals of the twentieth century the princes lost all their estates in Styria, Moravia and Slovakia. All that was left to the family was their sovereign principality in the Alps, tucked away in a corner between Switzerland and Austria and their palace in Vienna. It survived, almost, one could say, by oversight.

How different are the larger states, the so-called nation states of Europe from these two principalities? Not really all that different as they are made out to be. The Netherlands and Belgium were both integral parts of the German kingdom and the Holy Roman Empire, once upon a time. Religious persecution and heavy taxation, rendered even more unendurable because of the prosperity of the proud merchants, drove them to rebellion. Calvinism divided the northern provinces from the southern, who were mainly Catholic, and it was in Protestant Calvinism that the 'Republic of the Seven United Netherlands' found its peculiar 'national' identity. An attempt to integrate the southern provinces with the northern in 1815 (now, no longer a republic but a kingdom) failed, eventually leading to the creation of the kingdom of Belgium. But even that, linguistically divided between the Francophone Walloons and the Dutch-speaking Flamands, has had an uneasy history. Belgium has still to find its special national identity.

The Nation is after all a myth, part of the mumbo-jumbo of politics, a creation of propaganda, designed to secure the compliance of the ruled to the will of their rulers, who pretend to represent the nation. Patriotism–another name for nationalism–is, famously, as Dr. Johnson observed, the last refuge of scoundrels.

Let us first take up the case of France. In the Roman days it was known as Gaul and its borders spilled across the Alps Maritime to include north Italy. Gallia Cisalpina included modern Piedmont, Lombardy, Venezia and Emilia-Romagna. The ancient Gauls were a Celtic people, and they are personified in the popular imagination by Asterix and Obelix, the well-known comic creations of Goscinny and Uderzo. However, they soon gave up fighting the Romans and were accepted as Roman citizens. But in the course of the barbarian invasions of the fourth and fifth centuries they were completely overrun by various Germanic tribes, chief among them being the Franks. It was only in Brittany that the old Celtic culture survived, and indeed Brittany managed to remain a separate duchyindependent of the French crown till the sixteenth century.

France derives its name from the Latin 'Francia', or the 'Land of the Franks'. The Franks were one of the Germanic tribes who came to dominate northern Gaul and Germany south of Saxony, mainly along the middle and lower valleys of the Rhine and the Main. Their seat in the time of Merovech (from whom the Merovingians derive their name) was Tournai and the territory they commanded was called Austrasia. To their immediate south-west was the Roman outpost still held by Siagrius which was conquered by Merovech's grandson, the celebrated Clovis in 486. This came to be known as Neustria. Another twenty years later the Visigothic kingdom of Toulouse was added to the Frankish kingdom. Clovis also embraced Christianity–the Roman Catholic version as opposed to the Arrian creed which had been adopted by most of the other German tribes like the Goths.

The successors of Clovis continued their expansion and by the time of Charlemagne (800-14), the first ruler of the 'Carolingian' house, the Frankish kingdom embraced the whole of modern France (barring Brittany), the Netherlands, Italy (as far as Rome), and most of Germany. Charlemagne added more territories to the east, and the south across the Pyrenees. Of course, his greatest achievement was the acquisition of the imperial title as Holy Roman Emperor at the hands of the pope.

This Frankish empire included many other tribes like the Visigoths, Burgundians, Alemanii, Swabians, Frisians, Saxons, Thuringians and Lombards. It was only nominally a single state; in reality both under the Merovingians and Carolingians the territories would be repeatedly partitioned and repartitioned among the various princes or sub-kings. It was only briefly under Charlemagne that the empire had a single ruler. At the time of his accession he made his younger son Charles king of Neustria, another son, Louis the Pious received Aquitaine, while Carloman–renamed Pepin–received Italy. But Pepin and Charles died in 810 and 811, respectively, and Louis was made co-emperor in 813. Louis succeeded his father as sole emperor in 1814. Louis again divided his empire among his sons, but they could not get along and civil war broke out among them. After Louis' death there was the famous Partition of Verdun (843), to be followed by the Partition of Meersen in 870. Naturally there were yet further partitions, but after the death of Charles the Fat (885-8) the partition between West Francia (or France) and East Francia became permanent and the imperial title remained with the kings of the east. The notion of an East Francia still survives in the region known as Franconia, now divided between northern parts of Bavaria and Baden-Wurttemberg and the southern part of Thuringia. The old bishoprics of Bamberg, Wurzburg, Mainz and Speyer, besides the former petty states of Hesse, Nassau, Hohenlohe, the Rhenish Palatinate and the city of Frankfurt are also considered part of Franconia.

There was thus nothing particularly national about the kingdom of France. Although its rulers, from the time of the Merovingians, styled themselves 'Kings of the French' the kingdom was in fact a mishmash of various Germanic tribes who differed from their eastern cousins only in having received a strong strain of Celtic genes. The Gauls themselves have long since disappeared and survive today only in legend and comic strips, and as the Bretons of Brittany. Even today the latter consider themselves as distinct from the French; till the sixteenth century they managed to preserve a precarious independence under their own dukes, but after the death of Anne, their last duchess, in 1514,[7] every effort was made to deny the Breton identity. French 'nationalism' became particularly virulent during the revolution and when the Bretons, fiercely royalist and Catholic, rose in revolt they were suppressed along with the neighbouring

Vendeeans with genocidal ferocity. The Breton tongue is still not recognized as an official language in France, and with only an estimated 300,000 people (mostly above the age of 60) speaking it, it may be regarded as highly endangered.

The spoken language of Alsace was not French but German. After France regained this province in 1918 the use of the Alsatian dialect was vigorously suppressed, and a policy of Gallicization was actively pursued. Provence had its Provencal and Languedoc, its *langue d'oc*. Here the *oui* of the north becomes the *oc* of the south. There is a romantic separatist movement for the creation of 'Occitania' as well. Occitanian enthusiasts write and publish books in Occitanian in an effort to preserve their dying language. The old duchies of Aquitaine and Burgundy had been independent of the French Crown for many centuries. In the map appended to his *Compte Rendu au Roi*, published in 1781, Jacques Neckar, director-general of finances to the king of France, Aquitaine, Toulouse and much of the south are shown as 'foreign territories' of the French Crown. The Paris region, known as Ile de France, is the heartland of the French nation, and the metropolis has sought, over the centuries, to mould its dependent provinces in its own image. The Gallic mind, with its Cartesian logic, does not permit ambiguities and regional variations. There can be only one standard French language (the *langue d'oeil*, the dialect spoken in the Paris region), a standardized educational system, a uniform civil code, and it would very much have preferred to have only one standard religion as well. Of course, there could be no question of federalism. The French identity has been forged and imposed on the state through state–controlled schools with their standardized syllabi and approved textbooks. In short it is a remarkable achievement of state-inspired propaganda.

The other European nations were created by similar processes. German nationalism was born during the Napoleonic wars, and it became a tool of Prussian imperialism. Italy, hitherto a mere geographical expression, became suddenly aware of its national identity about the same time. Here Piedmont and the House of Savoy were the unlikely equivalents of Prussia and the House of Hohenzollern.

Europe has undergone thorough Germanization ever since the fifth century. Even if the peasantry has preserved some traces of their regional character and customs, the upper classes, particularly the higher nobility, were a transnational class. Their marriages were restricted by custom to their own class and nationality was usually of slight consequence. Usually fluent in several languages, it was not uncommon for members of the same family to be serving under different flags. Thus at the outbreak of the First World War a German prince happened, purely by chance, to be the First Sea Lord at the Admiralty in the United Kingdom. In 1914 *all* the ruling families of western and central Europe—except for the Bernadottes of Sweden—were of German stock and closely interrelated.

Even the Czar of Russia was a German. The male line of the Romanovs had died out with Peter the Great. His niece Anne who succeeded to the throne in 1730 was married to a prince of Holstein-Gottorp, then the ruling house of Sweden, and by origin a cadet line of the north German House of Oldenburg which had been ruling Denmark since 1448. She adopted an infant who was placed on the throne after her death under the name of Ivan VI. He was in fact the son of the *generalissimo* of the Russian army, Prince Antony Ulrich of Brunswick-Luneburg and Anna Leopoldovna of Mecklenburg-Schwerin, who was, through her mother, a granddaughter of Czar Ivan V. Thirteen months later as a result of a palace coup, Elizabeth, a daughter of Peter the Great was placed on the throne. Elizabeth never married, and she was followed by Peter III, the son of another Anne (this, a daughter of Peter the Great) who had married another prince of Holstein-Gottorp and died in childbirth in 1728. This young man was married to Sophia of Anhalt-Zerbst, who would be celebrated in history as the Czarina (or Empress) Catherine the Great of Russia. All succeeding emperors were married in German princely families. Three of the empresses came from Hesse, while the others were from Wurttemberg, Baden, Prussia, and Denmark. Thus the later Czars of Russia were Russian only by virtue of being rulers of Russia.

Even newly-created Balkan states, carved out of the decaying Ottoman Empire were presented with German princes as their rulers.

The first king of Greece was Otho of Bavaria. When the Greeks threw him out in 1862 the European powers presented them with another: this time, George of Denmark. The autonomous principality of Rumania started out with a native prince, Alexander John Cuza but after seven years he was overthrown in a palace coup and the European powers now presented Rumania with a new prince, Carol (Karl) of Hohenzollern-Sigmaringen, a distant collateral of the Prussian royal family. He was essentially a protégé of Napoleon III and it was he who recommended him to the notables of Rumania. The dynasty he founded would reign till 1947.

Bulgaria was created in 1879. Its first prince was Alexander of Hesse-Battenberg, who came to Bulgaria with the strong endorsement of the Czar. However, his relations with Russia soon soured and he was compelled to abdicate in 1886. His successor, Prince Ferdinand of Saxe-Coburg-Gotha was—naturally—also from Germany. His descendants weathered two world wars and the last, King Simeon (then aged nine) was forced into exile in 1946 when the Communists staged a coup during the Soviet occupation. Incredibly, after the collapse of the Communist governments of East Europe, Simeon returned to Bulgaria, founded a political party, and returned to power as prime minister in 2001! Some of the estates of the royal family were even returned to him. In the elections of 2005 his party got second place; he is therefore no longer prime minister, but even so his achievement is remarkable.

At the end of the Second Balkan War (1913) the Great Powers proposed an independent Albania. At first the princely crown was offered to Aubrey Herbert, a British MP who had championed the Albanian cause, but the British government dissuaded him from accepting it. It was then offered to Prince William of Wied, a nephew of Queen Elizabeth of Rumania, who accepted it in February 1914. However Prince William's reign was brief. The country was rocked by civil strife, then the world war broke out, and Prince William was forced to leave the country. He returned to Germany and fought in the German army under the pseudonym of Count of Kruja. The victorious Allies were hardly likely to restore a prince who had fought on the opposite side, and eventually in 1924 Albania was declared a republic. However, a few years later, in 1928, its president Ahmed Zogu declared himself king as King Zog I Skanderbeg III. At last a native of the Balkans had come into his own—the first after Milos Obrenovic of Serbia (1815-39). And this one was actually descended from Skanderbeg, the sixteenth-century hero of Albania! But being a native Muslim without any links with European aristocracy, King Zog was snubbed by European monarchs. His kingdom was unable to survive the storms of the Second World War though his son Prince Leka, 'King of the Albanians' still lives in Tirana.

The point of this lengthy survey of European kingdoms is mainly to emphasize that, notwithstanding the remarkable homogenization of the ruling families of Europe—and of its upper classes—it has not been able to achieve unity. The Germanization has been so thorough that it has even crossed the traditional cultural divide between Western Christendom and Eastern Orthodoxy—as we have seen in the Balkans and Russia. But a European—even a West European—unity has proved elusive, except in a roundabout way after the Second World War, through the Common Market and NATO, under the protective carapace of the United States of America. The trans-Atlantic republic is the equivalent of a modern day Macedon or Rome.

Why this was so difficult for Europe, but relatively easy for India—in spite of its far greater diversity—will be discussed in the subsequent chapters.

NOTES

1. John E. Morby, *The Wordsworth Handbook of Kings & Queens*, Wane, Herts: Wordsworth Editions, 1989, pp. 3-9.
2. Tacitus, *The Agricola and the Germania*, London: Penguin, 1970, pp. 114-17.
3. The Latin suffix 'ulus' signifies 'little' and it is here applied in a satirical sense. The correct style was of course Augustus, but since he was emperor only in name—and very young (only 14 years old)—the satirical variant was very appropriate and stuck.

4. Hodgkin, *The Barbarian Invasions of the Roman Empire*, vol. II, London: Folio Society, 2000, pp. 35, 292-4.
5. Surajit Sinha, 'State Formation and Tribal Myth in Tribal Central India', in Hermann Kulke (ed.), *The State in India 1000–1700*, New Delhi: Oxford University Press, 2004, pp. 305-18.
6. Louis L. Snyder, *Fifty Major Documents of the Nineteenth Century*, Princeton N.J.: Van Nostrand, 1955, pp. 16-18.
7. Anne, daughter of Duke Francis II of the House of Montfort, was married successively to two kings of France, Charles VIII and Louis XII, and her daughter Claude was in turn married to the heir to the French throne, the future Francis I. She had done her best to save her duchy and had in fact been married by proxy to Maximilian, then King of the Romans, in 1490 (he would become emperor-elect in 1493). But, by an earlier treaty between her late father and the French king, the latter's approval was necessary. So Charles VIII descended upon her capital, laid siege to it, and carried her away by force. Maximilian was busy fighting in Hungary and was unable to come to the defence of his wife. In a desperate attempt to avert the inevitable she arranged the betrothal of her daughter Claude to Charles of Habsburg, the future Emperor Charles V, but that too had to be broken off because it was unacceptable to her husband.

CHAPTER 3

Contrasting Wars

As pointed out earlier Indian wars are very different from European wars. The Wikipedia which is singularly unreliable gives a list of conflicts in Asia. I shall begin with the section dealing with India's 'medieval period'. It is as follows:

- Harsha's conquests 606-47
- Muslim conquests in the subcontinent
- Muhammad bin Qasim's conquest of Sindh 711-15
- Battle of Rajasthan 738 [?]
- Delhi Sultanate conquests 1206-1451
- Pala Empire conquests 750-850
- Medieval Chola conquests 848-1130
- Mongol Invasions of India 1221-1308

Of course, the list is most unsatisfactory and far from complete. The subsequent list of the 'Early Modern Period' is just as sketchy and unsatisfactory. The word 'conquest' does not figure in this list, but the wars listed here, such as 'Mughal Era conflicts', the Anglo-Mysore, Anglo-Maratha, Anglo-Sikh and Anglo-Burmese wars are simple straightforward wars of conquest too. By way of comparison, the list of European wars is far longer and much more detailed.

But even after conceding all these shortcomings, and a detailed reading of the actual published histories (as distinguished from virtual documents culled from the net) one notices that in Europe straightforward wars of conquest of the Indian or Asian variety are a relatively recent phenomenon, Napoleon being the first such conqueror in recent times. In the early period too, when the Danes and Norsemen went on their plundering raids, and the Teutonic Knights and Swedes were battling the 'heathen' Prussians and Lithuanians, there was a straightforward struggle for territory, but when the situation stabilized (by which time the Prussians had been exterminated and the Lithuanians baptized) new excuses had to be found for war. When civilizations mature, they do not necessarily become more peaceable, only their reasons for going to war get more complicated. On the border marches, however, where different civilizations meet, war tends to retain its barbaric character.

Interestingly, no European ruler since Alexander appears to have attempted, or even dreamed of world dominion–until we come to the time of Napoleon. The Roman Empire lasted much longer and extended over a wider area than the Macedonian, but it was built-up slowly in bits and pieces over a period of 300 years, and it took another two centuries to unravel in the West. Its eastern rump, also known as the Byzantine Empire, would linger for another 900 years! On the other hand, the nomads of the Asian steppes, uncouth barbarians though they may have seemed, appear to have routinely dreamt of world dominion. Chengiz Khan is only the best known among them, but Timur Leng (or Tamburlane) was almost as successful. And if you go back earlier there was Attila the Hun and, before him, the Avars. The last of the tribe was Nadir Shah of Persia, sometimes described as the 'Napoleon of the East'. After him the Orient was exhausted. It would take another 200 years to revive, starting with the British retreat from India. Japan, of course, is an exception. Forced 'open' by Commodore Perry's warships in 1854 it abandoned its policy of insular isolation and within 50 years had modernized itself to the extent of successfully challenging and defeating Imperial Russia, the greatest of the Eurasian land empires.

But this study is concerned mainly with the extant Western civilization which was born sometimes towards the end of the fifth century of the Christian era, and the modern Indian[1] civilization which was born about 200 years later. The Indians of this period did not attempt world conquest, nor did they even dream of it. They were content to live within their traditional geographical confines and were lucky to have escaped the ravages of the Mongol hordes of Chengiz Khan. During the latter's lifetime the Mongols never crossed the Indus. Later, for the next hundred years, Mongol[2] raiders would periodically sweep down the passes of the north-west across the plains of Punjab, occasionally as far as Delhi, and sometimes crossing into the Ganga-Yamuna Doab, but these were transient incursions. They would come in the winter season, ravage the plains, sack a few towns, and then, as the weather warmed up, retire to the cool hills of Afghanistan. There were at least 13 incursions between 1221 and 1350; and then, after nearly half a century, came the dreadful visitation of Amir Timur, who would be followed a hundred and twenty-five years later by Babur, his descendant in the fifth generation.

After the Turks and Mughals had established themselves in northern India they concentrated on extending their rule over the rest of the subcontinent. They had their hands full with this task, and notwithstanding their grandiloquent titles (viz., Jahangir, Shah Jahan, Alamgir, Shah Alam, etc.—all meaning conqueror or ruler of the world or universe) they were content with limiting their world to the subcontinent. Only occasionally would an embassy be sent to neighbouring Iran (or Turkey) to announce the accession of a new emperor, or to congratulate a new Shah or Sultan on his accession.

In Europe the tide of conquest had ebbed by the fourteenth century, by which time all Europe had become Christian,[3] and the barbarian or heathen 'other' had ceased to exist. Bohemia had embraced Christianity by the end of the ninth century, and Poland a hundred years later. Hungary became Christian around the year 1000 when 'good King Stephen' was its ruler. Lithuania was the last, and was Christianized only in the later part of the fourteenth century. But state-building in Eastern Europe was interrupted by the Mongol invasion of Europe which commenced in 1240. By the end of the thirteenth century the Mongol tide too had receded, and though the Khans of the Golden Horde, and Crimea would continue to harass the Poles and the Kievan Russians for several centuries, they had ceased to be a serious threat.

Poland, formerly a duchy, was revived as a kingdom in 1320. In 1386 Jadwiga, the sole heiress of King Louis the Great of the House of Anjou married Grand Prince Jogaila of Lithuania to constitute the 'Commonwealth of Poland and Lithuania'. This was also the occasion when the Lithuanians became Christians. Warfare would continue for a long time between the Poles and Lithuanians on one side and the various military orders on the other, the Teutonic Knights being the most important of the latter. The Swedes and the Russians were other actors, and, after the decline of the Teutonic Order, the principal ones on the other side. After Sweden left the stage following the disastrous wars of Charles XII (1697-1718) Brandenburg-Prussia stepped in, and ultimately the Polish Commonwealth would be partitioned between Russia, Prussia and Austria—with the largest share going to Russia. The Polish arms are a white eagle while each of the other three powers are represented by black eagles; the three black eagles (two of them double-headed) carving up a helpless white eagle made for powerful and evocative imagery. The treaty of Lowenwolde, or Berlin (1732), which was the first treaty between the three great powers regarding the future of Poland would be remembered bitterly by the Poles as the Treaty of the Three Black Eagles.

But while territorial ambition and simple aggression were the principal driving force behind the wars on the eastern frontiers of Western Christendom, a stable state system had been established in western and central Europe. Wars, of course, did not cease, only their causes were different. Conflict was inherent in the very nature of European feudalism. Once fiefs had become hereditary, kings lost control over their barons or tenants-in-chief. In the event of a failure of direct heirs of the body, brothers, uncles or cousins from collateral lines would lay claim to the vacant fiefs. Thus it often came about that one baron might hold different fiefs from different masters. A count holding a fief from the French crown, for instance, might become king of another kingdom. The county of Anjou was an outstanding example. Count Henry (1151-89) succeeded to the crown of England in 1154 because his mother was a daughter of Henry I, the last of the Norman kings of England. Two years earlier he had married Eleanor, the divorced wife of King Louis VII of France. Now Eleanor was duchess of Aquitaine in her own right, and by this marriage Count Henry became duke of Aquitaine and count of its dependent counties of Poitou, Toulouse, Saintonge and Limousin. Thus even before he had succeeded to the crown of England he was the first nobleman in the kingdom, overshadowing his nominal sovereign and liege-lord, the King of France. His pride and arrogance knew no bounds and after he had become king of England as well he tendered his homage to the French king most reluctantly. But pride cometh before a fall, and in the course of time, the English would lose the bulk of their French possessions in a series of wars, viz., the Norman war (1214), the Saintonge war (1242), and finally the War of Saint-Sardos (1324). Gascony was practically all that was left to them.

Soon, however, they were presented with a fresh opportunity to recoup their losses. In 1328 with the death of Charles the Fair, the Capetian house ran out of male heirs. Under the Salic law which was believed to apply to the Franks, women or their descendants could not inherit thrones and kingdoms, so the next heir was Philip, son of Charles of Valois, an uncle of the late king. But Edward III of England decided that this was a good opportunity to shake off his feudal subordination to the French crown once and for all, and since his mother was a sister of the late king, he staked his own claim to the throne of France. His claim was weak; under the Salic law he was debarred from the succession, and even if that law was to be ignored there were other heirs with better claims.

Nonetheless the war began in 1338, and with a few interruptions, it would continue for nearly a hundred years. This Hundred Years War had barely ended when England itself descended into civil war. This war, known as the War of the Roses, lasted thirty years, from 1455 to 1485. It was a struggle for the crown of England between two branches of the Angevin house, represented by the ducal houses of Lancaster and York. Both were descended from King Edward III (1327-77), the former from John of Gaunt, the third surviving son of Edward, and the latter from Edward of Langley, the fourth son. Henry IV, Henry V and Henry VI were all from the Lancastrian branch.

Henry VI proved to be mentally unstable and when he became insane in 1454 his cousin Richard, Duke of York, became regent with the title of Protector of the Realm. When the king's madness had passed, he relinquished the regency, but when King Henry raised his enemy, Edmund, Duke of Somerset, to power, Richard, apprehending a threat to his life, mobilized his army and struck hard at Somerset in the battle of St. Albans. Somerset was killed, the king taken prisoner, and Richard, once again, became Protector.

Henry, meek and gentle, might have reconciled himself to the situation, but his wife, Margaret of Anjou, continued to plot against the Yorkists, and the king's mental condition remained unstable. The queen's intrigues eventually forced Richard to assert his claim to the throne. In fact, he had a valid claim, for when Henry Bolingbroke had deposed Richard II and proclaimed himself king as Henry IV he had by-passed the descendants of Edward III's second surviving son, Lionel of Antwerp, the first Duke of Clarence, who eventually founded the rival House of York.

It is beyond the scope of this study to trace the fluctuating fortunes of the two factions in this long drawn-out civil war. It ended finally with the death in battle of Richard III, the last of the Yorkist kings, on Bosworth field in 1485. The Lancastrian champion was Henry Tudor, a grandson of Owen Tudor through Catherine of Valois, the widow of King Henry V to whom he was secretly married. His father Edmund, created Earl of Richmond, had married Margaret Beaufort, a daughter of John, Duke of Somerset, who was a grandson of John of Gaunt. Henry Tudor now ascended the throne as Henry VII, the first of the Tudor kings. His marriage with Elizabeth of York, the daughter of King Edward IV, unified the two warring houses and gave his children a stronger claim to the throne.

After the end of the Hundred Years War, and the Wars of the Roses, Europe had a spell of peace—except on its eastern fringes in Poland and Russia, and along the Ottoman frontier, where Constantinople had at last fallen to the Turks. The next cycle of wars between major European states within the Western group would be fought mainly in Italy, with France as the principal aggressor.

From 1494 to 1560 there were as many as seven wars in which French armies were deployed in Italy. The first two wars were over the succession to the throne of Naples. After the destruction of the Hohenstauffens the Pope had, in 1266, assigned Sicily (which included Naples) to Charles of Anjou, Count of Provence. But in 1282 occurred the famous uprising of the 'Sicilian Vespers' which resulted in the expulsion of the Angevins from Sicily, and the extension of Aragonese rule over that island. The Sicilians had solicited Aragonese assistance, for King Pedro III of Aragon was a son-in-law of Manfred, the last of the House of Hohenstauffen. As Pedro I he and his descendants remained kings of Sicily, and eventually in 1442, they succeeded in expelling Rene the Good, the last of the Neapolitan Angevins from Naples as well. Rene had no surviving sons, so the king of France, as his collateral cousin, could claim the throne of Naples.

The Aragonese claim was a valid one. The Salic law did not apply in Sicily. The Sicilian kingdom had been founded by Normans and the Hohenstauffens had acquired it through a woman, Constance, the last of the House of Hauteville, who married Henry of Hohenstauffen, King of the Romans. The Pope's claim to dispose of Italian fiefs and kingdoms was disputable; it was essentially an usurpation of imperial authority in the power vacuum that followed the fall of the Hohenstauffens. Rene had, however, bequeathed Naples to his nephew, Charles of Maine, by will. Charles had died in 1481 and he, in turn, had bequeathed his rights to Louis XI, the father of Charles VIII.

Throughout history, sunny Italy with its pleasant climate has held an irresistible attraction for the people of the north. Charles was a romantic and unbalanced youth, and King Rene's will provided him with the perfect *cassus belli.* He hoped to conquer Naples, and from there he planned to proceed eastwards to recover Jerusalem from the Turks.[4] In 1493 he proclaimed himself King of Sicily and Jerusalem, and in March 1494, crossed the Alps into Italy.

At first things went smoothly. There was little resistance, and by the end of February, the following year, Charles was in Naples. But then the diplomatic situation deteriorated. The Emperor, King Ferdinand of Aragon, and the Pope entered into an alliance, nominally against the Turk, but actually directed against France. Charles hastily concluded a peace with Ludovico Sforza, the duke of Milan, and returned home.

That was not, however, the end of it. Charles VIII died three years later, but Louis XII who succeeded him was determined to resume the struggle. Besides the old claim to the throne of Naples and Sicily, Louis, through his grandmother Valentina, the daughter of Gian Galeazzo Visconti, also laid claim to the duchy of Milan. His claim was opposed by Emperor Maximilian on the ground that the original grant of Milan to Gian Galeazzo by Wenceslas, King of the Romans, in 1395 excluded women from the succession, and Milan had thus reverted to the empire. The Sforzas had held it since 1450, and though usurpers, had been recognized as dukes by both Louis XI and Charles VIII.

Again the first part was easy. Venice, annoyed with Ludovico Sforza because he had concluded the Peace of Vercelli with Charles VIII without consulting it, had joined hands with France. The Milanese general, probably paid off by the French, quietly withdrew. Louis appointed a governor and returned to France.

The severity of the new governor and the insolence of the French garrison soon disenchanted the Milanese of their new rulers. Ludovico took advantage of the discontent and reoccupied the city, driving out the French. Louis collected a fresh army, and crossing the Alps, defeated Ludovico's forces at Novara. The latter was taken prisoner along with other members of his family. The power of the Sforzas was broken forever and Ludovico lived out the remainder of his life as a prisoner of the French in the chateau of Loches.

Encouraged by his easy success against Ludovico, Louis decided to advance further and seize Naples. Since the death of Alfonso V of Aragon (1416-58), Naples had been separated from Sicily and given to Ferrante, his illegitimate son. At the time of this second invasion it was ruled by his second son, Fredrick. On the pretext that Fredrick (on failing to get help from the Emperor) had sought an alliance with the Turkish Sultan who had attacked Venice and invaded its province of Friuli, Ferdinand of Aragon joined hands with Louis and agreed to a partition of the Neapolitan territories. Naples was to go to France, while Calabria and Apulia, the 'toe' and 'heel' of the Italian peninsula, were to go to Aragon, attached to the kingdom of Sicily.

But the peace was short-lived. Disputes soon arose between the French and the Aragonese in the southern foot of Italy and war flared up once again. This time fortune favoured the Aragonese, and by the beginning of 1504 Naples was again lost to the French and the great fortress of Gaeta surrendered.

But the Italian wars did not cease. There was the War of the League of Cambrai (1508-10) and the War of the Holy League (1511-13). These would be followed by Louis' third invasion of Italy in 1513 which culminated in the catastrophic defeat of the French on the field of Novara (6 June 1513). Two years later Louis XII died, but his successor took up the struggle again. In his first invasion he was lucky. At Marignano he won a decisive victory over the Swiss, and an incursion by the Emperor Maximilian ended in an ignominous retreat by the latter. The peace of Noyon (13 August 1516) at last gave the Milanese to Francis. France, however, would occupy it for only five years.

There were three other Italian wars, during which the French suffered another catastrophic defeat at the Battle of Pavia, and the Eternal City itself was sacked for eight dreadful days in 1527 by the mutinous soldiers of Charles III, Duke of Bourbon, Count of Montpensier, and Constable of France. The Constable had broken with his royal cousin over the question of the succession to the estates of his late wife, Suzanne, who had been Duchess of Bourbon in her own right. The estates were being claimed by the Queen-Mother, Louise of Savoy, on the basis of being the nearest in blood, and the king, naturally, favoured his mother. The duke then entered into a conspiracy against the king, and, switching sides, entered the imperial service. Unfortunately, the troops that were placed under his command by the Emperor were mainly German Lutherans. They had been starved of pay and provisions, and desperate for plunder, they forced the duke to march on Rome. The duke himself was killed in the assault before the walls, but his army succeeded in storming the city which was then subjected to probably the worst sack in its history, surpassing even the horrors perpetrated by Alaric the Goth in AD 410. With their commander killed, and no one to control them, the soldiers ran amok; churches and convents were plundered, nuns raped, and it was almost a month before order could be restored.

The cycle of Italian wars ended in 1559 with the peace of Cateau-Cambresis which finally put paid to France's Italian ambitions, and left Habsburg Spain and Austria as the dominant powers in Italy and Europe. The Venetian republic, the Pope, other minor Italian states, even England, Scotland and the Ottoman Turks—besides the Empire—were participants in most of these wars. Besides Italy, Germany, Hungary, Navarre and Scotland were also the scenes of fighting. The original dynastic claims to the Duchy of Milan and the Crown of Naples became irrelevant in the general struggle for Italian domination in which every power, major or minor, sought to strengthen its position. The Habsburgs were the only gainers, but it must be remembered that this cycle of wars, spread over sixty years, had its origins in the French claims to the Duchy of Milan and the Kingdom of Naples, based on the ordinary laws of inheritance.

How the Habsburgs built up their sprawling empire by carefully crafting strategic marriages is well known. The process was largely peaceful, and, even though many of their crowns were theoretically elective, the electoral principal was successfully subverted—as in the case of the Holy Roman Empire itself—usually by arranging the election of the successor (usually the son or brother) in the lifetime of the reigning monarch, or by pushing through a resolution in the concerned diets declaring the succession hereditary in the House of Habsburg. Of course, this was not a Habsburg innovation; earlier dynasties like the Saxons, Salians, Hohenstauffens, and the Luxemburgers had done the same, as indeed had the Arpads of Hungary, the Piasts of Poland, and the Premysls of Bohemia.

Even before the cycle of Italian wars had ended, religious questions had come to the fore. In Germany the Reformation began with Martin Luther in 1517 when he nailed the '95 Theses' on the door of the church of Wittenberg. John Calvin had been born only a few years earlier (in 1509) but by the late 1530s he too had established his base in Geneva and his harsher puritanical teachings soon won him considerable following in Switzerland, France and northern Germany. But Bohemia had had its religious Reformation more than a century before Martin Luther, and the Cathars had led a peaceful movement against the corruption of the Catholic Church in southern France as early as the fourteenth century. Catharism had been suppressed in a sea of blood with mass burnings of 'heretics' but two hundred years later, Calvinist 'Huguenots' would find the south a fertile ground for their doctrines. Besides the disturbances and minor wars arising from the religious stirrings, there were also several uprisings by peasants and the minor nobility, who were in distressed circumstances because of the decay of feudalism.

In 1522 there occurred the Knights' War in western Germany. It was a rising of the imperial knights (the *Ritters*), usually holders of a single castle–or fractions thereof, who lived partly by brigandage and partly by the levying of extortionate tolls. The Church had lost its old respect and veneration; its properties excited only the cupidity of the impoverished (and often Lutheran) Ritters. In Denmark there was the similar Counts' War from 1533 to 1536.

The Peasants' War (1524-5) was a much more serious uprising in Germany. It was marked by massacres and arson; and castles were torched in the countryside as in the *jacqueries* of revolutionary France, two and a half centuries later. Had Luther lent his support to the movement the fires may well have become uncontrollable, but the prudent monk shrank from revolution and the uprising was ruthlessly suppressed by the princes. The embers continued to glow for a few years more in the mountain valleys of the Tyrol. Slovenia too had had a peasants' revolt in 1515, and the Counts' War in Denmark also expanded into a peasant uprising. Across the straits in southern Sweden, the rising known as the Dacke War (1542-3) was also essentially a peasant uprising. It started as a protest against increased taxation by the king who had recently converted to Lutheranism. Anti-clericalism was an element in the revolts of both peasants and knights.

In Germany Luther's teachings found a responsive chord, and the Elector of Saxony, the Landgrave of Hesse, and the Duke of Wurttemberg were the main leaders of the Protestant party. They formed the League of Schmalkalde in 1530 and ultimately, after the Emperor (Charles V) had secured the election of his brother Ferdinand as King of the Romans, war broke out between the Protestant and Catholic parties. Imperial diplomacy was able to ensure that it remained a limited one; the rivalries and divisions between the Protestant princes were cleverly exploited, but it was not until 1555 that the religious question was finally settled in the Peace of Augsburg. According to the terms of this peace it was left to the princes and the Imperial cities to decide whether they would be Catholic or Lutheran. Thus true religious freedom was still a distant reality. The principle adopted was that of *cuius regio, eius religio*–the people must follow the religion of their rulers.

The Reformation never became a people's movement in France. Paris remained staunchly Catholic but there were pockets of Calvinist 'Huguenots' everywhere, particularly in the south where the old Cathar sentiments still lingered in the Cevennes. Persecution began in the reign of Francis II, and 23 Huguenots were burned at the stake in the course of six months in 1534-5. About 3,000 Vaudois were massacred in 1545, and it is estimated that 200,000 may have been massacred in the years immediately preceding 1581. The great nobles were divided between Catholics and Huguenots, the Duke de Guise and the Constable Anne de Montmorency being the main leaders of the Catholic party, while the latter's two nephews, Coligny, Admiral of France, and D'Andelot, Colonel of the Infantry, were leading lights of the Huguenots. The Prince of Conde, the Duke of Vendome, and the King of Navarre (in right of his wife), both from the powerful House of Bourbon, were the nominal chiefs of the Huguenot party.

There were as many as nine religious civil wars, with the first starting in 1562, and the last concluding in May 1598. In all there were twenty years of war and during this period France had ceased to be a factor in European diplomacy. In 1572, in a seeming reconciliation, the Huguenot prince, Henry, King of Navarre, was married to Marguerite de Valois, the sister of the French king. But six days after the wedding there occurred the notorious Massacre of St. Bartholomew (so-called because it happened on the feast-day of that saint), in which Coligny, the Duke of Rochefoucauld, and at least 2,000 others were massacred in the streets of Paris. The newly wedded bridegroom barely escaped with his life. In the provinces thousands more were slaughtered, the estimates ranging from 20,000 to 100,000. The Guises and the Queen-Mother, Catherine de Medici, were suspected of having inspired this massacre.

With the death of King Henry III on 2 August 1589, the male line of the Valois came to an end. The evil Queen-Mother had died some months earlier in January, and the Duke of Bourbon-Vendome, King Henry of Navarre, the husband of Marguerite, was now the strongest claimant to the French throne. But his title was challenged by several rivals, and it was only after a long civil war (and after his adoption of Roman Catholicism) that Henry of Navarre was finally crowned in February 1594 as King Henry IV. Four years later, in order to retain his support among the Huguenots, the Edict of Nantes, established freedom of worship in the kingdom and freed the Huguenots from most of the disabilities from which they had suffered.

In England King Henry VIII had broken with the Roman Church over the rather discreditable matter of his divorce. During the reign of his daughter Mary (1553-8), who was married to King Philip of Spain, the Catholic Church was restored, and there were the usual burnings and executions. Her sister Elizabeth, who succeeded her, restored her father's Protestant Anglican Church, and now it was the turn of the Catholics to be persecuted. Savage penal laws were passed against Catholics and other Non-Conformists. In Scotland, John Knox, a disciple of Calvin, founded the Presbyterian Church of Scotland. The Catholic faith survived only in the Highlands, the Lowlands were solidly Presbyterian.

The three Scandinavian states of Denmark, Norway and Sweden had been united in the Union of Kalmar under the House of Denmark since 1397. The Lutheran faith first gained popularity among the Swedish nobility. King Christian II, in an ill-advised attempt to suppress the movement, landed troops in Sweden and there followed the notorious Bloodbath of Stockholm (1520) when 90 of the leading Swedes (mostly nobles and clergy) were executed as heretics. Sweden revolted, its nobles elected Gustavus Vasa as their king, and Sweden seceded from the Kalmar Union. Thereafter the Lutheran doctrine spread rapidly in the kingdom and eventually in Norway and Denmark as well. As happened in England, Gustavus (1523-60), though himself Catholic, had no scruples in helping himself to church property for paying off the debts of Sweden.

Thus apart from the Franco-Italian wars which ended in 1559, much of Europe was in religious turmoil for most of the sixteenth century. But the fighting was confined to Italy and Germany, and it was limited in nature. The following century would witness the Thirty Years War (1618-48) which for a long time, remained unsurpassed in savagery. It devastated central Europe, particularly Germany, and it is estimated that in some parts, like Brandenberg and Bohemia, the population declined by as much as two-thirds. The death-roll of the Napoleonic wars may have been greater, but the battles of Napoleon were fought over a much wider area. The Napoleonic theatre of war stretched from Moscow to Spain and Syria, whereas in the Thirty Years War the battles were fought in Germany and Bohemia.

The cause was partly religious. The Peace of Augsburg had made no provision for Calvinists; it recognized only Lutherans and Catholics, so the Calvinist princes banded together to form the league of Evangelical Union under the leadership of the Elector Palatine. In Bohemia the Protestants (mainly Hussites) were uneasy. Emperor Rudolf had assured them that their religious rights would be respected, but by 1617 it was evident that the Emperor Matthias would die without a direct heir, and the prospect of his cousin Ferdinand succeeding to the throne filled them with disquiet. The latter who was the heir-apparent had been educated by the Jesuits, and suspected of being a bigot, eager to apply the principle of *cuius regio, eius religio.*

Matthias was able to secure the election of Ferdinand to the throne of Bohemia during his lifetime, but when the latter sent his representatives to take over the administration in Prague, high words were exchanged with some of the Bohemian nobles who had gathered to receive them in the Hradčany Castle. Ferdinand had prohibited the construction of a Protestant Church on a piece of land because the Catholic clergy had claimed that the land was theirs. One thing led to another, and the royal emissaries were eventually thrown out of the castle window in what became famous as the 'Defenestration of Prague'. Amazingly none of the three men were seriously hurt, though the drop from the window was nearly 30 metres. Their fall is supposed to have been cushioned by a large heap of horse-manure in the castle-moat, directly below the window.

Relations between the Bohemian nobles and the new Emperor (and King of Bohemia) Ferdinand II rapidly deteriorated. The Bohemian Estates disavowed their allegiance to Ferdinand and offered the Bohemian crown to Fredrick V, the Elector-Palatine, whose late father had been the leader of the Protestant Union, a defensive alliance of Protestant princes in Germany. He accepted. This was rebellion, for the Habsburgs could, under no circumstances, allow Bohemia to slip from their hands. Thus apart from the religious undertones and the power politics of France and Sweden and Denmark, the question of succession to the Bohemian throne was the immediate spark that fired the powder-keg that was Europe in 1618.

The war left France as the dominant power in Europe. The Emperor (now Ferdinand III) was forced to cede Alsace to France; at last the French had reached the Rhine. Germany had been devastated by war, famine and pestilence. The Emperor had been forced to recognize its princes as sovereign, thus ensuring that the empire would never be anything more than notional. Spain had bankrolled the war; it had poured out its blood and treasure from the mines of Mexico and Potosi in support of its imperial cousins, even though Spain had nothing to do with Bohemia. The independence of the United Provinces of the Netherlands had also been recognized, bringing the Eighty Years War to an end as well.

In the subsequent century France would endeavour to exploit its dominant position by encroaching on the Spanish Netherlands and reducing the princes of western Germany to the position of clients. It believed that the river Rhine was its 'natural' border, so its long-term objective was to annex the Spanish Netherlands, Alsace and Lorraine.

Although the war in Germany ended with the Peace of Westphalia, the Franco-Spanish conflict dragged on for another ten years. Finally after the Spanish defeat at Dunkirk in 1658 in what is known as the Battle of the Dunes, a peace was negotiated. France gained Roussillon in the south, making the Pyrenees the border with Spain, and Artois in the north, along with some adjustments in Luxemburg and Flanders. A marriage was also arranged between the young Louis XIV and the Spanish Infanta, Maria Theresa. According to the treaty Maria Theresa renounced all claims to the Spanish throne, and in return was to receive 500,000 gold ecus by way of dowry. This dowry was never paid, and this failure would lead to other wars.

When Philip IV of Spain died in 1665, Louis, as the husband of Maria Theresa, laid claim to the duchies of Brabant and Limburg along with their dependencies. The claim was asserted because of the failure of Spain to pay the promised dowry, and because the local laws of Brabant gave Louis a tenuous legal base. According to the local laws the children of a first marriage had prior and exclusive claims over the children of a second marriage, and since Maria Theresa was a daughter of Philip through his first marriage, her claims (at least in Brabant and Limburg) were superior to those of her brother Charles (now King Charles II) who was born of the second marriage. Her earlier renunciation was held to be void because of the failure to pay her dowry, and the succession to Brabant and Limburg now 'devolved' upon her. Thus began what is known as the War of Devolution (1667-8).

The war was over in less than a year. Lille, Charleroi, Tournai and Douai and some towns were taken. The opposing Spanish forces were weak and the garrisons undermanned. The Franche-Comté (or the county of Burgundy) was overrun, Dole and Besancon were taken, but then the diplomatic situation changed to the detriment of France. The Dutch were alarmed by the rapid advance of the French in Flanders and Brabant. They themselves had no ambitions in that quarter (Louis had proposed a partition to William) and were anxious to preserve the Spanish Netherlands as a buffer between their state and France. William III, the Dutch Stadtholder, entered into an alliance with England and Sweden and warned Louis that while they granted Louis the territory he had initially demanded, they were not prepared to countenance the annexation of the Spanish Netherlands.

The Treaty of Aix-la-Chapelle (May 1668) brought the war to an end. France was obliged to evacuate the Franche-Comté, but it retained twelve towns in the Netherlands, the most important being Lille, Tournai, Charleroi and Armentieres. Louis was, however, determined to have his revenge against William, whom he regarded as a betrayer. Four years later the Franco-Dutch war (1672-8) broke out which was essentially a continuation of the earlier war.

This time England and Sweden were allied with France, along with the ecclesiastic states of Cologne and Munster, while the empire and Brandenburg supported the Dutch Republic. In spite of some early successes the war soon ground down to a tiresome war of attrition. The Treaty of Nijmegen finally gave the Franche-Comté to France besides some additional territory in the Netherlands.

Ten years later the French and the Dutch were again at war. This is known by various names, the Nine Years' War (1688-97), the War of the League of Augsburg, the Williamite War, and sometimes as the War of the Palatine Succession or of the English

Succession. Prior to this there had been another short conflict known as the War of the Reunions (1683-4), which again was a continuation of the earlier conflict. The Treaty of Nijmegen had not defined the territory to be ceded to France too precisely, hence differences arose and Louis set up 'Chambers of Reunion' to ascertain whether any dependent villages had been left out. Though short, the war was brutal, with the French laying waste the Rhenish Palatinate by destroying crops and burning villages.

One of the excuses for the Nine Years' War was Louis' claim to the Palatinate. The Elector Palatine had married his daughter to the Duke of Orleans, brother of King Louis XIV, in the hope of securing a powerful ally against the Emperor. But when he died in 1685 without a male heir, Louis claimed the Palatinate—even though the Salic law prevailed in the Palatinate (as in France) and the lady in question had never given her consent for pressing the claims. This is why the war is sometimes also described as that of the Palatine Succession.

In 1688 William had also received an invitation from notable English noblemen, including the Bishop of London to depose his father-in-law James II and become king himself. A few months earlier James' consort, Mary of Modena had given birth to a male heir, threatening a Catholic dynasty, a prospect which the Catholic-phobic English found most distasteful. James himself was Catholic but until the birth of this infant it was assumed that he would be succeeded by his daughter Mary, who was married to William of Orange, the leading champion of the Protestant cause in Western Europe. But now since a male child had been born to a Catholic, Italian-born queen, the great Whig peers were anxious to be rid of James at the earliest. So in November William landed with a small army and the king, taken by surprise, fled to France. Louis supported James, and when he sailed a few months later to Ireland he sailed with the blessings of Louis with a small French detachment. Thus the war is also known as the War of the English Succession.

The war was fought in the Spanish Netherlands, in Germany, in Italy, in Catalonia, Ireland and Scotland (where there was a Jacobite uprising in the Highlands). It was also fought in the American colonies and on the high seas. The Treaty of Ryswick which ended the fighting restored the status quo. All territorial gains were surrendered but for Strasburg (which had been seized by France before the war during the proceedings of the Chambers of Reunions). The French recognized William as King of England, and promised they would not actively support the deposed James. The Emperor was able to arrange for the election of his son as King of the Romans, and his candidate, Augustus of Saxony, was elected King of Poland, defeating the French candidate, the prince of Conti. All the belligerents were anxious to conclude the war, and prepare for the next one, the long awaited war of the Spanish Succession for it was evident that King Charles II was dying, and with him the line of the Spanish Habsburgs would come to an end.

The sick, misshapen and mentally feeble Charles finally died three years later. The direct heir was Louis, the Dauphin, the eldest son of Louis XIV and Maria Theresa, the half-sister of the deceased King, but on the other hand Maria Theresa had renounced her rights at the time of her marriage. The position was further complicated by the fact that the renunciation was considered invalid as her father had never paid the promised dowry which was part of the marriage contract. The alternative candidate was Emperor Leopold himself. He was the first cousin of the late King, but this would reunite Spain and Austria, a prospect as unwelcome to France as a Franco-Spanish union was to the Emperor. There was yet a third candidate, Joseph Ferdinand, the son of the Elector of Bavaria, Maximilian II. His mother Maria Antonia was a daughter of the Emperor, through another Maria Theresa of Spain, this one the *real* sister of Charles II. But in 1699 the Bavarian prince, who was the most favoured of the three candidates, succumbed to smallpox. The king, shortly before his death, decided to bequeath all his lands to the Dauphin's second son, the Duc d'Anjou. Should Anjou chance to inherit the French crown the Spanish crown would go to his younger brother, the Duc de Berri, and only if Berri failed to beget an heir, would Archduke Charles of Austria succeed.

But Austria wanted a share of Spanish lands, particularly its possessions in Italy, so ultimately, as soon as Charles died, war broke out. Britain, the United Provinces, Savoy and Portugal, besides Prussia and a host of minor German states sided with the Emperor, while France, Spain and Bavaria were on the other side. The war was fought in Spain, the Netherlands and Germany—besides colonial North America (where it was known as Queen Anne's War)—and for once the imperial side was favoured with a set of remarkably capable commanders, namely, Prince Eugene of Savoy, John Churchill (who would become a duke by the time the war ended) and the Margrave of Baden. The victories of Blenheim, Ramillies, Oudenarde and Malplaquet established the reputations of Prince Eugene and Marlborough as two of the greatest commanders of the times. But in 1711 Marlborough fell from grace at home; charges of corruption were brought against him and he was recalled. This gave France a reprieve, the expected invasion of France never materialized and eventually Britain and the United Provinces made a separate peace by the Treaty of Utrecht in 1713. France made peace with the other powers in the treaties of Rastatt and Baden. Spain, however, did not ratify the treaties until 1720, by which time it had been defeated once again by all the powers in the War of the Quadruple Alliance.

By the peace treaties the Duc d'Anjou was recognized as King Philip V of Spain. He renounced his rights to the French throne and ceded the Netherlands, Naples, Milan and Sardinia to Austria, Sicily and parts of the Milanese duchy to Savoy, and Gibralter and Menorca to Britain. Thus although a Bourbon now sat on the throne of Spain, Louis XIV had been downsized, the Habsburgs strengthened, and the balance of power restored with Britain acquiring strategic outposts in the Mediterranean.

Spain had lost all its Italian possessions but its king, who had just lost his first wife had, in the same year as the Treaty of Utrecht, got married to Isabella Farnese, a niece of the childless Duke of Parma. The marriage was therefore pregnant with future possibilities for Spain in Italy. A move by the powers to transfer Sicily (which had been assigned to Savoy) to Austria was the immediate provocation for the next war. Spain landed troops in Sardinia and Sicily. A British fleet attacked Vigo, landed troops and pushed some distance inland. As a result, Spain, realizing its vulnerability quickly made peace with the allies at the Treaty of the Hague (February 1720). The status quo was restored, but the allies recognized that the children of the Spanish queen had the right to succeed to the ducal thrones of Parma and Piacenza after the death of her childless uncles, Francesco and Antonio. Eventually her son Charles would succeed to Parma in 1731.

In 1733, following the death of Augustus II of Poland the stage was set for another European war. The Polish throne was elective and the Diet had elected Stanislas Leszczynski as his successor. But Austria and Russia favoured the son of Augustus, so some of the nobles, acting under the directions of Russia and Austria, held another election and declared him elected. He was recognized immediately by Russia and Austria as Augustus III, King of Poland. The war that followed was fought in Poland, the Rhineland and Italy, and though, at the end of it, Stanislas was obliged to step down in favour of Augustus, the war went badly for Austria. Stanislas (who was the father-in-law of Louis XV of France) was compensated with the duchy of Lorraine, which would, after his death pass to France, through his daughter. The former duke of Lorraine was compensated with the promise of the duchy of Tuscany where the once great house of Medici was on the verge of extinction. Gian Gastone, the last grand-duke, childless, possibly homosexual, and married to the monstrously fat princess of Saxe-Lauenburg was an introverted alcoholic with no interest in governance. As Tuscany was considered an imperial fief, the Emperor was in a position to effect the exchange. Out of deference to Gian Gastone's wish it was, however, decided to preserve its separate identity, though as a hereditary possession of the House of Habsburg-Lorraine. The duke was the Emperor's son-in-law, having married the Emperor's elder daughter and heir-presumptive, the Archduchess Maria Theresa, in 1736, and it was the latter's succession to her father's numerous thrones that provoked the next cycle of European wars.

The extinction of the male line of the Spanish Habsburgs had been a warning to the Austrian branch. While the Spanish war was still in progress the Emperor Leopold I tried to establish an explicit law of succession to provide for succession by females in the event of the failure of a male heir. The family compact was signed by the Emperor and his two sons, Joseph and Charles, both destined to become emperors after him. Hungary and Croatia voted their 'Pragmatic Sanction' accepting female succession after the extinction of the male line. Charles, however, complicated matters by executing a will which specified an order of succession which differed from the original compact of 1703, giving precedence to his own daughters over those of his late brother. This was read out in 1713, and duly accepted by the diets and estates of the various units which constituted the Habsburg realm. Most of the other European powers also accepted it, but as soon as Charles VI died in 1740, many chose to renege on their word. Maria Theresa could not, however, be elected empress, for the imperial election was governed by the constitution of the empire and could not be amended by a family compact. Charles Albert, the Bavarian Elector who happened to be a son-in-law of Maria's uncle, the late Emperor Joseph, announced his candidature. He denounced the Pragmatic Sanction of 1713, and laid claim to all the Habsburg lands in the name of his wife who would have had priority over Maria Theresa according to the original compact of 1703. He joined hands with France and Spain and invaded Upper Austria and Bohemia where he was crowned king. In January 1742 he was elected King of the Romans by the imperial electors, and in the following month, after the imperial coronation he assumed the title of Holy Roman Emperor. But after his early spectacular success, he suddenly fell ill and died. In the election that followed in 1745, Maria Theresa was able to get her husband elected, and he assumed the title of Emperor Francis I.

Fredrick II of Prussia laid claim to Silesia. It is generally assumed that Fredrick's seizure of Silesia was just a cynical move to acquire some choice real estate and that he had no real right to it. Silesia had been part of the kingdom of Bohemia, and when the Habsburgs acquired Bohemia, Silesia came with it. But in reality, ever since the fourteenth century, Silesia was divided into a number of duchies held by members of the Piast family, the ruling dynasty of Poland. After the Mongol withdrawal from Poland, the Polish dukes and kings had encouraged colonization by Germans in the depopulated country and the Silesian Piasts accepted the suzerainty of Bohemia. At that time Bohemia was the stronger state, and protected by the mountains in the north it had been spared the Mongol visitation. But in the seventeenth century the Piast dukes were on the verge of extinction. As they died, one by one, the duchies were incorporated into the kingdom of Bohemia. In 1537, however, the Piast Duke Fredrick II of Liegnitz (Legnica), Brieg (Brzeg) and Wohlau had concluded a treaty with the Elector of Brandenburg according to which Brandenburg would inherit the duchy on the extinction of his line, but the treaty was rejected by Ferdinand of Habsburg, then King of Bohemia and Holy Roman Emperor. The Piasts of Liegnitz died out in 1675; the Elector persisted in pressing his claims, and the Emperor continued to be evasive. Finally in 1686 he persuaded the Elector to abandon his claims in return for the little enclave of Schwiebus. An added sweetener was a subsidy of 250,000 gulden. The urgency at that time was to secure the military assistance of Brandenburg-Prussia against the Turks. However, Prussia felt that it had not been dealt with fairly, and now in 1740 as France and Bavaria were preparing for war, Fredrick decided that this was the most appropriate time for reviving his family's claims to the Silesian duchies. No doubt his unprovoked descent on Silesia, without even the formality of a declaration of war, has been condemned as outright robbery, but it had its roots in an old unsatisfied claim to that province.

The War of the Austrian Succession lasted eight years, from 1740 to 1748. Prussia was, however, largely an independent actor. In these eight years there were two Silesian wars, the first from 1740 to 1742, ending with the Peace of Breslau, and the second from 1744 to 1745, being concluded with the Treaty of Dresden. The Seven Years War (1756-63) was essentially a continuation of the earlier war. During it Prussia fought the Third Silesian War (1756-63). But for the timely death of the Czarina Elizabeth and the accession of Czar Peter III, an ardent admirer of the Prussian king, Prussia may well have been destroyed. It was a very close fight. Britain, France and Russia were the other belligerents, and as in the case of the Spanish succession, the battles were fought in Germany, Bohemia, the American colonies, the Caribbean and India.

However, the Seven Years War was the last of the wars of succession. The next war was the War of American Independence (1775-83), but this was only a colonial rebellion of the Thirteen Colonies which succeeded. In the later years of the war, France, Spain and Holland would also enter the lists against Britain, and France would even send troops to America to assist the American rebels, but these developments were an outgrowth of the American war, and of France's desire to obtain satisfaction for its loss of Canada in the previous war and the failure of its designs in India.

The next cycle of wars was ignited by the French Revolution and fuelled by the ambitions of Napoleon, who aspired to be another world-conqueror in the line of Alexander, Chengiz Khan and Amir Timur. Of course, it was not put that way. The European powers were at first genuinely alarmed at the revolutionary actions of the French. The restraints placed on the king by the Estates General alarmed the European dynasts, then basking in the sun of 'absolutism'. The events in France seemed a real threat to the international order, in the same way as the Russian revolution of 1917 appeared to threaten international capitalism. As a counter-blast the French sought to export their revolution. The king's abortive flight resulted in his deposition and eventual execution, the proclamation of the republic, and the Reign of Terror. Revolution was successfully exported, and the Cisalpine, Roman and Parthenopean republics were set up in Italy. The Swiss Confederation was replaced by the Helvetic Republic, while the Batavian Republic replaced the United Provinces of the Netherlands. These proved ephemeral because

Napoleon, who was soon supreme in France, had imperial ambitions of his own, and soon new kingdoms and grand-duchies would replace the fledgling republics.

The subsequent wars of the nineteenth and twentieth centuries were all part of a struggle for the mastery of Europe and indeed the world, and the language used by the rulers made no bones about the fact that these would be pitiless wars.

There was, however, one little question of 'succession' after the old pattern which gave rise to three minor wars in the nineteenth century. These concerned the succession to the duchies of Schleswig and Holstein, whose duke happened to be the King of Denmark. The death, without issue, of King Christian VIII of Denmark in 1848 sparked off the first war of Schleswig-Holstein (1848-51). There would be a second war in 1864, followed by a third war, known as the Austro-Prussian or the Seven Weeks War. The belligerents were Denmark, the German Confederation, Prussia and Austria. Apart from the intricacies of the succession the main cause of the war was the growth of nationalism. Schleswig and Holstein were both part of the German Confederation (which had replaced the old empire in 1815), but while the population of Schleswig was Danish, that of Holstein was predominantly German. The succession dispute was exploited by Bismarck, the Prussian chancellor for the purpose of humiliating Austria, and ultimately (in 1870) to dissolve the Confederation and usher in a new German Empire under the auspices of Prussia, rather than Austria.

The rhetoric of the Revolutionary and Napoleonic wars was bad enough, but it is only when one comes to the age of the German Kaiser that one realizes that the world had changed dramatically. The West was now supremely confident of its superiority over the Oriental and other non-European states, and Kaiser Wilhelm, whose 'Second Reich' was a relative upstart among the Great Powers, very aptly exemplified the crude spirit of the new age of 'blood and iron'. While addressing troops who were about to embark for China where the Boxers had attacked the foreign legations and murdered the German minister, the Kaiser exhorted his soldiers thus:

> ...when you come upon the enemy, smite him. Pardon will not be given. Prisoners will not be taken. Whoever falls into your hands is forfeit. Once, a thousand years ago, the Huns under their King Attila made a name for themselves, one still potent in legend and tradition. May you in this way make the name German remembered in China for a thousand years so that no Chinaman will ever again dare to even squint at a German![5]

Thanks to this impulsive and impromptu speech the Germans would henceforth be associated with the Huns. That is what the English called them during the First World War, though then this epithet was probably undeserved; the German armies behaved no worse than those of the other warring states, but in the Second World War Hitler deliberately inculcated the spirit of pitiless ferocity. The Waffen SS, who were supposed to be the finest of the German troops, were expected to behave with savage brutality, regardless of the rules of war and the Geneva Conventions, and on the Eastern Front they probably outdid Attila and the Huns.

The concept of an 'unconditional surrender' as opposed to the negotiated peace treaties of earlier, and more civilized times is again indicative of the moral certainties and the spirit of bigoted righteousness which marked the new age. In 1918 Germany did not surrender unconditionally; there was an armistice followed by a peace conference and the Treaty of Versailles, but the terms were unusually hard. Germany was forced to accept responsibility for the war, and savage reparations were recovered from it to expiate that guilt. But after the Second World War there was no peace treaty at all; neither in the case of Germany nor Japan.

Roosevelt declared that the Japanese attack on Pearl Harbour would be remembered as a date which would 'live in infamy'. What hurt him particularly was that Japan launched a surprise attack, without a formal declaration of war, while the two states were still engaged 'in conversation' for the maintenance of peace in the Pacific. Two years earlier Hitler had launched his attack on Poland after a faked attack on a German border post. In 1964 the United States would begin its bombing of North Vietnam after an almost equally fake 'incident' in the Gulf of Tonkin, where it claimed that a US destroyer had been attacked by North Vietnamese torpedo boats. In fact, it was claimed that two incidents had occurred, the first on 2 August, and the other two days later. It is now conceded that in the first incident the Americans were the aggressors (only one machine-gun bullet hit the US destroyer in the supposed attack), while the second was almost entirely imaginary. But the United States was looking for an excuse to intervene in Vietnam; the CIA was already supporting covert operations by South Vietnamese and Laotian mercenaries in the North, and this allegedly 'unprovoked attack' came handy. Haiphong was bombed by US planes immediately after the 'second' attack, and President Johnson was authorized by Congress to assist any South-East Asian country whose government was perceived as being under threat by 'communist aggression'. Some 50,000 Americans and several million Vietnamese, Laotians and Cambodians would die, and three countries would be devastated as a result of this American version of the Goebbelsian Big Lie.

Twentieth-century diplomacy, whether at the time of the two world wars, or in the Cold War, was brutally simple. And the wars of Kuwait, Iraq and Afghanistan have shown that things have not changed much. When 'Great Powers' wish to go to war, they fight regardless, however, flimsy the reasons. Notwithstanding the rhetoric, the United Nations Charter and the proliferation of international bodies created ostensibly for the promotion of international cooperation, the world is a far more dangerous place than it was in the eighteenth century.

NOTES

1. Or Hindu–if you must. That is what Toynbee called it, to distinguish it from the earlier 'Indic' civilization which was predominantly Buddhist in its last 1,000 years.
2. Or Mughal–they are one and the same thing. In Persian the name is spelled as Mughal. It is only a convention of history that reserves the word 'Mughal' for the dynasty founded by Babur.

Of course, Babur himself was a Turk descended from Timur, only his mother was a Chaghtai Mughal. But for more than a hundred years the invaders from the north-west had been Mughals, so the name was applied to even to the Turkish Timur and his descendant Babur.

3. Much of Spain was under Muslim rule, and some parts would remain so for another two hundred years.
4. The late René the Good, among other dignities, was the titular king of Jerusalem.
5. http://www.h-net.org/~german/text/gtext/kaiserreich/china.html

CHAPTER 4

Feudal Lords and *Mansabdars*

After the Germanic tribes had overrun the Western Empire, Europe was reorganized, socially and politically, on the basis of feudalism. Except for the towns which were usually outside the control of feudal lords much of western Europe was divided into manors or lordships. Some of the land was set aside as 'crown land' for the maintenance of the royal dignity, and some, no doubt, was left with the original 'Roman' inhabitants, at least in Italy, Gaul and the other provinces of the erstwhile empire. But even these were placed under the control of the notables of the old regime–the remnants of the senatorial and patrician families–on the same terms as the new baronial class.

These manors were held on the condition of military service, the holder being obliged to furnish a certain number of mounted knights (chevaliers) or men-at-arms for a specified period in a year. Very soon these lordships became heritable, and these 'lords of the manor' constituted the gentry class, the holders of single estates or manors being knights, while the holders of plural lordships were barons. Not all barons held their land directly from the king, but those who did were called 'tenants-in-chief' and many of them were soon raised to higher dignities like those of a count or an earl, and they held executive charge of 'counties'. Later on other grades would be introduced. Those holding border counties were known as 'marcher lords', or marquesses in England. In France the marquess became a marquis, while in Germany he was called a margrave, while the ordinary count or earl was a graf. The highest grade was that of duke, and very often this rank was reserved for the sons and brothers of the king.

In Norman England the lords held their estates in absolute proprietorship; in France only the 'home farms' of the estates were held as such, but all inhabitants of an estate were liable to various feudal dues, and the lord enjoyed certain monopolies like the right to hunt and fish in the forests and streams. All peasants were obliged to grind their grain (for a fee) at the lord's mill, and only the lord could set up a mill on the estate. He might, however, for a consideration allow others to do so also. Very early in history the baronial estates, and the offices of count or earl, as well as other grades became hereditary. Gradually their functions became more decorative and the actual administrative duties came to be performed by salaried officials who were usually of middle-class origin. Very often these attorneys and tradesmen had purchased their offices. They viewed it as an investment with the salary and other 'traditional' perquisites as legitimate profit. However, the nobility took its military responsibilities seriously, and even when the feudal levies were replaced by professional standing armies in the sixteenth century, the officer class remained overwhelmingly noble. In fact, right up to the First World War military and naval officers belonged overwhelmingly to the nobility or untitled landed gentry.

Somehow this never happened in India. While the *mansabdars* of Akbar—or the *khans*, *begs*, or *amirs*[1]—were essentially military officers, like the barons of medieval European rulers, their offices never became hereditary except under exceptionally weak governments. They remained working officials subject to periodic transfers, like the civil and military officers of modern times. Hence they could never become as powerful as their European counterparts, while Oriental rulers, however, they styled themselves—as sultans, *padishahs* (*badshahs*), ranas, maharanas, or mere rajas—evolved into the stereotype of the Oriental Despot, often with a Chief Executioner in constant attendance at court. The stereotype is, as is often the case, exaggerated, but at times the reality did approximate to the caricature, and instances of high-ranking officers being attacked and killed in open court, often in the presence of the monarch himself, are not entirely unknown. This was, however, more typical of the courts of Central Asia or of the Grand Seignior of Istanbul, than that of the Great Mughals.

Like the baronial nobility of western Europe, the *omrahs* of the Indian emperors derived their income from land, but while the European barons were granted landed estates in full or partial proprietorship, the Indian nobility were paid from assignments on the land revenue of particular estates known as *jagirs*. On the other hand, there was no concept of land revenue in Britain and Europe. In India the land was supposed to belong to the king,[2] and the land revenue was the rent which the cultivators paid to the monarch. Even today the word *lagaan* is applied indiscriminately to both the land revenue payable to the state,[3] and to the rent paid to the landlord. The monarch would temporarily assign this rent by way of emoluments to his nobles or *omrahs*. In normal times the revenue would be collected by the officials of the monarch and deposited in the provincial treasury from where it was drawn by the officer concerned–or more usually by his agent. Very often this agent would be the officer's banker who would actually advance the requisite funds to the officer and later recoup himself from the receipts of the *jagir*. To further safeguard against the possibility of the officer developing a vested interest in the estates or *mahals* constituting his *jagir*, the assigned estates would also be changed periodically.[4] As a general principle the *jagir* was usually far from the place of the officer's posting. Say, for instance, if the officer was posted in Malwa or the Deccan, his *jagir* might be located in Bengal or Punjab, 1,000 km away.

Thus while the European aristocracy was firmly rooted in the soil, the Indian *omrahs* were rootless. They rarely lived on their estates. They were rich, but their wealth and continued prosperity was entirely dependent on imperial favour. 'A prince today, a beggar tomorrow', such sudden and rapid turns of the wheel of fortune were not unheard of. What is more, the wealth accumulated by a great noble was liable to escheat when he died.[5] In Ottoman Turkey and Safavid Iran the great officials of the state were often slaves in the literal sense, and the property of a slave is legally heritable by the master. In India this was not usually the case, but some of the practices of the Mughal court were reminiscent of the slave empires of the Middle East and Central Asia. Some scholars have disputed whether there was actually any right of escheat. The supposed escheat, according to them, was the outcome of an audit of the funds advanced to the officer from the treasury during his lifetime,[6] but since this detailed audit was usually held only after he had died (when he could not defend himself) the result was the seizure of all his moveable and immoveable property, save for a modest subsistence allowance allowed to his family and other dependents, as an act of grace. Of course, there were many exceptions and there are recorded instances of Aurangzeb ordering that the debts of deceased *mansabdars* be written off when he found that the payment was causing hardship to some families,[7] but this was exceptional. In the eighteenth century one often reads of the houses of deceased *omrahs* being 'raided' by officials, mansions being sealed and of floors dug up in search of concealed treasure. Acting very much like the income tax officials of today, or the Vigilance Department and the CBI.

There was thus a world of difference between the European nobility and the Indian official class, notwithstanding the apparent wealth of the latter. The Great Mughal was an absolute ruler who could govern untrammeled by the rights of local magnates. There were in fact no 'local magnates' in the core area of the empire who could claim old traditional rights. There were no local representative bodies at all except for village and caste panchayats at the lowest level and these normally concerned themselves with petty matters in which the monarch was not likely to have any interest. There were no institutions comparable to the parliaments, diets or 'estates' (with two, three or even four chambers) of European states, which were a serious brake on the executive authority of kings and emperors. Thus the powers of a European monarch in matters of waging war and levying of taxes were severely circumscribed.

By the later seventeenth century most European monarchs had found ways of circumventing these limitations, and some kind of 'absolutism' had become fashionable. When the French Estates General, for instance, were summoned in 1789 they were meeting after 175 years! But the very fact that they had to be summoned at all, demonstrates the limitations of royal absolutism. Established institutions can be circumvented only up to a point.

In India, however, there were no such institutional constraints on the authority of the ruler. Regional consciousness and identity was also extremely limited. The administrative boundaries of *sarkars* and *subas* were drawn purely according to administrative convenience. In contrast the boundaries of the county of Flanders and the duchy of Brabant have remained virtually unchanged since their creation in the tenth and the twelfth centuries. Thus, when wars were fought, the bargaining blocks were historic units, counties, lordships or duchies. The partition of Luxemburg in 1890 on the basis of nationality and language marked the end of an era, and the beginning of another and far more brutal phase.

The right, to property is fundamental to Western liberties. In India, on the other hand, there was no respect for property. In theory, everything belonged to the ruler, and could be resumed at any time, for whatever reasons. This applied particularly to landed property. In Europe, on the other hand, it is remarkable how, in spite of innumerable bloody wars and violent revolutions, how much of the land still remains in the hands of the old families. In the event of civil wars or rebellions like the Jacobite uprisings in the Scottish Highlands, where the offence was high treason and the punishment death with confiscation, it is remarkable that in most cases the confiscated estates would be transferred to a younger brother or a close cousin, provided he could prove that he did not participate in the rebellion.

Castles and palatial country houses set in the middle of parks and lush gardens are inseparable from the image of the English and European nobility. They are often the seat of ancient families who might have been residing in the same mansion (frequently rebuilt or renovated) for generations, going back hundreds of years. For an Indian nobleman of the Mughal period, a set of tents–preferably a double set—was far more important. In addition he would require palanquins, horses, camels and elephants for his and his family's personal transport, besides a small army of servants, draught animals and carts. Mughal *mansabdars* and *omrahs* were almost constantly on the move. The family home, if it existed at all, would be fairly modest. If posted at the capital and occupying a powerful post the nobleman might be able to get one of the escheated mansions allotted to himself. If his rank was modest he would probably have to buy or rent a house from a local resident.

Even great *taluqdars* and zamindars in Bengal and Awadh, often controlling hundreds of villages, might be found living in small forts built of rammed earth or sun-dried bricks. There would be very little furniture in such houses, apart from bedsteads and a few chairs. Indians preferred to sit on the floor, and white sheets spread over a few mattresses with bolsters and cushions usually sufficed for the principal audience chamber. There would be no pictures or tapestries decorating the walls. There was a world of a difference between the lifestyle of *badshahs* and these rural zamindars, the equivalent of the English squirearchy.

One wonders at this striking contrast between the European and Indian ruling class. The former—whether Frankish or Norman—would immediately set about building castles and manor houses, and these were of solid stone construction. Many of them are still standing today. In India, on the other hand, we have very few examples of secular construction from those times. We have old forts and the remains of palaces, but there are scarcely any early examples of the private residences of ordinary middle-level noblemen. Perhaps race had something to do with it. The Germans were an agricultural people. Even the Scandinavians—notwithstanding their propensity for plundering raids across the seas—lived in permanent villages back home. The Turks and Mongols, on the other hand, were semi-nomadic; they lived on the usufruct of the land, but they did not cultivate it. The Eurasian steppe was arid when compared with the sheep and cattle regions of western Europe, and the herds had to keep moving. It was not simply a matter of moving them from one meadow to another. For the Eurasian nomads, tents were the only viable option.

The nomad does not therefore have that strong attachment to a particular piece of land as a farming community has. Thus, except for the sultans and *badshahs*, the houses of the lesser nobles were fairly non-descript. And while the European nobility identified itself, and derived its titles from specific territorial estates held in perpetuity, the Mughal *omrahs*—and the Tartar nobility of Asia—was content with a cash *jagir* derived from estates which were liable to frequent changes. The value of the *jagir* was fixed, the estates from which it was derived were variable. Their titles, instead of being territorial, were honorific, like *Asaf Jah*, meaning 'Of the Exalted Dignity of *Asaf* (the prime minister of King Solomon), or *Nizam-ul Mulk* meaning 'Administrator of the State' and *Safdar Jang* or 'Vanquisher in War', and so on.

It was only after the British government granted full proprietary rights to these former tax farmers that they started building large mansions and furnishing them in the European style, in a frank imitation of the European landed gentry. By that time Indians had ceased to hold important positions in the public service, except in the Princely States. The new landed gentry in the provinces of British India were only landlords, holding at best the post of honorary magistrates (usually with only 'second class' powers). Their wealth, however, enabled them to dominate elective posts in municipalities and district boards. Some of the big landlords who had cultivated close relations with the bureaucracy could hope to find themselves nominated to bodies like the Governor-General's Executive Council, where the Indian notables filled what were essentially decorative and symbolic positions. Those who had acquired a suitable education might be able to secure appointments in the lower rungs of the bureaucracy, as *tahsildars*, or in the provincial civil service, or the police.

Under the British Raj the function of the newly created landed gentry was essentially decorative. They sported titles like that of *Khan Bahadur* and *Rai Sahib*. A few were even given titles like that of raja, nawab, or maharaja, and some of them would pass themselves off as princes of 'native states' during visits to England. In reality, of course, even the mightiest 'native prince' ranked lower than the junior-most baron in the peerage of the United Kingdom. Otherwise, they were good hosts to the British bureaucrats, and entertained governors, financial commissioners and deputy commissioners to lavish *shikar* parties, dinners and *nautches.*

The British tried to inculcate among Indians the same respect for property and wealth which was customary in Britain. But when India became free in 1947 socialism was in the air, and even Britain had a Labour government. Pandit Nehru was a socialist by conviction, so among the first acts of the new government was the passage of a slew of agrarian legislations by which 'intermediary tenures' like those of zamindars and *taluqdars* were abolished and ceilings imposed on the amount of agricultural land an individual could own, the excess (if any) being acquired by the state at a fraction of the market valuation for distribution to the landless. This draconian legislation was, quite naturally, challenged, and the courts upheld the rights of the landlords and large proprietors. The government promptly amended the constitution and placed the impugned legislation beyond judicial scrutiny. And when even that proved inadequate, the constitution was once again amended and the right to property itself deleted from the chapter on Fundamental Rights!

Of course, the agrarian reforms were not easy to implement and many large proprietors were able to retain large tracts above the legal limit by circumventing the law in various ingenious ways, assisted, of course, by clever lawyers, a corrupt executive, and a dilatory judiciary. But the old intermediary tenures were abolished and even if some ingenious zamindars were able to hang on to a few hundred, or even a few thousand acres, it was no longer possible for single individuals to retain control over scores and even hundreds of villages, as had been the case formerly. Many of these former *taluqdar* and zamindar families are still wealthy and influential in politics, but nobody believes that the old order can ever be restored. The change that has occurred is accepted as irreversible. That is why one is astonished that even after half a century of Communist rule, people like the von Schwarzenbergs were able to get back even a part of their confiscated estates in Bohemia. Of course, the law of restitution under which these estates were returned is hedged in with many restrictions—agricultural lands, for instance, cannot be restored. What has been returned is, for the most part, forest and castles.

Even so, what has happened—even in the few isolated cases—is almost incredible. The von Schwarzenbergs, von Liechtensteins and others like them represented the German Catholic ascendancy which was established in the kingdom of Bohemia after the Battle of the White Mountain. For about a hundred years the Habsburgs had been kings of Bohemia. They did not acquire the Bohemian crown (or the Hungarian crown for that matter) by conquest, but by carefully arranged marriages, negotiated treaties, and managed elections. The Bohemian diet retained its independence and Bohemia had its own laws which the Habsburgs were obliged to respect. But in the intervening century Bohemia had become largely Protestant—a mélange of Utraquists, Lutherans and Calvinists—and the rule of the Catholic Habsburgs was beginning to be resented.

The reigning Emperor Mathias was old, ailing and childless. He was also King of Bohemia. In 1617 he was persuaded to step down from the Bohemian throne in favour of his cousin Ferdinand. The Bohemian crown, like that of the empire, was elective and though Ferdinand had the reputation of a bigot, for want of a better candidate and a failure of leadership among the Protestant nobles, he was accepted.

Within a year, however, the Czechs had revolted and the Bohemian estates invited Fredrick, the Elector Palatine to accept the crown. He was crowned in November 1619, thus setting off the Thirty Years War. The Protestants were, however, decisively defeated in November 1620 at the Battle of the White Mountain. The consequences were horrendous. The 'Winter King', as Fredrick was derisively called, fled, but 27 Protestant nobles were summarily executed in the principal square of the capital. Five-sixths of the Bohemian nobility went into exile and their properties were confiscated, while all Calvinists and non-Lutheran Protestants were ordered to quit the realm in three days. The confiscated estates were bestowed on German Catholics on whose loyalty Ferdinand could depend. Thus the changes wrought in Bohemia were even more drastic than those which followed the Battle of the Boyne in Ireland. It is estimated that there were 151,000 farming homesteads before the war, but their number came down to 50,000 after the war, and the population shrank from 3 million to 800,000.[8]

With this historical background it is astonishing that a former ascendancy nobleman like Karl Johannes Nepomuk von Schwarzenberg should be able to recover his ancestral castles and even become foreign minister of the Czech Republic. That the prince of Leichtenstein should have the gall to go to court against Slovakia is no less astonishing.

Because the European nobility was secure in its estates it was able to stand up to arbitrariness. The Magna Carta of 1215 is supposed to be the foundation of English liberty. It was, in fact, no such thing. It was forced upon a reluctant king by his nobles and barons, and if it guaranteed anything at all, it was primarily the rights of the barons. The succession to feudal fiefs held in chief from the king was guaranteed, even when the heir was a minor. Up to this time the king could arrange the marriages of heirs—including widows and daughters—often, virtually selling them for a profit! The Charter limited this right, a widow of a nobleman could, if she wished, remain unmarried, but in case she wished to remarry she was obliged to obtain the assent of the king. Certain other clauses protected the nobles and barons from arbitrary arrest and trial, from which are derived the writ of habeas corpus and the right to trial by a jury composed of one's peers.

King John who is also known in history as 'John Lackland' because of his poverty (he was his father's youngest son) was driven to various dubious expedients for the purpose of raising money for his wars. This was the immediate cause of the barons' defiance of his authority and the provocation for forcing him to acknowledge their rights in the Magna Carta.

In India rulers rarely had to face such acute financial distress, as John and most other European rulers had to face, at some time or the other, because of their undisputed right to the land revenue. In Britain and western Europe there was no comparable tax or levy. Indian rulers collected the land revenue because they owned all the land in theory. In feudal Europe, on the other hand, the kings owned only the royal demesnes or the crown lands. The rest of the land was owned by his nobles as tenants-in-chief of the Crown—or by free cities and towns, known as 'boroughs' in Britain, or by the Church. Thus the king's income was extremely inelastic. Whenever the king needed more money to finance his wars he had no option but to summon his Grand Council, or other representative bodies like parliaments and diets, and seek their approval to the taxes he proposed to levy. In India there was no need for such parliaments. For extraordinary requirements, like war, there were usually accumulated hoards of gold and silver to draw upon.

It is the natural tendency of kings and emperors to be despotic. Human nature in the West is no different from that in the East, and given half a chance the monarchs of Europe would have been no different from their eastern counterparts in Asia or India. The Emperors of Rome and Constantinople had been 'absolute' rulers too. But the German tribes that overthrew the Western Empire were relatively unsophisticated in political terms. Their kings or chiefs did not claim divinity; they were raised to the chiefship by popular acclaim. 'Such hearing is given to the king or state-chief as his age, rank, military distinction, or eloquence can secure—more because his advice carries weight than because he has the power to command', observed Tacitus. The observations of this Roman historian are remarkably acute even though the *Germania* was written more than 700 years before the time of Charlemagne. 'If a proposal displeases them, the people shout their dissent; if they approve, they clash their spears.'[9]

With chiefs who were little more than *primus inter pares* they divided among themselves the land which they conquered. Their chiefs or kings were as far from absolute rulers as it was possible to be. It was only when Charlemagne was crowned by Pope Leo III and acclaimed as 'Carolus Augustus, crowned by God, mighty and pacific emperor', that the seeds of a divinely ordained kingship were planted.

But notwithstanding the rise of the notion of the Divine Right of Kings and royal absolutism in the seventeenth and eighteenth centuries the European nobility remained rich and powerful. And even though the British House of Lords has long since been reduced to the position of a mere historical relic, some of its members are still the greatest landowners in the country. The Duke of Buccleuch still owns estates totaling 270,000 acres, while the Duke of Westminster owns 120,000 besides a large slice of the West End of London. The Duke of Sutherland, who still owns 90,000 acres in Scotland, owned 1.5 million acres in 1820, 'an area not equaled in the British Empire'.

Respect for property and the rule of law are responsible for the persistence of the noble families of Europe. The latter again became ingrained in the European consciousness because the power of the nobility was an effective counterfoil to royal tyranny. Besides there was the lingering influence of Roman law on the continent which had been codified by the Emperor Justinian (527-65) and forms the basis of the civil and criminal codes of most European countries, including the famous Code Napoleon of France. In Europe law never became personalized. The king could not interpret or modify it at will, as a Mughal emperor could. It was preserved by learned professionals for whom it became a source of livelihood. The phrase 'vested interest' has a derogatory connotation, but it was the vested interest of the property owning nobility and of the legal profession which prevented the rise of lawless and arbitrary tyrants which are the rule rather than exceptions in Indian history—and indeed, in the history of Asia.

The relative weakness of the Indian *omrah* would lead to other consequences, desirable in some respects, but on the whole undesirable. They were little more than 'yes men' who were wary of giving honest advice to their masters. This was noticed by European visitors to the court of the Great Mughal. Edward Terry, chaplain to Sir Thomas Row, the English ambassador to the court of Jahangir remarks in his journal:

> And this tie of theirs upon the King's favour, makes all his subjects most servile flatterers; for they will commend any of his actions, though they be nothing but cruelty; so any of his speeches, though nothing but folly.[10]

Flattery flourished no doubt in the court of Saint James as well, but no English or French nobleman ever felt obliged to abase himself to the level which was normal in the court of the Grand Mughal. No European nobleman would have ever 'gone up into a tower and cast himself headlong into the sea' merely because the emperor had commanded him to do so, or laid 'hands of violence upon his son, or the son upon his father . . . thus forgetting nature, rather than subjection'.

NOTES

1. The term for the superior officers of the state in Mughal times was *umara* or *omrah*, which is the plural of the word *amir*. As the plural form is regarded as more respectful it was more commonly used than the singular, except when it was prefixed to the name, as in 'Amir Khusro'.
2. Francois Bernier, *Travels in the Mogul Empire*, Delhi: Low Price Publications, 1989, p. 5.
3. In those states where land revenue still exists. Many states have abolished it, as a populist measure. The populism is entirely sham, because it had long since ceased to be a burden on the peasantry.
4. Irfan Habib, *The Agrarian System of Mughal India*, New Delhi: Oxford University Press, 1999, p. 301.
5. Bernier, op. cit., p. 204.
6. Ishtiaq Husain Qureshi, *The Administration of the Mughul Empire*: Delhi: Low Price Publications, 1990, p. 110.
7. Ibid.
8. Anon., *Nase Rodina,* St. Paul, MN, vol. 15, no. 4, June 2003, pp. 125-9. www.Family-lines.cz/html/Articles/30-war.htm

9. Cornelius Tacitus, *The Agricola and the Germania*; Penguin, 1970, p. 111.
10. Edward Terry, *A Voyage to East India Etc.*, London: Wilkie, Cater & Hayes, 1777, pp. 392-3.

CHAPTER 5

Continuity in European History and Society

One of the most striking features of European history is its continuity—in spite of all its violence and the fearful wars. One would have thought that nothing could be more disruptive than the Russian Revolution, but after the civil war, famines, deportations and purges, and the horrors of the Gulag Archipelago, the so-called 'dictatorship of the proletariat collapsed' in less than 75 years. True the Romanovs have not been restored but the Orthodox Church has revived, and the churches and cathedrals are again full of worshippers. The double-headed eagle and the old imperial tricolour are back, the Red Star of the atheistic USSR dimmed forever.

Likewise Spain became a republic in 1931 when King Alfonso fled the country and civil war broke out. In 1939 a Fascist dictatorship was established, but 40 years later in 1975, with the death of the dictator there was a peaceful restoration of the Bourbon monarchy. The French revolution of 1789-92 was just as violent as the Spanish—possibly more—and it sparked off a series of wars which kept Europe in turmoil for twenty-five years. But after experimenting with a Consulate, a Directory and Empire, and trying to replace Catholic Christianity with the Worship of the Supreme Being and Reason, the Bourbons returned in 1815. There would be more revolutions in the decades to come, another Napoleonic Empire, and then finally the Third Republic. The present republic passes as the Fifth, and though there has been no royalist restoration after the collapse of the Second Empire a certain Count of Paris still pretends to be the rightful king of France!

One may almost say, the more things change, the more they remain the same. Of course, that is not quite true, but compared to Europe, change is far more drastic in Indian history. The village may indeed give the impression of a timeless continuity. The people may still worship at the semi-ruined temple which was built perhaps 600 years ago, the rituals performed before the deity may appear to be timeless, and are indeed incomprehensible mumbo-jumbo for most of the worshippers, but in fact the Indian world is in many ways much more dynamic than the European. The United States of America—as one would expect of a marcher state—is of course an exception. For the past 400 years it has been in continuous flux. The flux, however, is not chaotic. There is a pattern to the change, though the elements of the design are constantly changing. One is tempted to use the simile of the kaleidoscope but even that would be inaccurate. In a kaleidoscope the constituents of the design are the same, as one turns the scope the fragments re-form and arrange themselves to make new patterns. But in the USA the elements of the design have been constantly changing. At one time we have an influx of Dutch emigrants, then Anglo-Saxons, followed by Germans, Irish, Italians, Mexicans and other assorted Hispanics, not to mention the Africans imported as slaves. You have Arabs, Turks, Russians, Poles, Greeks and all varieties of Indians and other South Asians, besides Chinese and Japanese. One may safely say that every nation, race and religion is represented in substantial numbers in the USA today. It is said, for instance, that the metropolitan area of Chicago has the largest Polish population in the world after the city of Warsaw and the Jewish population of New York exceeds that of Tel Aviv. And they still keep coming.

Europe, on the other hand, was a relatively closed society with very little immigration until fairly recent times. But after the destruction wrought by the Second World War and the resultant shortage of manpower, 'guest workers' had to be imported from overseas. But even before the two world wars, population growth rates had been declining, so much so that in the 1960s and 1970s many European countries, including the largest, France, started showing a decline in population. In Britain and France the labour shortfall was met by immigration from the former colonies and overseas dominions, from the Caribbean and South Asia in the case of the

UK, and in the case of France mainly from Africa, particularly Algeria, Senegal, and the Sahelian countries. Now all European metropolises have considerable foreign populations.

The Slavic East has seen many more changes than western and central Europe, principally on account of the social engineering attempted by communist governments in the last century. The changes wrought by the First World War were political rather than demographic with the Austro-Hungarian Empire breaking up into its national components, and the white eagle of Poland rising from the ashes after an eclipse of 125 years. The Russian Revolution did lead to a considerable exodus of 'White Russians' but there was no major movement of population, except in the Balkans where the collapse of the Ottomans led to an exchange of populations, mainly of Greeks from Asia Minor, and Turks from Thrace and Macedonia. The Armenians had been largely liquidated or dispersed before and during the war.

After the Second World War the demographic changes were much more drastic. The Polish state was pushed westward to the line of the Oder-Neisse and there was a wholesale expulsion of ethnic Germans from Russia, the Ukraine, the Baltics, Poland, East Prussia, Pomerania and Silesia. And of course most European Jews had been exterminated by the Germans as part of the 'Final Solution of the Jewish Problem'. With the communist takeovers in Czechoslovakia, Hungary and the Balkans there was another exodus of old aristocratic families. The Lobkowitzes, Kinskys, and Schwarzenbergs finally abandoned Czechoslovakia; so too the great magnate families of Hungary. Some resettled in Vienna (where many of them had town houses) while others scattered further west, to the USA, Canada and Latin America.

While Britain has been an active participant in most of the major European wars of the last 300 years it has been spared the usual horrors, since no war has actually been fought on British soil. The last full-scale invasion by a foreign prince was that led by William the Conqueror in 1066. Some of the oldest families in the peerage of the United Kingdom go back that far. Not all the titles themselves are that old, however. For instance, the present Duke of Northumberland is only the tenth member of the family to bear the title, but the family traces its descent from a certain William de Percy who came to England with William the Conqueror. In the fourteenth century one of his descendants was created Earl of Northumberland and in 1766 the earldom was raised to a dukedom. Their principal seat, Alnwick Castle, was acquired by the family in 1309 and they still own more than 100,000 acres.

The present Earl of Derby is the eighteenth Stanley to bear the title but he traces his descent from another Norman knight, Adam de Adithley who also crossed the Channel with William the Conqueror in 1066. The last Earl Fitzwilliam was only the eighth earl (the title became extinct in 1979) but the family is ancient and indeed claimed descent from the Conqueror himself. The Dukes of Devonshire, whose wealth was legendary in the eighteenth century, descend from one Sir John Cavendish, a fourteenth-century knight, but the first Cavendish was made a peer as late as 1605. Later, in the course of the century, they acquired an earldom, then a marquisate, and finally, in 1694, the dukedom.

One could go on like this. Naturally, not that many of the 500 odd peers can trace their families back to the eleventh-century knights and barons who came with the Duke of Normandy; many more were Tudor creations, others were ennobled by the Stuarts, while others became peers only in the eighteenth, nineteenth or the twentieth centuries. Descent through male primogeniture was the usual rule for old baronies and earldoms, only rarely could the title be passed on to women, so in course of time most titles tended to die out. But even if the title became extinct the property could still be inherited by a cousin or, in the case of a woman, passed on by marriage to her husband. Thus the ordinary law of inheritance facilitated the accumulation of wealth. For instance, the fourth Duke of Sutherland who died in 1913 was master of nearly 1.5 million acres in Scotland and England–that is, over 2,400 sq miles, or two and a half times the area of the Grand Duchy of Luxemburg! His holdings comprised the lands of the earldoms of Sutherland and

Stafford, and the extinct dukedom of Bridgewater. A series of marriages to heiresses by members of the Leveson-Gower family (whose original title was that of Marquess of Stafford) made the Dukes of Sutherland the largest landowners in the United Kingdom.

The amazing thing is that no one seemed to regard such accumulation of acres as obscene. There was never any movement for enabling tenants to become owners—even though a Land League had been established in neighbouring Ireland for the express purpose of financing tenancy purchase. Ireland had a history of agrarian violence, and many of the original owners had been forcibly evicted from their lands as late as the seventeenth and eighteenth centuries. This was not the case in England, where it was seemingly taken for granted that it was in the natural order of things for gentlemen to be landlords and peasants to remain tenant-farmers.

It was impossible for any private gentleman in India, even if he happened to be the highest *omrah* of the empire to accumulate such wealth, particularly in land, and even if he did, to pass it on to his heirs. Every European visitor has remarked on the wealth of the *omrahs* of Mughal India, and how freely it was expended in lavish display and the splendid *nazars* that were offered to the emperor on ceremonial occasions. Well they might, for they knew full well that as soon as they died the *diwan* of the Department of Confiscations and Escheats (*Buyutat*) would send his *sazawals* to seal their mansions and draw up a detailed list of all their property, moveable and immoveable. All that their widows and dependent children could expect was a modest subsistence allowance, and in the case of sons, the offer of employment, though they would have to start from the lowest *mansabs*, and future promotions would depend entirely on their own merits.

When the British East India Company became the paramount power in India things changed. They started remoulding Indian institutions after their own notions. Since they had been so successful against the Indian powers, they took it for granted that European—and specifically British—ways of doing things were intrinsically superior to those of the 'natives'. Thus under the

Permanent Settlement of Bengal the zamindars were made proprietors of the estates they had earlier held in farm, and the revenue demand was fixed in perpetuity. Likewise under the Taluqdari Settlement of Awadh the *taluqdars* became proprietors of the lands and villages they held, though this time the settlement was temporary rather than permanent, with the land revenue rates subject to revision at intervals of thirty years.

Under the old Mughal system the provincial *subedars* and their subordinates, the *faujdars* of *sarkars*, were subject to transfer every three or four years, but after the Nadir Shahi incursion of 1739 the Mughal administration more or less collapsed. Strong governors were able to resist transfer, and in Punjab, Bengal, Awadh, and the Deccan Viceroyalty the *subedars* soon assumed the character of provincial dynasts. The process had in fact started much earlier in the century. The English also started dealing with them as if they were sovereign entities, and after the second Anglo-Maratha War (1803-5) which left the Emperor Shah Alam a ward of the British, the latter started referring to him as the 'King of Delhi' instead of Emperor of India, which he, technically, still was.

The transfer of power from the Mughals to the British was an abrupt break with the past. It was not as sudden and as abrupt as that which followed the battle of Tarain in 1193, for the British Empire in India was a gradual accretion spread over fifty odd years. Then between the capture of Delhi in 1803 and its recapture by storm in 1857 there was the 'golden calm' of fifty odd years. But with the city's final sack in September 1857 the Indian world changed entirely. The pageant court of the poet-king was wound up; and the make-belief emperor deported to Rangoon. Half his courtiers had been killed in the massacres and executions that followed, those that survived sank into destitution and anonymity.

Fragments of 'Old India' survived in the courts of the Princely States which still covered two-fifths of the area of India. But they were mere fossilized relics of a world that had passed away, and unable to stand up to the bullying tactics of the new dominions. Within weeks of the transfer of power in August 1947 all but a handful of princes had signed Instruments of Accession with one or the other of the successor states of India and Pakistan. The last recalcitrants were forced to accede in October 1949.[1] Military intervention was necessary in only four states, viz., Junagarh, Jammu & Kashmir, Kalat and Hyderabad. Twenty-two years later the privy purses which had been granted to the rulers of some 400 states at the time of their accession—ostensibly in perpetuity—were abolished along with the princely order. It led to a split in the Congress party, but that was about all. Today, but for a handful of former princes (or rather, their sons and grandsons for most of the original princes have died by now) who are still wealthy, most of the princely families have sunk into oblivion. The transition from the British Indian Empire to the Indian Republic has been a much more drastic break with the past than anything in Europe.

Of course, one reason for the drastic breaks is the fact that our last few Universal States were set up by foreigners. The first Turkish Sultanate was set up by invaders from what is now Afghanistan. The founder of the next was a Timurid prince from Samarkand, while the last was the handiwork of a company of merchant adventurers who had come to India for the purposes of trade. Britain and Europe, on the other hand, had to suffer only one wave of largely German and Scandinavian invasions (the Avars, Huns and the Arabs were the exceptions) spread over four hundred years. Hence even the most sanguinary of the European wars and revolutions did not cause as much disruption in the long term as the Ghurid, Mughal and British conquests.

Another explanation for the persistence of the same families over hundreds of years in European history was the respect for property and the custom of primogeniture which kept the original estate intact, and facilitated its enlargement because, inevitably, some branch of the family would sooner or later become extinct and its property would be merged with that of the nearest cousin. When the heir happened to be a female, provided the original grant by which the fief was held allowed females to inherit, the marriage of the heiress would result in the merger of the estate with that of the husband. Marriage thus became a convenient method for aggrandizing family fortunes.

What applied to the nobility and gentry applied equally to sovereign princes. The most well-known case is that of the Habsburgs of Austria who built-up a considerable empire mainly by carefully arranged marriages. The most celebrated of the Habsburg monarchs is the Emperor Charles V. An abbreviated list of his titles is as follows:

> King of the Romans, Emperor Elect, Ever August, King of Spain, Sicily, Jerusalem, the Balearic Islands, the Canary Islands, the Indies, and the mainland of the far shore of the Atlantic; Archduke of Austria, Duke of Burgundy, Brabant, Styria, Carinthia, Carniola, Luxembourg, Limburg, Athens and Patras, Count of Habsburg, Flanders and Tyrol, Count Palatine of Burgundy, Hainault, Pfirt, Roussillon, Landgrave of Alsace, Count of Swabia, Lord of Asia and Africa.

He was the heir of four of Europe's leading dynasties, the Habsburgs of Austria, the Valois of Burgundy, the Trastamara of Castile, and the House of Aragon. To this sprawling agglomeration his brother Ferdinand added the kingdoms of Bohemia and Hungary by marrying Anne, the daughter of Vladislas II, King of Bohemia and Hungary.

Burgundy and the other counties and duchies of the Netherlands had been acquired by his grandfather Maximilian who had married Mary of Burgundy, the heiress of Duke Charles the Bold. Spain and the Indies and 'the far shore of the Atlantic' came from his mother Joanna the Mad, the heiress of Ferdinand and Isabella, who had married his father Philip the Fair.

Some of the titles like that of 'Duke of Athens and Patras' were only of historical interest because these territories had been conquered by the Ottomans about fifty years earlier. Charles' claim to the title derived from his Aragonese inheritance. For a few years in the later part of the fourteenth century after the Fourth Crusade they had held these territories. They soon passed to the Venetians and a Florentine family before being recovered briefly by the Byzantines. The claim to the Kingdom of Jerusalem derived from the

Angevin kings of Naples who had purchased it from Mary of Antioch in the thirteenth century. Mary's grandmother had actually been a queen of the Crusader Kingdom of Jerusalem. The other German territories like the counties of Swabia, Habsburg, Tyrol, Carinthia and Carniola were old possessions of the family. A series of carefully arranged marriages and fortuitous deaths had made this agglomeration possible.

But even before the Habsburgs there had been the so-called Angevin Empire. The counts of Anjou, from which place the dynasty derives its name, eventually succeeded to the throne of England after the twenty troubled years that followed the death of King Henry I of the Norman house in 1135. Later the English Angevins acquired the huge territories of Aquitaine when its duchess, Eleanor, the divorced consort of King Louis VII of France, married King Henry II of England. The duchy with its dependent counties covered more than half of France. The acquisition of these territories, held nominally as fiefs of the French crown, would lead to constant friction with the French kings and what is known as the Hundred Years War. Ultimately almost everything would be lost.

During the course of these wars the French kings had dispossessed the English Angevins (or Plantagenets as they were also known) and in 1247 Louis VIII gave the county to one of his younger sons Charles, thus launching the Counts of Anjou of the Second Creation. By Louis' marriage to Beatrice, heiress of Raymond Berenger IV of Provence, he had already became Count of Provence. On an invitation from the Pope who was at the time engaged in a struggle against Emperor Fredrick II of Hohenstauffen, he conquered Sicily (which Fredrick had inherited from his mother Constance) and received it in fief from the pope, thus becoming King of Sicily in 1266. About forty years later his great grandson Charles set out to win the Hungarian crown. His grandmother Mary was a daughter of King Stephen V of Hungary (1270-2). The Arpad house of Hungary was on the verge of dying out and the Hungarian magnates were in search of a successor. Mary was invited to accept the throne. First she proposed to send one of her sons but he died before he could set out. Then she sent her grandson Charles. Charles was successful and this dynasty of Hungarian Angevins lasted from 1307 to 1395. One of them, Louis (1342-82), known as 'the Great', was also able to get himself elected to the Crown of Poland in 1370. His mother Elizabeth was the daughter of King Wladislaw I, last but one of the House of Piast, another royal house which was fading out. He and, after him, his daughter Jadwiga, ruled Poland for twenty-nine years. Jadwiga married Jogaila, the Grand Duke of Lithuania, and their descendants ruled the Commonwealth of Poland and Lithuania for nearly two hundred years.

Nothing comparable can be found in Indian history. Because a ruling prince or emperor was invariably polygamous with a well-stocked *zenana* there was little danger of the royal line ever dying out. And because the *zenana* was a very private place it was not very difficult to induct a spurious infant and pass him off as a genuine son, should the need arise to do so. While the usual practice was to follow primogeniture, the death of the ruler would often be followed by a short fratricidal struggle with the fittest succeeding to the throne. In the absence of a direct heir any prince–any son, grandson or great-grandson–would do.

Among the native Hindu princes who still ruled in their principalities in Rajasthan, central and south India, the usual practice was to adopt a suitable heir. Of course, this happened only when the ruler died suddenly and the principal or favourite consort had been unable–for whatever reason–to introduce a spurious infant in the harem. It was not necessary that the adopted heir should be from the immediate family. Sometimes a 'search committee' would be constituted, and the widowed queen would be guided in her choice by wise and able councillors. Often the adopted heir was a mature and grown up man rather than a child, as happened in the case of the house of Holkar after the death of Malhar Rao in 1766. His only son Khande Rao had died in 1754, and had left a child by the name of Malhi Rao. This boy was of weak intellect, and in the words of his mother, the saintly Ahalya Bai, a 'perfect demon'.[2] Fortunately, before long he too died, and in 1767 Ahalya Bai selected one Tukkoji Holkar as her adopted 'son'. Tukkoji was a grown man, had commanded the *paigah* or household troops and was quite unrelated to the family. The mother was actually younger than her adopted son!

Thus Indian states could be self-perpetuating, but unless the circumstances were exceptional they tended to remain small. The usual method of expansion in Europe—by convenient marriages with heiresses—was not available in India, simply because there were no heiresses with heritable territorial estates!

Property and principalities could only be transmitted through men. Only one case comes to mind where a principality passed peacefully from one family to the other, that of the kingdom of Delhi, which passed from the Tomaras to the Chauhans some time in the later half of the twelfth century. Anangpala Tomar was the last of the Tomara kings of Delhi and he is supposed to have adopted his daughter's son Prithvi Raj, Raja of Ajmer, as his son. But the facts are not clear, and it may well have been an usurpation by the grandson.

In India the only way in which a state could expand was by naked aggression. It was necessary to provoke a war on any pretext, demand submission, and force the other party to its knees.

The present Indian republic has no connection with any previous Indian state. Its ceremonies and rituals have no resemblance with those of the Mughal court—or of any other Indian princely court for that matter. In fact, one can question whether there is any ceremonial at all. There is no prescribed 'court dress' and the modern Indian politician is conspicuous only by the shabbiness of his appearance. The Rashtrapati Bhavan is a worthy palace; some of the pomp and circumstance of the old British viceroys still lingers in its halls, in the uniformed ADCs, the mounted bodyguard, and ceremonies like Beating the Retreat. But official functions are chaotic and eminently forgettable. While some decorum is observed in Delhi, in the states, the Governor's Garden Party given on the occasion of Independence and Republic days gets over in half an hour, with the majority of the guests as non-descript as imaginable.

Pageantry and style went out of fashion the day we became independent. There is virtually no link with tradition.

NOTES

1. Interestingly the last states to accede to India were Manipur and Tripura. They signed merger agreements as late as October 1949.
2. John Malcolm, *A Memoir of Central India*, London: Parberry, Allen & Co., 1832, p. 158.

CHAPTER 6

Aristocracy in Europe and in India

Territorial aristocracies and landed gentry may be parasites; they serve little or no economic purpose, but they do lend a certain grace and stability to society. They also lend colour to what can otherwise seem a drab and utilitarian world. It was only in the twentieth century that these terms acquired a derogatory connotation. Till then it was taken for granted that they were indispensable pillars of the state and society.

In the UK, members of parliament were the unpaid legislators of the kingdom and its overseas possessions, including India. The government, that is, the ministry, was drawn largely from its ranks. So were the bulk of the army and navy officers, the civil services, and the magistracy. Except for the members of the House of Commons who had to stand for election, the others were appointed by the exercise of patronage, on the basis of family connections. It was taken for granted that membership of the landowning class, and public school or university education was sufficient qualification for governing the state. It was only in the 1850s, after the setting up of the Civil Service Commission on the recommendations of the Northcote-Trevelyan Report of 1854, that patronage gave way to competition, and thus the doors were gradually opened to the sons of the middle class.

But the transition was gradual. The position of the landed gentry as the power elite rested on popular sanction. Until the industrial revolution class conflict in the Marxian sense was practically unknown in Britain. As Cannadine observed, the majority of the people unquestioningly accepted the gentry's right to rule.

> Landowners had leisure, confidence, experience, expertise: they had time to govern, they were expected to govern. The business of busi-

nessmen was business; the business of landowners was government. For generations, and in some cases for centuries, the same gentry and noble families had sent representatives to Parliament.... To most people this was the natural order of things: it had been ever thus.[1]

In no other European country was the domination of the landed classes as complete as in the United Kingdom. The British aristocracy was the smallest, the most exclusive and the richest of all continental nobilities. In any other European country its untitled landed gentry would have passed as nobility. Even as late as the last quarter of the nineteenth century the UK was dominated by great estates. Sixty-six per cent of the area of the UK was comprised of estates of 1,000 acres or more—and in Scotland this percentage was as high as 93 per cent! By themselves the 525 peers of the United Kingdom owned about 15 million acres, the 28 dukes, alone owning 4 million.[2]

In France the revolution had had its effect. It is estimated that in nineteenth-century France only about 20 per cent of the land was actually owned by the descendants of the old feudal nobility. Before the revolution the percentage was about 25 per cent.[3] In Prussia the *junkers* owned about 40 per cent of the land while in backward, reactionary Spain the percentage reached the figure of 52. In Europe the size of the average estate was also much smaller. In pre-revolutionary France most noble holdings varied between 200 and 400 acres.[4] Only in Austria-Hungary do we find estates which are comparable to those of the higher nobility of the United Kingdom.[5] There were about two dozen aristocratic families in Austria with over 250,000 acres apiece, with the Prince von Schwarzenberg lording over 360,000 acres. In Hungary the Esterhazy family held close to a million acres, followed closely by the Andrassys, Karolys and Schonborns.

However, in Europe the great magnates tended to dominate particular regions. In Germany, the *junkers* were dominant east of the Elbe. In Cis-Leithanian Austria large estates were predominant in Bohemia and Moravia, while in Trans-Leithania great magnates were to be found in Hungary and Slovakia. In Italy great landlords were the rule in Sicily, Calabria and the Romagna. In the south they were also usually absentees.

But in spite of the relatively small nobility the greatest concentration of large proprietors was to be found in Britain. One might expect from this pattern that the British peasantry would be the most oppressed in Europe, and that agrarian unrest, with its usual accompaniments of arson and murder, would be the bane of the British countryside. But curiously–apart from Ireland and to some extent Scotland–the British Isles presented a picture of relative peace and stability. In the same period, France underwent three revolutions, and practically every German and Italian state was shaken by revolution in 1848.

There was indeed agricultural distress in the English countryside. In Scotland thousands of crofters were evicted from their tiny smallholdings so that the landlords–some of them the greatest magnates in the country–could replace them with sheep, but oddly enough there was no revolution. There was only the so-called Peterloo massacre of August 1819 in which 15 people were killed and about 500 injured when cavalry was used to disperse a crowd of perhaps 50,000 demonstrators–most of them industrial workers agitating for a broader franchise.

The variations in the aristocratic and landed classes in the different countries of Europe are not very important, for even in Europe, in spite of the numerous revolutions, at the end of it the social order did not change all that dramatically. If primogeniture was not the usual custom in Europe, it only meant that the numbers of noblemen were much greater than in the UK.[6] They were also, naturally, much poorer with far smaller estates.

A noble class with its power based on landownership is a force for stability, because of its determination to defend its property. The European nobilities derived their strength from their landed estates. Royal favour was courted because court favours and appointments enabled the nobles to increase their income by which they could acquire additional estates. Occasionally, if one was lucky, a grateful monarch might shower a successful general with titles, decorations and palaces. Thus John Churchill, a scion of minor gentry, who started life as a page of King Charles II, rose ultimately to become the first Duke of Marlborough, a Knight of the Garter, *and* of the Golden Fleece, and to cap it all, a Prince of the Holy Roman Empire!

The rise of Arthur Wellesley, Duke of Wellington, by birth a younger son of a minor Irish earl and the victor of Assaye and Waterloo, was scarcely less spectacular. He was a mere colonel when he arrived in India in 1797. Five years later he was a major-general; on his return he was appointed a Knight Companion of the Bath. After his victories in Portugal and Spain he received dukedoms from both governments, and was created, successively, a baron, a viscount, and finally a duke by his own king. In 1810 he had been voted a pension of 2,000 pounds per annum, and again, on two separate occasions, grants of 400,000 and 200,000 pounds to enable him to acquire estates to support the dignity of his noble titles. Then he was honoured with the Knighthood of the Garter by his own monarch, with the Order of the Golden Fleece from Spain, besides other chivalric decorations from Austria, Prussia and Russia.

The king and his nobles lived in a state of mutual interdependence, and there was little danger of a noble family being destroyed by the arbitrary confiscation of its estates by the crown. Only in the event of a civil war, or disputed successions when a noble might choose the wrong side, or persist in refusing to acknowledge the new dynasty, do we read of confiscations by the passing of 'Acts of Attainder'. The violent overthrow of King James II in 1688 and the dogged loyalty shown by some families to the 'Jacobite' cause are an interesting example. After the seizure of the English throne by William of Orange (albeit on the invitation of Parliament) Ireland rose in support of the deposed king. The uprising was crushed ruthlessly in a sea of blood. There would be further risings in the Scottish Highlands in 1715 and 1745, and a number of noblemen accompanied the fallen monarch into exile (some were even executed), but interestingly, most of the confiscated estates of the attainted nobles were re-assigned to other members of the same family who had not compromised themselves.

For instance even though the Earl of Derwentwater was attainted and beheaded for participating in the Jacobite rebellion of 1715, his son John, who had not been compromised in the rebellion was, allowed to succeed to his title and estates. The title, however, became extinct with him, because he died issueless and the next in line, his uncle Charles, who had been living in exile on the continent was executed in 1745 on his capture while on the way to join the rising of the Young Pretender, Prince Charles Edward Stuart. He had been condemned for his role in the rising of 1715, and he was beheaded in execution of the sentence passed in 1715.

Lord William Gordon, sixth Viscount Kenmure, was the other peer who suffered execution along with Derwentwater. His estates were declared forfeit, but when they were put up for auction his widow was able to buy them back, and pass them on to her son Robert when he came of age. His nephew who was a captain, was elected to Parliament and was able to restore his family honours by means of a private bill which he was able to see through Parliament. Several other attainted peerages were successfully revived by the passing of similar private acts of Parliament, but the process was slow and expensive.

On the whole remarkably few noblemen paid the supreme penalty in these Jacobite rebellions. Only two peers were beheaded in 1715, and three in 1745. The number of commoners executed was much higher—being 120 in 1745-6. Nearly 1,000 were transported to the colonies.

We observe a similar sensitivity for the rights of foreign princes and nobles. When the Polish kingdom was partitioned between Russia, Prussia and Austria there was no general scramble for Polish lands among the nobility of these states. Except for the nobles who accompanied Kosciusko into exile, or who were deported to Siberia, the rest of the Polish nobility remained secure and undisturbed in their estates. The Norman conquest of England in 1060 is the solitary example where the overthrow of a dynasty led to a wholesale expropriation of an earlier aristocracy. But those were the Dark Ages.

France experienced a bloody revolution towards the end of the eighteenth century. The Reign of Terror was followed by the counter-revolution of Thermidor, which installed the Directory in power. The latter, in turn, was replaced by the Consulate which in turn evolved into the Empire of Napoleon. After that had collapsed and the emperor had been transported to St. Helena, the Bourbons returned to power. But within fifteen years another 'bourgeois' revolution resulted in the installation of Louis Philippe of the Orleans branch in place of Charles X. Eighteen years later there was yet another revolution which ended ultimately with the revival of the empire under another Napoleon. Interestingly, Napoleon III recognized all noble titles. Thus in the Second Empire there were some nobles of the *ancien regime* with titles dating prior to 1789, others who were the creation of the First Empire, then came the Orleanist creations, and finally, the new nobility of the Second Empire.

The Second Empire lasted less than twenty years. But even though the Third Republic (which replaced it) reiterated the principles of equality it did not attempt to actually abolish titles of nobility. They had been abolished in 1789, and again in 1848. In 1852 they were restored by decree but in spite of the collapse of the Second Empire and the proclamation of the Third Republic they were never officially abolished. They are still in use today. There is, however, no office comparable to the College of Heralds to regulate the use of titles, but anyone wishing to use his title can apply to the minister of Justice, who can, after investigation, confirm his right by an order.

It is a little strange that so little animus exists against the nobility today. Once upon a time Louis de Rouvroy, Duc de Saint-Simon (1675-1755) had claimed that the French nobility was descended from the Frankish conquerors of Roman Gaul, and therefore racially distinct from the common people. During the debates of the National Assembly the Abbe Sieyes is quoted as having questioned: 'Why does not (the Third Estate) send all these families who still make the crazy claim that they are descended from a race of conquerors back to the forests of Franconia?'[7]

As a matter of fact, whatever may have been the origins of the French aristocracy, in the eighteenth century the majority of noble families were of middle-class origin. As compared to England the French nobility was much more open. There had never been a proper registry of the French nobility,[8] and patents of nobility could be obtained by purchase if an applicant could prove that his family had held certain specified offices for a specific number of generations. Even though the offices were supposed to be a monopoly of the noble class, rich bourgeois were ready to pay large sums for long-term benefits, and a venal administration was eager to connive at the fraud. The new creations which were the result of this process were officially distinguished from the old nobility, *la Noblesse de l'Epee*, as *la Noblesse de la Robe.* Since the middle classes had long aspired to the rank and status of nobility, once the revolutionary fervour had passed aristocratic titles again became *la mode.* Thus ultimately all titles of nobility were accepted by a republican France, irrespective of the regime that had granted them. It is true, however, that by that time titles had become merely decorative, an affectation of social snobs. Perhaps that is why no one objected to them.

In India the landed interest was destroyed by the agrarian reforms of the early 1950s when all 'intermediary' tenures like zamindari, *taluqdari* and *ala-malkiyat* were abolished. Subsequently ceilings were imposed on the amount of land an individual could own. While the first phase of reforms was relatively easy to implement, the second phase of the ceiling legislation proved much more difficult and was widely evaded. But with the passage of half a century one can safely say that, by and large, there are no large proprietors left. There are indeed a few large holdings but these are stud farms, orchards and private forests for which special exemptions were provided by most states. Some enterprising smallholders also lease in substantial acreages from a large number of small and marginal farmers, but even these farms are small when compared to the *latifundia* of Canada, the United States, Latin America and Australia. The huge holdings of the *taluqdars* of Awadh and Bengal zamindars—which often extended over tens of thousands of acres comprising scores or even hundreds of villages are gone forever.

All these great estates came up during the British Raj. Under the Mughals land *per se* had little value. There was no properly developed land market. Some of the older zamindari and *taluqdari* estates were old and ante-dated the British conquest, but the zamindars and *taluqdars* of that period did not claim to be actual owners of the land. They only held the zamindari rights. At that time these were true intermediary tenures. The zamindar was responsible for collecting the land revenue from individual cultivators and depositing it in the government treasury through the collector, who was then known as the *nazim*, *faujdar*, *chakladar*, or *aumil.* For this purpose he maintained a network of petty officials who maintained the records, and to cover his expenses he retained a percentage of the collections. In addition he was entitled to rent-free land (known as *nankar* in north India) in the village. This was the equivalent of the home farm of the British and French lord of the manor. If there was no actual home farm in the village he, nonetheless, made a further deduction on its account in his favour. Sometimes the zamindar was actually the descendant of an ancient chiefly lineage which had been allowed to perform these functions by virtue of the influence which his family might still be exercising in the area. More often he would be the scion of an old court official who, by corruption and mani-pulation, had acquired the 'farm' of the estate in the event of a default by an earlier intermediary.

When the East India Company first acquired the *diwani* of Bengal from the Emperor in 1765 there was no immediate change in the administrative arrangements of the province. The *diwan's* duty was the collection of revenue and only he could authorize disbursements from the collections, even for the ordinary expenses of administration. The *subedar* or *nazim* was the executive authority of the province, its chief magistrate and police officer. This was the standard Mughal practice, particularly in the larger and richer provinces, to ensure that authority in the provinces remained divided and rebellion was impossible except in the unlikely event of both the *subedar* and *diwan* joining hands.

Murshid Quli Khan, also known as Jafar Khan, was appointed by Aurangzeb as *diwan* of Bengal. At the time the Emperor's grandson, Azim ush-Shan, was the *subedar* of the province. Azim was killed in the fratricidal struggle that followed the death of his father, Shah Alam Bahadur Shah in 1712. When Azim ush-Shan left for Lahore he had left his son Farukhsiyar behind at Patna. When the news of Azim ush-Shan's death was received at Patna, Farukhsiyar raised an army and set out, up the country to challenge the accession of his uncle. Since then Jafar Khan and his descendants had ruled unchallenged in Bengal, holding both the offices of *diwan* and *nazim*.

With the appointment of the 'Company Bahadur' to the *diwani*, the two offices were again separated, but under the changed circumstances the system became unworkable. The Company and the Nawab-Nazim were by no means equals. The Company was now a king-maker; it had defeated the emperor himself the previous year and the latter, lodged in the fort of Allahabad garrisoned by the Company's soldiers, was its virtual prisoner. The *nawab-nazim* was a mere 'phantom', a 'man of straw'. His standing army had been so emasculated that it was bereft of all offensive potentiality. It was in fact no other than his *suwarry* of which the number of sepoys and peons was limited by the Company. 'Nor can the Nabob have occasion for an army, who has no possessions to lose, and who is protected in the place he holds by the forces of another power, which the Company, by the treaty which has been produced, have undertaken to protect him in.'[9]

In the later part of Aurangzeb's reign, particularly during the *diwani* of Murshid Quli Khan, a number of large zamindars came into prominence, and during the lax administration of his successors the power of these mushroom zamindars continued to grow. When the Company took over the *diwani*, about half of Bengal was held by half a dozen large zamindars. Most of them were from relatively new families. Foremost, among them was the Raja of Burdwan. The family traced its descent from a Punjabi Khatri of the Kapoor clan who had come to Bengal during the reign of Jahangir and set himself up as a banker and trader. Under the Permanent Settlement the Burdwan *raj* was assessed at Rs. 40,15,109. The second largest estate was that of Rajshahi, which in the lifetime of its founders had swollen to extend over 13,000 square miles with a rent-roll of over Rs. 27 lakh.[10]

The Bengal Presidency also included Bihar, which was also famous for its great zamindari estates. The largest of them all was the Darbhanga *raj*. Its chief who initially bore the title of Raja, was later raised to the rank of a Maharaja. In due course he was conferred the even higher dignity of *Maharajadhiraja*. The zamindari covered over 2,400 sq miles (or 1.53 million acres), comprising 4,495 villages in Bihar and Bengal, and employed about 7,500 officials. The zamindars were brahmins and traced their fortunes to one Pandit Mahesh Thakur who was appointed by Emperor Akbar in 1577 as governor or zamindar of Mithila in north Bihar, which had been in a state of chronic anarchy ever since the Afghan uprising in the reign of Humayun. Since Mithila had a large brahmin population, the emperor hoped that another brahmin would be able to bring order to the region. His expectations were not belied, and the power of Mahesh Thakur's descendants continued to grow. In 1947 Darbhanga was arguably the biggest zamindari in India.

Another great magnate was the Raja of Ramgarh, now in the state of Jharkhand. The Ramgarh *raj* was spread over three districts and comprised 3,672 villages, but its income of Rs.15 lakh was derived more from mining than agriculture. The Ramgarh family was one of the oldest families of the region, and it traced its descent from one Baghdeo who established himself in the area around the end of the fourteenth century. The Gaya Kothi estate extended over 1,550 villages; its zamindars were also an old family, tracing their descent from an officer of Sher Shah Suri who established himself in the area in the sixteenth century.

Under the Mughal revenue system the zamindar was only a tax farmer contracted to collect and pay a specified sum for the *parganas* under his charge. Under ideal conditions, as visualized in the *Ain-i-Akbari* there ought to have been no revenue-farmers and the state was expected to collect the revenue directly, on the basis of a proper settlement, from the cultivators through their representatives. This system was known as *amani.* But with the breakdown of administration and increasing corruption in the later part of the seventeenth century harassed *subedars* found it expedient to farm out the revenue to speculative contractors, sometimes also known as *ijaradars.* Bids would be invited with the original figures of Todar Mal's settlement serving as a guide, and the contract would be awarded to the highest bidder (and doubtless who also offered the maximum kickbacks). When the *ijaradar* had become sufficiently established he would be recognized as a zamindar, the zamindari right being essentially the right to collect the land revenue. This at least was the system that prevailed in Bengal.

For some time the British continued with the prevailing system, farming out the revenues on ten year leases known as Temporary Settlements, but recognizing that the prevailing system was a bad one and ruinous to the peasantry the thinking gradually veered round in favour of a Permanent Settlement. At the same time Lord Cornwallis replaced Warren Hastings as governor-general. The latter, a Suffolk landowner, decided to reform the revenue system of Bengal by making the zamindars actual owners, like English landlords, and fixing the land revenue once and for all.

The same thing happened in the south after the annexation of Malabar following the defeat of Tipu Sultan in 1792. The petty chiefs or *janmis* who had exercised authority and collected the revenues on behalf of Haidar Ali and Tipu, and earlier on behalf of the Zamorin, the Kollattiri or Nambiar chiefs of that area were traditionally entitled to a well-defined share of the produce, or the land revenue, for their pains. But post-annexation, they were constituted the lords of the soil to the detriment of the actual tillers or *ryots.*[11]

Cornwallis probably had the English example of improving landlords in mind when proposing the Permanent Settlement. He would have been familiar with the agricultural improvements being effected at Holkham Hall by Coke of Norfolk, by way of crop rotations and animal husbandry. Norfolk, after all, was a neighbouring county, to the north of his native Suffolk. Coke was not alone in his experiments; there were many improving squires like him, but being a notable Whig parliamentarian, with friends like Charles James Fox, he was the most well known.

But the hopes of the reformers were belied. The settlement rates were pitched much too high. Many of the great zamindaries defaulted and were broken up and put to auction. The great Rajshahi *raj* all but disappeared, so did the Dinajpur zamindari. The Rajas of Nadia, Bishenpore and Cossijurah also lost great swathes of their lands. Burdwan alone survived, but only just. In about 15 years few of the original zamindars with whom the Permanent Settlement had been made retained their properties which were sold and resold to merchants and speculators.

The government's demand had been fixed notionally at tenth-elevenths of the rent paid to the zamindar by the cultivating *ryot.* At such high rates only the most careful management could have enabled a zamindar to meet his instalments on time, and zamindars, by temperament, were not good bookkeepers. If the intention of government had been to break up the largest estates for political reasons, that, certainly, was achieved.

About ten years later a series of Anglo-Maratha wars resulted in a slew of new territory being annexed by the Company Bahadur. The hapless Nawab of Awadh had also been forced to cede his Doab districts to satisfy the Company's claims for alleged arrears of the subsidy payable by him to defray the cost of the military force maintained by the Company, ostensibly for his protection. British territory now extended right up to Delhi and the Himalayan foothills. The question of how to settle these 'ceded districts', which came to be known as the North-Western Provinces of Agra, now agitated the Bengal government.

Disillusionment with the supposed benefits of a landlord-oriented settlement had set in after seeing the unhappy results of the Permanent Settlement. The settlement of this province was therefore pro-peasant and anti-landlord. Where zamindari or *taluqdari* rights were claimed by chiefly families, a very high degree of proof was demanded. Most *taluqdars* were uneducated and documentary evidence was seldom available. For them the trenchant sword spoke louder than pieces of paper. Thus great estates were broken up and disappeared. The great Mainpuri *raj* shrank to a mere 40 villages—about a fourth of its original extent. When the rump state of Awadh (Oudh) was annexed in 1856 the trend was still anti-landlord.

In England too Benthamite 'Utilitarianism' was the fashion of the day, and seen through its spectacles landlords served no useful purpose. Their Indian counterparts, zamindars, *taluqdars*, etc., had even less justification. The chief commissioner was directed to proceed to the formation of a temporary settlement, to be made 'village by village with the parties actually in possession, but without recognition, either formal or indirect, of their proprietary right'. It was declared 'as a leading principle, that the desire and intention of the Government is to deal with the actual occupants of the soil, that is, with the village zamindars or with the proprietary coparcenaries which are believed to exist in Oudh, and not suffer the interposition of middlemen, such as *taluqdars*, farmers of the revenue, and such like,' whose claims, 'if they have any tenable claims, might be more conveniently considered at a future period.'[12]

In the first summary settlement after the annexation, out of 25,543 villages held by *taluqdars* at annexation, 13,640 were settled with them. Thus the change was by no means as radical as it was intended to be, but nonetheless the area under *taluqdars* was nearly halved. But very soon the policy would be reversed. The Mutiny, which broke out shortly after, shook the British. As a consequence the East India Company was swept away, and its rule replaced by the direct rule of the Crown.

It was felt that one of the reasons for the violence of the Mutiny in Awadh was the new post-annexation administration's perceived hostility towards *taluqdars*. It was also observed that in no part of Awadh had the annexation produced less change in the status quo than in the trans-Ghaghra districts of Gonda and Bahraich where very few villages were lost by *taluqdars*. Yet in no part of Awadh did the latter join more readily in the revolt. It was also observed that so many villagers whom the Summary Settlement had recognized as independent landholders, cut their own throats by joining the *taluqdars* by whom their lands had been absorbed, thus putting at the service of the upholders of the *taluqdari* system an argument which, under the circumstances, was so nearly irresistible that one cannot be surprised at its success.

'The people,' it was argued, 'evidently regard the *taluqdars* as their natural leaders. Why then, should we go out of our way to force on them a more democratic system for which their own conduct shows them to be unfitted? Let us make terms with the *taluqdars*, and the country will be pacified.'[13]

Whether or not they were natural leaders might have been debatable, but the die had been cast in their favour. Military expediency urged an early conciliation, the prospect of a summer campaign in the malarial grasslands and forests of the Terai against an elusive enemy who employed guerrilla tactics was daunting. Once the main centres of the rebellion, namely Delhi and Lucknow, had been reconquered, Lord Clyde (Sir Colin Campbell), the British general commanding the field armies, had no stomach left for the inglorious and heart-breaking task of besieging numberless forts and losing men at every one. If undertaken it would have cost many lives and prolonged the fighting for another year.

Lord Canning, newly arrived in the country as governor-general and viceroy, sincerely believed that a *taluqdari* settlement would be in the interest of tranquillity and would materially assist in the re-establishment of British authority. Perhaps he believed in what he said; as a landed nobleman he would naturally be inclined to favour the restoration of the *taluqdars*. Indeed he went so far as to assert that the *taluqdari* system was the 'ancient, indigenous, and cherished system of the country'.

A proclamation was published declaring that with the exception of six named estates, the 'proprietary right in the soil of the province is confiscated to the British government, which will dispose of that right in such manner as to it may seem fitting'. This was speedily followed by another calling upon all *taluqdars* to come to Lucknow and receive the *sanads* of their estates from the hands of the chief commissioner. Hesitantly at first, the *taluqdars* trooped in and were pleasantly surprised at the liberal terms being offered. A second summary settlement was rushed through, and the status quo ante was largely restored. Only those *taluqdars* who had participated in acts of violence against Europeans lost their estates. Otherwise it was practically a general amnesty.

There were differences in detail between the Permanent Settlement of Bengal and the Awadh *taluqdari* system. Unlike the former this was *istamrari* or temporary, and subject to revision every thirty years. It was similar insofar that the Awadh *taluqdar* and the Bengal *zamindar* were both made actual proprietors of their estates; they were no longer mere tax farmers.

The spirit behind the new settlement is revealed in the concluding paragraph of the *sanad* which was given to the *taluqdars* which stated that it was 'another condition of this sanad', that the *taluqdar*, would to the best of his power, try to promote the agricultural resources of his estate, and if there happened to be any holders of 'subordinate rights' on the estate they would be 'preserved in their former rights'. The pious intention was therefore to transform the turbulent taluqdars into 'improving landlords' like the squires of rural England.

Pious intentions like these usually remain intentions, and the condition of the peasantry did not improve. In fact, in most cases it deteriorated as their 'subordinate rights', where they existed, were, by and large, ignored. As Irwin observed, occupancy rights with fixed rents were respected, if at all, only where the tenants (for such indeed was the position to which they had been reduced) belonged to the superior castes, namely Rajputs and Brahmins—who were 'the most idle and least improving classes of the agricultural body'. The *taluqdars* themselves were mostly Rajputs and they looked down upon the Kurmis, Muraos, and Kachhis who were far more industrious and hard-working. These were at an extreme disadvantage in establishing their rights, for the person who had to adjudicate upon their claims was very often the landlord himself. *Taluqdars* had in many cases been vested with magisterial and judicial powers—just like the English landlords who sat on the county bench and functioned as Justices of the Peace.

Even in Britain and Europe the baronial and knightly class who held the manorial estates in the early Middle Ages took a long time to transform themselves into 'improving landlords'. They were the ones who had reduced the peasants to serfdom in the first place, and their greed for land had resulted in the enclosure movement which resulted in the expropriation of the rights of the petty peasantry in the village commons. In many estates the enclosed commons became the nobleman's park or hunting preserve, and this process was still going on in the eighteenth century.

In the Scottish Highlands it would continue well into the nineteenth century when great magnates like the countess of Sutherland, William Chisholm of Strathglas, Alistair Ranaldson of Glengarry and a score of others evicted their tenants by the thousands—replacing them with sheep because sheep paid better. The horrors visited by them upon their tenants and crofters were no less than those visited by Raja Darshan Singh and his sons Raghubar Dayal and Man Singh[14] upon the peasants of Gonda-Bahraich and Daryabad-Rudali where they served as *nazims*. The manner in which the great Mehdona estate (later renamed as the Ayodhya estate) was put together by force, fraud, favour and coercion makes most unedifying reading.

Until the Highland chiefs cleared their land of their tenants and replaced them with sheep they had been feudal chiefs. The cash rents which they received from their 'tack-men' and crofters were pitiful. Macdonnel of Glengarry, for example, held 600 sq miles of territory which yielded only 300 pounds of rentals—but he could, when required, raise 1,000 swordsmen. The Highland chiefs reckoned their strength by the number of swords they could command, rather than in terms of pounds sterling. But when greed overcame them and they became capitalists, they heartlessly turned on their tenants, not hesitating to evict them, even in the middle of winter.

The *taluqdars* and zamindars of Awadh and Bengal were by no means feudal chiefs. A few—*very few*—were indeed the descendants of ancient ruling dynasties, but most were former courtiers and officials who had entered upon the risky, but often highly lucrative, *métier* of a revenue farmer as a business venture. Under the *nawabi* their tenures whether as *aumil* or *ijaradar* were uncertain, but suddenly in 1858 they found they had become owners of the estates they had formerly held in farm—owners in perpetuity.

It had taken several centuries for the descendants of brutal baronial lords to be transformed into improving landlords in England. May be with time the landlords created by the British in India might also have achieved a similar transformation. But within a hundred years of the British annexation of Awadh the British Indian Empire had collapsed, and *zamindari*, *taluqdari* and other similar intermediary tenures had also been abolished.

The English had tried to create an Indian landed nobility after their own pattern in the British Isles. It was a new experiment which did not last, but curiously the old Mughal *mansabdari* system had certain resemblances to the Russian nobility. With a few exceptions the status of Russia's peerage derived not from territorial rights but from loyal and extended service to the Czar. While many of the patents of nobility had included grants of landed estates, the great majority of Russian nobles were completely landless. There was a table of ranks consisting of fourteen parallel grades for military and career civil servants, with emphasis on time served rather than merit. Until 1896 military officers of non-noble origins acquired hereditary noble status upon entering the fourteenth or lowest rank while civil officers had to rise to the eighth grade to reach that distinction. Later nobility was restricted to the top seven military ranks and the top five civil grades. One is reminded of the esteem with which 'gazetted officers' and government pensioners used to be regarded in India during the British Raj. The main difference was that in Russia nearly half the nobles bore hereditary titles.

Thus, in 1858 there were around 610,000 hereditary nobles in the 50 provinces of European Russia. By 1897 their number had risen to 886,000 besides 487,000 Czar-appointed personal nobles. In all there were 1,373,000 of both sexes, of whom about 55 per cent owned land. But just as in Mughal India there were others besides the public service nobility—there were about 800 distinguished families of princes, counts, and barons, mostly in Georgia and Poland, and among them there were about 40 princely families claiming descent from the ruling houses of Kievan Russia.[15]

In India in 1947 there were about 562 princely or 'native' states, nominally independent, but whose relations with the Imperial Government were governed by treaty. The largest among them, like Hyderabad and Kashmir, were as big as the larger European states, while the smallest, like some chiefs and *thakurs* in Kathiawar and Bundelkhand, extended over only a few hundred acres. Less than a third of these were of ancient lineage with genealogies going further than the eighteenth century. Then there were several thousand so-called landed gentry, known variously as *taluqdars* and zamindars. Some of them bore titles like that of Raja and even Maharaja; consequently they are sometimes confused today with the former ruling princes. But even though their estates were sometimes huge, much bigger than many 'native' states, they were, in law, private gentlemen. By and large they were creations of the British Raj, though again, a few of them claimed to have enjoyed some sort of chiefly status as revenue-farmers as early as the fifteenth or sixteenth centuries.

These older *zamindari* and *taluqdari* families could be equated with British and European nobility. At least the larger magnates were as rich as any of the European nobles. But a court is necessary for the sustenance of an aristocracy. The Mughals were steadfast in their refusal to treat them as anything more than mere zamindars. Even the princes of Rajasthan were never treated as tributary kings. They too are consistently described as mere zamindars and were co-opted into the imperial bureaucracy and given ranks of 4,000 or 5,000 *zat* or *sowar* as the case may be—like any other imperial *mansabdar*.

The British tried to build them up—along with other large landowners—along the lines of its own nobility in Britain. Elaborate lists of district, divisional and provincial *durbaris* were maintained. These were the notables who were entitled to invitations whenever the governor or governor-general held a public *durbar* (or reception). This helped to maintain their prestige in the public eye. But the prestige was largely artificial. When the republic was established in 1950 and their economic base destroyed by the agrarian reforms, not many regretted their passing. Some of them have no doubt succeeded in retaining some local influence, and many are in politics but they are rarely leaders of society. The republican spirit has triumphed. It is the Laloo Yadavs, Mulayam Singhs and Mayawatis—people of humble origins—who dominate the political scene in the states. In Delhi the tone may be a little higher, but neither are Manmohan Singh, Sonia Gandhi, or Montek Singh Ahluwalia, members of the old gentry—not by a long shot.

So ignorant is the general public and the media that these *taluqdars* and zamindars are often confused with the former princely families. It is assumed that anyone who is called a Raja or Maharaja is former 'royalty'. The Mughals were careful not to accord that rank to anyone outside their own immediate family, and even the British ensured that no one—not even His Exalted Highness, the Nizam of Hyderabad, the King-Emperor's Most Faithful Ally—was anything more than a prince. In Germany there were many princes entitled to the honorific of 'Royal Highness' but in British India there were none. Only Hyderabad was allowed the privilege of the additional honorific of 'Exalted'.

NOTES

1. David Cannadine, *The Decline and Fall of the British Aristocracy*, London: Papermac, 1996, p. 15.
2. Arno J. Mayer, *The Persistence of the Old Regime*, New York: Pantheon, 1981, p. 25.
3. R. Forster, 'The Survival of the Nobility during the French Revolution', *Past & Present*, 37(1): 71-86, p. 1.
4. Ibid.
5. Cannadine, op. cit., pp. 9-21.

6. In France, according to Bluche, the number of nobles in 1789 is estimated at 140,000. In Prussia their number is estimated at 40,000, while in Austria-Hungary their number is estimated at 250,000. By way of comparison in the UK, the number of nobles was only 580 in 1880!
7. Guy Chaussinad-Nogaret and William Doyle, *The French Nobility in the 18th Century*, Cambridge: Cambridge University Press, 1986, pp. 1-2.
8. Which explains why the estimates of the numbers of the French nobility are so variable, and one only has estimates and not precise figures.
9. W.K. Firminger, *Historical Introduction to the Bengal Portion of the Fifth Report*, p. xvii.
10. Ibid., p. xxvii.
11. Logan, *Malabar Manual*, vol. 1, Madras, 1951, p. 495.
12. Irwin, *The Garden of India or Chapters on Oudh*, p. 179.
13. Ibid., p. 187.
14. The last named would later be honoured with the dignity of a Maharaja and the Knight Commandership of the Star of India.
15. Mayer, op. cit., pp. 120-3.

CHAPTER 7

Our Medieval Sultans

I had always been struck by the quick succession of relatively transient dynasties in the Sultanate period. The comparison is with the dynasties of the petty kingdoms of Rajasthan as well as the royal dynasties of western Europe. The conventional list of the dynasties of the Sultanate of north India is as follows:

1. The Slave Kings (1206-90)
2. Khalji Sultans (1290-1320)
3. Tughluq Sultans (1320-1414)
4. Sayyid Sultans (1414-51)
5. Lodi Sultans (1451-1526)
6. Suri Sultans (1540-55)

Not one of them lasted even a hundred years. Further, the Slave kings actually constituted three dynasties: the house of Aibak, the house of Iltutmish and the house of Balban. The progenitors of all three were slaves, purchased from the bazaar, and only two of them, Iltutmish and Balban, had reigns of twenty years or more.

The Mughals who succeeded them were truly exceptional. Even if we exclude Babur and Humayun, they reigned for more than 200 years. They are also the only dynasty in Indian history to have made a comeback after being overthrown and expelled.

Ibn Khaldun, the celebrated Arab historian, the only one with an analytical mind, has made some interesting observations regarding Muslim dynasties. He was of the view that dynasties had a natural lifespan like individuals and that this seldom exceeded three generations, or 120 years. Over this time-span the dynasty usually becomes senile. The later kings—assuming the dynasty does not become extinct by then—are *fainéants* or 'do-nothings'. Their *wazirs* or ministers become all-powerful and the kings are reduced to symbols, performing ceremonial functions only.[1]

His logic is simple. The founders of dynasties are strong, powerful men, used to a hard life, and capable of endurance and privation. They are usually succeeded by people who have been brought up in comparative ease and luxury, but since they have seen some of the times of hardship and have had personal contact with the founder and have learnt from his example, they understand how political power is won and maintained. The third generation would not have any knowledge or memory of the early days of hardship. They delude themselves with imagining that ease, comfort, and royalty are their birthright; their wazirs encourage them in their delusions, they cease to identify themselves with their subjects or fellow-tribals and the latter feel alienated from their rulers. What Ibn Khaldun describes as 'group-feeling' has all but evaporated and the time is ripe for a regime change.

Qutb ud-Din Aibak was the first of the Slave kings. He had been purchased by his master, Sultan Muiz ud-Din Muhammad bin Sam of Ghor and had risen solely by virtue of his merit to be appointed viceroy of his Indian conquests. The Sultan had no sons, so he was succeeded by his slaves whom he regarded as his sons. Aibak, who was the most capable, overcame the others and made himself master of Delhi. But his reign was brief–only four years. He was succeeded by one Aram Shah who has been described as his son in some histories, but he proved incompetent, and within a few months was replaced by Iltutmish, another Ilbari Turk who had been first offered by slavers to the Sultan at Ghazni. Muhammad Ghori, however, declined to buy him as he felt the price demanded was too high. The slavers then offered him to Aibak at Delhi and the latter bought him. He would be one of the most successful of the Slave kings.

Iltutmish reigned for 24 years. After his death his son Rukn ud-Din Firoz Shah succeeded him but proved incompetent, being weak, licentious and utterly worthless, dominated entirely by his mother Shah Turkhan, a vindictive woman of low origins. After six months he was killed and replaced by his sister Raziyya who had been initially recommended by her father to the nobles as his designated heir. In spite of her ability and talents Raziyya's reign was also short and disturbed by rebellions. Sultan Raziyya and her husband Altuniya were also killed and she was replaced by her brother Bahram.

The Delhi court was at this time controlled by a clique of powerful nobles numbering about forty (and known therefore as the *chahalguni* or *chalisa*), who divided the principal offices of the empire between themselves. They also made and unmade kings. Bahram was not particularly intelligent and after a short reign of two years was overthrown and killed by the 'Forty'. His brother Masud replaced him but after five years the Forty turned against him as well. He too was put to death and replaced by an uncle Nasir ud-Din Mahmud, a youth of about seventeen.

The new king had a long reign of twenty years, and he wisely left all the details of government to his minister, the sagacious and ruthless Balban. The latter, though well-born, had been enslaved by the Mongols, and eventually acquired by Iltutmish. He had been a leading figure among the Forty and was father-in-law to the young sultan, his nominal master. He ruled with an iron hand, and on the death of his master (who died issueless) ascended the throne unchallenged. He ruled, now as sultan, for another twenty years.

His eldest son and heir-presumptive, Muhammad Khan, an accomplished prince was unfortunately killed in an ambush by the Mongols in one of their invasions. His second son Bughra Khan, governor of Bengal, preferred to remain there, and even the offer of the throne could not lure him back to Delhi.[2] Balban had designated his grandson Kaikhusrav, the son of the deceased Muhammad Khan as his heir, but he was ignored by the nobles who instead placed on the throne Kaiqubad, the son of Bughra Khan, who was in Delhi.

Kaiqubad had had a strict upbringing at his grandfather's austere court, but now released from all restraints, he plunged into a life of unbridled debauchery. Within three years his health broke down and he was struck by paralysis, the throne passing to Jalal ud-Din

Firoz Khalji, governor of the frontier province of Samana. The paralytic sultan was rolled up in his bedding and thrown into the river Yamuna which flowed below the walls of the palace-fort. His infant son Kayumars who had been proclaimed sultan by a faction of the nobles also disappears from history, while Kaikhusrav was murdered earlier on Jalal-ud-Din's instructions. The House of Balban too had become extinct.

So far the history of the Slave kings of Delhi conforms to the typical pattern outlined by Ibn Khaldun. There were three capable sultans. All three were purchased as slaves and rose to royalty by sheer merit. But their successors proved either incompetent, or unfortunate (as in the case of Raziyya, who, as a woman, had the odds stacked against her), or hopeless drunkards and debauchees.

One need not go into the details of the other dynasties that constitute the Sultanate of Delhi. The Khalji sultans are usually numbered at five, but only two, Jalal ud-Din Firoz (1290-5) and Ala ud-Din Muhammad (1295-1315) were of any account. Two, Ibrahim Shah and Shihab ud-Din Umar were blinded. Mubarak Shah's reign was a little longer; four inglorious years were passed in dissipation and debauchery, until finally he was murdered by his favourite Khusrav Khan, who ascended the throne as Nasir ud-Din Khusrav Shah. This last had no connection with the Khalji house; he was a neo-Muslim of low origins who had completely dominated the infatuated Sultan. In a few months, this upstart too received his just desserts, and the throne passed to the house of Tughluq.

The line of sultans of the House of Tughluq is much longer. We have as many as eleven rulers covering 92 years. But here again only the first three are of any consequence accounting for as many as 68 years. The Syeds who followed lasted less than 30 years, and produced four rulers, of whom the first, Khizr Khan (1414-21) never assumed the royal title.

The Syeds had taken over a ruined state. Timur had sacked Delhi in 1398, massacred much of its population, and much of the Punjab and the Ganga-Yamuna Doab had been laid waste by his army. The Sultanate had shrunk to Delhi, Punjab and the Doab. Given the best of men, the restoration of royal prestige would have been an uphill task, and the Syeds were only average men. While Khizr Khan showed some vigour, and even the second Mubarak Shah (who was murdered) at least tried to rule, the last two were but feeble shadows. The last, Alam Shah, tamely abdicated in favour of Bahlol Lodi who allowed him to retire to Budaun.

The Syeds were followed by the Lodis—a dynasty which produced three kings and ruled for 75 years. Of the three, Bahlol was doubtless the most capable, but neither Sikander nor Ibrahim could be accused of being weak and incompetent. It was just bad luck that Ibrahim lost to the small but disciplined army of Babur, the latest adventurer to try his luck at conquering India.

Among the provincial Muslim dynasties the position is a little different. Most of the dynasties ruled for a hundred years or more. The Bahmani sultans reigned 179 years, the Adil Shahs 197, the Farukhi Khans of Khandesh 200, the Qutb Shahs 175 and the Gujarat sultans for 186 years. In Bengal the House of Ilyas Shah ruled for 206 years.

But while they do not conform to the model of Ibn Khaldun as closely as the Delhi Sultanate, there is a pattern nonetheless. Of the eighteen rulers of the Bahmani Sultanate as many as seven were either murdered or blinded. Of the first eight, three were transients who reigned for only a few months, and from Ahmad Shah I (1421-35) onwards, the ministers are more important than the sultans. The last four were raised to the Turquoise Throne of the Bahmanids by Amir Barid, who had dominated the court of Bidar ever since 1504 when he succeeded to his father's offices. He had put to death Ala ud-Din Shah and Wali Ullah, and when Kalim Ullah feared that he would suffer a similar fate (his secret correspondence with Emperor Babur being discovered) he fled the kingdom. The field was now clear for Amir Barid to dispense with puppets and ascend the throne himself, although it was his son Ali who first assumed the royal style of Barid Shah.

The sultans of Malwa belong to two dynasties, the first were Ghoris and the second Khaljis. They numbered only seven but as many as five died unnatural deaths, four of them by poison. The first of the Ghoris reigned only four years, and like most of the founders of these successor states he preferred the modest style of 'Khan' to the regal 'Shah'. He was poisoned by his son, Sultan Hoshang Shah who was an energetic warrior and fought wars with his neighbours, and raided as far as Jajpur in Orissa, the object of his raid being to procure elephants. Of the second house, only the founder Sultan Mahmud Shah (1436-75) was notable, and even though he ascended the throne by poisoning his predecessor, who happened to be his sister's husband, he was undoubtedly the greatest of the Malwa sultans. It may be added, by way of partial exoneration, that his predecessor was a monster who had started his reign with the murder of three brothers and the blinding of a nephew, and that he was an alcoholic who left affairs of state entirely in the hands of his ministers.

The Gujarat sultans numbered fourteen, and as many as seven of them died unnatural deaths. But there were several capable rulers among them, the most celebrated being Sultan Mahmud Begarha (1458-1511), while the last three were but shadowy *fainéants*.

The kingdoms of Berar and Bidar, ruled by the Imad Shahs and Barid Shahs, were fated to be annexed to Ahmadnagar and Bijapur, respectively.

The list of Bengal sultans is long. Of the House of Ilyas (1339-1481) out of twelve kings only two, Shams ud-Din Ilyas Shah (1339-58) and Nasir ud-Din (1442-59) were notable. Of the House of Husain Shah only the first, Ala ud-Din Husain Shah was of any eminence. We have the usual parade of sadistic monsters and sensualists, and the brief episodes of the House of Raja Kans (1409-31) and of the Habshi sultans (1486-90). Raja Kans (or Ganesh) was a Hindu chieftain who managed to seize power and converted to Islam along with his son in order to become more acceptable to the largely Turkish and Afghan nobles who had dominated Bengal since its conquest in 1202. The first of the Habshi kings, Sultan Shahzada Barbak, was an Abyssinian eunuch. Sultan Rukn ud-Din Barbak Shah (1459-74), the second ruler of the restored house of Ilyas, had chosen to entrust his personal security on a corps of Abyssinian slaves imported from Africa, whose power and insolence waxed as the character and vigour of their masters declined. Shams ud-Din Yusuf Shah was an eccentric bigot who insisted on the rigid observance of Islamic law while his successor Sikander Shah was so deranged that he was almost immediately deposed in favour of his great-uncle. Jalal ud-Din Fateh Shah, the great-uncle who succeeded, was wise and well-meaning but his attempts to curb the excesses of the Abyssinian *mamlukes* provoked the conspiracy and usurpation of Shahzada Barbak.

The Muslim rulers of the time were almost invariably of foreign origin. Of the ruling dynasties the Nizam Shahs of Ahmadnagar alone were Indians, being descended from a Deccani brahmin family. And in spite of the fact that the Turkish conquest of the Deccan was fairly recent, the rulers of the Deccan Sultanates chose to base their power on foreigners, either slaves or adventurers. Malik Ambar and Mahmud Gawan—both Abyssinians—were the finest ministers of the Nizam Shahs and the Bahmani sultans. Yusuf Adil Shah, the founder of the Bijapur state, was probably an Ottoman prince. Sometimes one cannot resist the feeling that the situation in medieval India was not very different from that obtaining in sixteenth-century Mexico and Peru. The ruling elites were almost as foreign as the Spanish conquistadores.

But yet, not quite, for this was also the period when the regional languages of India flowered. The earlier Hindu kings were dominated by brahmins and Sanskrit enjoyed the status of a classical language. But these new rulers, whether Turkish, Iranian or Afghan, had little regard for this language which was entirely alien to them. They communicated with their subjects in their vernaculars, and songs and hymns in these languages acquired a respectability far faster than would have been the case otherwise. Kabir, Surdas, Tulsidas, Nanak and Namdev belong to this period. A little later, in the reign of the great Akbar, the *Ramayana* and *Mahabharata* would also be translated into Persian.

But I am digressing. The object of this study is to compare the history of Europe with that of India. Both were conquered territories. Just as Western and Mediterranean Europe had been conquered by Germanic tribes, India had been conquered by the Turks who were followed by a medley of Afghans, Persians, Mughals, and the odd Arab. The old rulers were overthrown and new dynasties founded, but in India there persisted, for a long time, a strong element of instability which is absent in the European dynasties.

It isn't that the European dynasties were more durable. A quick perusal of John Morby's *Handbook of Kings and Queens* will reveal that few European dynasties lasted more than two hundred years. But the transition from one ruling house to another was usually smooth. In contrast, in India the change was invariably accompanied by violence and war. It will also be observed that all the kings of France, whether Capetians, Valois or Bourbons, were the descendants of Hugh Capet (987-96). But for the two brief intrusions of the Bonapartes and the republican interludes, France was ruled by the same family from 987 to 1848. And Hugh Capet happened to be a grandson of Robert I of the Carolingian dynasty, thus connecting him directly with Charlemagne. In the case of England the succession is not so clear; on several occasions the 'legitimate' heir has been set aside, ignored or deposed in favour of another, but *all* the kings, William the Conqueror (1066-87) onwards, whether Plantagenets, Tudors, Stuarts or Hanoverians were closely related.

The Muslim rulers of India on the other hand had no such concept of legitimate succession. They did try to stick to primogeniture as a general principle, but this was often substituted by that of the fittest, and a contested succession was by no means unusual. Aurangzeb succeeded his father even though he was the youngest of his three brothers, albeit after a bitter fratricidal war. Likewise, Farukhsiyar successfully challenged the succession of his uncle Jahandar Shah, who was the eldest son and had won the throne after another bloody contest with his brothers. Yet their legitimacy as rulers was never questioned. The Ottomans and the Indian Mughals partially solved the problem by killing their surviving brothers after seizing power. Later, the surviving brothers and other descendants of former emperors would be kept in close confinement. But no such cruel and barbaric expedients were felt necessary in European dynasties. The rules of succession were well known and accepted; there was no question of plural marriages, and the sons of royal mistresses, though they might often be given titles of nobility, could never hope to succeed to the throne.[3] In European royalty—and even among the not quite royal but 'sovereign' princes of the Germanies—the marriages of princes were closely regulated by law. A prince or a king could not marry just anyone he pleased. There was no question of a Cophetua making a beggar maid his queen. If he did the marriage would be deemed 'morganatic' and the children of that union would be barred from succession, the throne going automatically to the next in line.

The Turks were similar to the Arabs in many ways. Both were dwellers of deserts and steppes, and strangers to royalty and kingship until the rise of Islam in the case of the latter, and of Chengiz Khan in the case of the former. I have here treated the Turks and Mongols as different tribes of the same people, and so have they been regarded by most historians. At different periods and in different parts of the steppes they have been known by different names—Turks, Tartars (or Tatars), Uzbegs, Kalmucks, Kazakhs, Kirghiz, Uighurs, Mughals (or Mongols)—whatever the name by which they may be known, as a race they are very much the same people. Ibn Khaldun has made some interesting observations about them, and though his study is concerned essentially with the Arab people, what he says applies equally to the Turks of Central Asia.

Ibn Khaldun clearly rated the Caliphate (or Imamat) higher than mere kingship, because the former also included a religious responsibility. It was the duty of the Caliph to ensure that the religious law prevailed. He led the Faithful in their prayers, and was the final judge not merely in matters of religious law but also in all matters not covered by the *shariat*. The early Caliphs were easily accessible; any Muslim could approach them with his problem or complaint. Abu Bakr, the first Caliph, was noted for the purity of his life, and he is known as *al-Sadiq*, or the Truthful One. Muslim historians distinguish the reigns of the first four Caliphs as founded on faith, from those of the later ones, as based on the world and its passions and vanities, and while there is no doubt about the goodness of Abu Bakr, worldly considerations had certainly come into play in the politics of Osman and Ali. Omar, Osman and Ali, all died unnatural deaths.

Muhammad nominated Abu Bakr as Caliph, not king or sultan. The Arabs had not known any kings so far, and the Arabian peninsula was dominated by Bedouin tribes with a few scattered towns in the oases. The Bedouins were not amenable to royal authority—as Ibn Khaldun observed 'the Bedouins are of all nations the one most remote from royal leadership'.[4] The Prophet himself censured kings and their representatives. He blamed them because of their enjoyment of good fortune, their senseless waste, and their deviations from the path of God. Royalty was suspect and regarded as worthless.[5]

The shelves of libraries sag with the weight of history books, but in the popular imagination few sultans or *padishahs* figure as heroes. Most have been deservedly forgotten. The people remember only the saints and mystics, and maybe the odd *ghazi* who attained martyrdom, like Masaud Salaar. Kings are only a necessary evil. Some may be more evil, others less, but they are all evil nonetheless. In the exercise of royal authority the Holy Law is almost invariably violated, even by the best of kings. The honorific *alqabs* of some of these rulers may be impressive. Almost all of them are Commanders of the Faithful (originally associated only with Caliphs), the Refuge of the World, and even, most presumptuously, the Shadow of God on Earth, but no one ever took these pretensions seriously. Unlike the Christian West there never was an Islamic version of the Divine Right of Kings. Kings were to be endured, to suggest that they had a divine right to oppress their subjects would have been adding insult to injury.

Through the Caliphate Islam tried to combine the religious and secular functions, but very soon the former were superseded by the latter and the Caliphate survived only in name, the Caliph being indistinguishable from any other secular royal authority. Christianity, in contrast, was born in the heart of the Roman Empire. There was no way that Jesus Christ could have assumed the secular leadership of his followers, and when questioned on the point he urged his followers to give Caesar what was his due. At the time the Christians were just another Jewish sect, and, in any case, the Jewish people already had in the Herodian dynasty a royal authority. That Herod and his descendants were Roman clients was entirely another matter.

So Christianity started with two distinct authorities, one secular and the other religious. When the Roman emperors embraced the religion of Christ they attempted to dominate the church, but the bishops and patriarchs who were the religious authorities resisted the imperial efforts to make them subordinates. Instead there developed an uneasy partnership. In the West where there were no emperors after 475 the Bishop of Rome who held the See of St. Peter's acquired an unusual degree of independence and in due course assumed the character of a prince in Italy. In the East where the Byzantine emperors were to continue for nearly a thousand years, the church was never able to acquire the same degree of independence, since both Patriarch and emperor had their respective palaces in Constantinople. This was the basic reason for the split between the Roman Catholic Church of Rome and the Eastern Orthodox churches. There were other finer points of difference based on doctrine, the Greeks being notorious for theological hair-splitting, but in general the Orthodox churches were much less independent of the secular arm than the Roman Church.

When Ibn Khaldun wrote his work the Eastern or Byzantine Empire was in terminal decline. Within fifty years of his death it would pass into history. Two centuries earlier its capital had been sacked by a Frankish army of supposed Crusaders; most of the Balkans and Greece were in the hands of the Turks while the islands of the Archipelago were largely held by the Venetians. Ibn Khaldun was familiar with the various Christian sects, but he rightly considered the Roman Church (which he describes as the Melchites) whose patriarch was called the Pope, as the most important. He discusses the relationship between the Pope and emperor thus:

> It is the custom of the Pope with respect to the European Christians to urge them to submit to one ruler and have recourse to him in their disagreements and agreements, in order to avoid the dissolution of the whole thing. His purpose is to have the group feeling that is strongest among them (concentrated upon one ruler), so that he has power over all of them. The ruler is called 'Emperor'. (The Pope) personally places the crown upon the head of (the emperor), in order to let him have the blessing implied (in that ceremony).[4]

Thus while in Christian Europe there were clearly two separate authorities which tried to support and collaborate with each other, in the world of Islam there was no such split. In theory there was only one supreme head–the Caliph or Khalifa. But by the time of Ibn Khaldun the Caliphate was long dead. As already discussed soon after the first four Caliphs, the Caliphate had become indistinguishable from any royal authority, the later Caliphs being more and more involved in the affairs of the world. With the transfer of the Caliphate from Damascus to Baghdad the Caliphs assumed more and more the character of the Persian monarchs of old, and the later Abbassids were mere puppets in the hands of their ministers, and the only function left to them was that of a fount of honours. They alone could legitimize royal authority by grant of *firmans* or letters patent–which they happily did for a consideration. But even this residual function ceased after the destruction of Baghdad by Hulaghu Khan in 1258. Three years later a survivor of the Abbassid house set himself up at Cairo under the protection of the Mamluke sultans of Egypt, and it was from a descendant of one of these that the Ottoman sultan, Selim I purchased the dignity in 1517 after he had defeated the Mamluke power. The Caliphate of Cairo is, quite appropriately, called the 'Shadow Caliphate'.

The Ottomans were a very formidable military power as compared to their predecessors–indeed for over two hundred years they were the greatest military power in Europe and West Asia. But they were primarily emperors, the Caliphal title was just another dignity which they had acquired–and indeed Selim 'the Grim' who had two brothers and five orphaned nephews strangled on the occasion of his accession to his father's throne, had none of the qualities which one would associate with a religious authority. Except for their durability and wealth, there was nothing to distinguish the Ottomans from any of the shahs, sultans and amirs that lorded over the unfortunate lands of *dar ul-Islam*. They were as despotic as any of the dictators that rule those countries today. Kingship, or the secular authority was never able to acquire the legitimacy which it was able to acquire in Europe. The papacy for all its sins and worldliness, its cynical simony and the sale of indulgences was incapable of atrocities on the scale of secular princes, and whenever it came in conflict with the emperor, it was the Pope that triumphed. Muhammad had ignored the royal authority because he saw it only as an evil. He tried to substitute it with the Caliphate or Imamate, but that too proved impractical. The wealth that fell into the hands of the Caliphs within a few short decades of the death of the Prophet ensured its speedy corruption and dissolution.

In pre-Islamic (essentially Hindu) India the position was quite different. Sri Ramchandra of Ayodhya and Sri Krishna of Dwarka are not merely two of the most revered figures of Hinduism. Their historicity is irrelevant, it suffices that most Indians believe they did exist at some time (however, remote). What is even more interesting is that they are worshipped today as demi-gods in most lists of the ten incarnations of Lord Vishnu. Most Rajput clans and ruling dynasties trace their descent from either one or the other–or from some other equally impressive progenitor. The former kings of Nepal were also regarded as incarnations of Vishnu.

Islamic rulers, on the other hand, were unable to forge a similar mythology. The rulers of its kingdoms, whether located in India or West Asia, were never regarded as anything more than human. The Islamic creed was strictly puritanical. As Ibn Khaldun points out, in the early days the Muslims refrained even from beating drums and blowing trumpets in their armies because they despised pomp and wanted to avoid 'the coarseness of royal authority'. The first Caliph to use a throne was the fifth, Mu'awiyah, and he did so only after asking the people's permission as he was too corpulent and had difficulty in getting up from the floor.[7]

Curiously, the Sikhs, a relatively young community, have a similar abhorrence for hereditary kingship. Recognizing only their ten Gurus and their sacred book as their true sovereign or *Sacha Patishah* they have regarded monarchical pretensions with extreme suspicion. Although they became all-powerful in the Punjab after 1763, they were unable to come up with a stable monarchy and for a long time remained divided among a host of petty chiefs, each claiming to be independent. Even today, the Sikhs like to say that Ranjit Singh, their most famous ruler, popularly described as the Lion of the Punjab, never really called himself Maharaja. That was a title foisted upon him by the British—he himself preferred to be addressed simply as *Sarkar*. The Sikh coinage never bore the name of either Ranjit Singh or any of his transient successors. Just as the coinage of the early Caliphs and sultans of Muslim states gave primacy to the *kalima*, the Muslim profession of faith, the legends on the coinage of the Lahore Durbar only contained the names of Nanak and Gobind Singh, their first and last gurus.

Needless to say the brief history of the Lahore Durbar was as violent and unstable as that of any Muslim state. The few Sikh states that survived in the Cis-Sutlej tract were able to do so only because they accepted the *Pax Britannica* early on, in their anxiety to secure themselves against the transgressions of the wily Ranjit, the Lion of the Punjab.

NOTES

1. Ibn Khaldun, *The Muqaddimah*, translated and abridged by Rosenthal and Dawood, Bollingen Series, Princeton: Princeton University Press, 1989, pp. 136-8.
2. He had in fact been summoned to Delhi by his father after the death of his elder brother, but after some time, unable to put up with the depressing atmosphere of his father's austere court, left for Bengal without permission.

3. There were exceptions, like William the Conqueror who was a bastard, but none after the Middle Ages.
4. Ibn Khaldun, op. cit., 2.27, p. 120.
5. Ibid., 3.26, pp. 160-1.
6. Ibid., p. 188.
7. Ibid., pp. 214-16.

CHAPTER 8

State Building in Europe and India

In both India and Western Christendom there exists the concept of a universal state which should, ideally, embrace the entire civilization. But in Europe the empire was very soon confined to Germany[1] and Italy, and finally to Germany alone. By the end of the eighteenth century it had been reduced to a historical curiosity; in the oft-quoted phrase, 'neither Holy, nor Roman, nor an Empire'. By the turn of the century this phantom had been pushed aside by the fast expanding frontiers of Napoleonic France. Finally, acting on the directions of the Corsican upstart, the Holy Roman Emperor Francis II wound up the old empire and reinvented himself (with singular lack of imagination) as 'Francis I, Emperor of Austria', while Napoleon had himself crowned 'Emperor of the French'.

The French Empire, though much more real than the one it replaced, proved ephemeral; France reverted to its pre-Revolutionary borders and its former status of a kingdom after the debacle of Waterloo, and after the brief revival of the Second Empire (1852-70) under Napoleon III, ultimately reverted to a republic. The Austrian Empire, however, lingered on. In 1866 it again reinvented itself as the Austro-Hungarian Empire (also known as the Dual Monarchy), which would finally collapse in 1918, along with all other European empires—German, Russian, and Turkish. It is only now that the European Union appears to be close to achieving some semblance of political unity.

Fareed Zakaria has suggested that geography may have something to do with it. Western Europe is broken into small units cut-off from each other by mountain ranges, and even though the mountains are not very high when compared to those of Asia, countries have a tendency to expand to their 'natural' limits. In the case of France these were the Pyrenees to the south, the Alps and the Vosges to the east, and to the north the forests and hills of the Ardennes and the marshes of the Rhine-Maas delta.[2] Spain, Italy and the Scandinavian countries have similar well-defined borders. Only in the case of Portugal and Spain is the border based entirely on old feudal fiefs. The German-Polish border too has no mountain ridges to distinguish it, so Germany fades gradually into the plains of Poland. Until the population movements that followed the Second World War there had always been a sprinkling of Germans in the east, concentrated mainly along the Baltic shore, in the old Hanseatic cities and East Prussia, once the home of the Teutonic Order.

In India, on the other hand, we have the vast swathe of the Indo-Gangetic plains, and if the Indus basin was not particularly fertile and only sparsely inhabited by pastoral tribes (at least until the advent of canal irrigation in the nineteenth century) the Gangetic plain amply made up for it. There were no natural barriers for an invading army, and once the border kingdoms of Lahore, Delhi or Agra had been broken the conqueror was able to extend his sway with relative ease right up to the Bay of Bengal. At a time when the land revenue constituted the principal income of the state, the dense population and intensive cultivation of the basin placed unmatchable resources at the disposal of any would-be ruler with imperial aspirations. Thus the Gurjara-Pratiharas with their base at Kanauj were soon able to extend their control over much of northern and central India. Likewise, when Muhammad Ghori conquered Lahore and Delhi in 1186 and 1192 respectively, he and his lieutenants were able to extend their control right up to Bengal, which they reached in 1202. In little more than a hundred years the Deccan plateau and much of the peninsula had been penetrated and made tributary to the sultanate of Delhi by the armies of Sultan Ala al-Din Khalji and his eunuch general Malik Kafur.

The Khalji Empire was, however, a house of cards. Less than fifty years later, during the reign of Sultan Muhammad bin Tughluq of the succeeding dynasty, it started to crumble. Revolts broke out all over and by the time the Sultan died in 1351 independent kingdoms had been established in the Deccan and the Delhi Sultanate was once again confined to the Indo-Gangetic plain. The next notable imperial dynasty was the Mughal, whose founder Babur established himself at Agra in 1526. Although the north and centre were subdued swiftly enough, the conquest of the south was a more gradual process. Starting with Akbar (1556-1605) it was not completed until the reign of Aurangzeb (1658-1707), and even before its completion the Marathas had started the unraveling process. But this time the disintegration was a much more gradual process, the provincial governors, and the other regional powers that emerged being content, for the most part, with virtual independence while still acknowledging the notional authority of their sovereign in Delhi. At the same time the ultimate successors of the Mughals, the British, had started spreading their wings. Starting from their three bases at Calcutta, Madras and Bombay, by 1803 they had reached Delhi and were virtual masters of the subcontinent. In another few decades their *de facto* control was formalized into *de jure dominium* when the rule of the East India Company was superseded by the direct control by the British crown. In 1876 Benjamin Disraeli, in an inspired moment, had Queen Victoria proclaimed Empress of India, or *Qaisar-i-Hind*, making the bond much more real. The princes of India had long been familiar with Mughal emperors, and Disraeli was hoping to make British rule more acceptable to the Indian masses and elites. And indeed, as long as she was alive, this diminutive widow acquired a larger than life image. For the Indian masses and the princes she became a sort of mother figure.

But less than seventy-five years after the memorable Durbar of 1876, this latest of Indian empires had also wound up. The British left and India became an independent republic, but before that could come about a new state, Pakistan, was carved out of it. The latter would also split, in due course, to give birth to Bangladesh, but that is another story. What is significant is that the centre of power in India has always been located in the northern plains. During the British Raj the capital was at first located in Calcutta, later it was transferred to Delhi. In Mughal times, Agra, Lahore and Delhi had all, at one time or the other, been the seat of empire. Still earlier, the capital had been Kanauj on the Ganges, and in ancient times it was Pataliputra, or modern Patna. Because of its demography and agricultural wealth the north has always dominated. The country has always been conquered from the north, never from the south. The Marathas tried to reverse the course of empire in the eighteenth century, but their base at Poona, in the largely rain-fed Deccan, was too poor to support an imperial enterprise of that magnitude.

In contrast there has been no such easily identifiable power centre in Europe. Rome used to be the seat of the Roman emperors, to begin with. Later, in the fourth century, Constantine the Great would move the capital to Byzantium, the ancient Greek city which he renamed Constantinople or New Rome. Later when the empire was partitioned into the eastern and western, Rome lost its primacy, and while the eastern capital remained Constantinople the western capital was Ravenna for some time, and later Milan. Charlemagne's capital was Aachen in the Rhineland, while the revived Ottonian empire had no proper capital at all. Since the Emperor was first of all a German prince, and emperor or king only after that, the seat of his principality was his main capital. The election was, however, usually held at Frankfurt, while the first coronation as King of Germany (or, more properly, of the Romans) was at Aachen where the imperial regalia was kept. Sometimes there would be a second coronation at Rome by the Pope. Only after that was he properly an emperor. Until then he was only Emperor-Elect, or King of the Romans. The German Diet usually met at Regensberg (Ratisbon) but it often met in towns like Nuremburg and Augsburg as well. Later when the title became virtually hereditary in the Habsburg house the capital was essentially Vienna (for a time Prague too was the capital under the emperors of the Luxemburg house, as well as under Rudolf II of the House of Habsburg) but the Diet itself never met in Vienna.

During the brief term of the Napoleonic empire the capital was Paris. Situated in the heart of the fertile Ile de France, Paris is ideally situated to be a power centre–which Berlin, in the infertile, glaciated province of Brandenburg most definitely is not. Thus the old dream of a single emperor dominating Europe proved elusive, and instead we had a multi-polar reality, with four Great Powers, three with emperors (an empress in the case of Britain) at their head, and the fourth (France) a republic.

In the east there was the vast sprawling empire of the Czar 'of all the Russias' while in the south-east there was the Turkish empire, terminally sick, or so it was supposed, for most of the past hundred years. Ironically, it managed to last as long as its two inveterate enemies, Austria and Russia. In fact, it actually did much better, because unlike the other losers of the world war, it refused to accept the draconian Treaty of Sevres, and after fighting a second victorious war was able to negotiate much better terms in the Treaty of Lausanne.

Until the reign of Peter the Great (1682-1725) Russia had been relatively isolated from the rest of Europe, being preoccupied with wars on its southern frontier with the Khans of the Golden Horde and Crimea, and with Poland and Sweden to the west. But with the accession of Catherine II (1762-96)—by birth a German princess and a daughter of the Enlightenment (she corresponded with Voltaire)—it became a major European power. The Revolutionary and Napoleonic wars had brought Russian armies into the heart of Europe—to Italy, Bohemia, Germany and France. For several decades it was part and parcel of the Concert of Europe, the system designed by Metternich to keep Europe secure from the sedition of revolution. The system broke down in the Crimean War, and in the subsequent decades the old fault-lines between Western Christendom and Eastern Orthodoxy became manifest by way of disputes and differences between Russia and Austria-Hungary in the newly emerging Balkan states.

Thus we have two strikingly contrasting narratives. While both India and western Europe cherished the dream of a universal emperor holding sway over their respective civilizational spheres, in India the dream was realized with relative facility—at least thrice within a span of 1,200 years. Europe, on the other hand, never quite managed it even once; only now it seems tantalizingly close to achieving it through the slow, boringly deliberative processes of the European Union. In the eastern Orthodox world, Russia has been the torch-bearer of universal empire. At first, of course, was the Byzantine empire, where the Greek Byzantines were soon supplanted by the Muslim Ottomans–who too, like the Christian Greek dynasties before them, saw themselves as Romans, and styled themselves as *Qaisar-i-Rum*, or Emperors of Rome. But while the power of the Byzantines declined, Orthodox Christianity spread among the Slavic people of the northern steppes, as well as in the Scandinavian or Varangian settlements which had developed along the waterways of Russia. Ivan the Great (1462-1505), Grand Prince of Moscow, who had greatly expanded his principality, and had espoused Zoe Palaeologue, a niece of the last Byzantine emperor in 1472, began to see himself as the successor of the Byzantine emperors. Moscow was proclaimed to be the 'Third Rome' and the double-headed eagle of the Byzantines was adopted as the insignia of the princes of Muscovy who would soon declare themselves as Czars or emperors.

There were no natural barriers to the expansion of the principality of Moscow. As the Mongol power (to which the princes of Muscovy had once been tributary) decayed, the Russian power expanded, and when in the nineteenth century the Ottoman empire, in turn started to break-up, the new Balkan states became virtual protectorates of Russia. The history of the Russian (or the Eastern Orthodox) universal state is, in a way, much more similar to that of India.

But Western Christendom was witness to the rise of a different type of dynastic empire, a type which has no parallels in India, or the Orient for that matter. This was an empire put together by strategic and well-planned marriages rather than military conquest.

The story of the Habsburgs is well known, but there were several other family empires which rose in the Middle Ages, which did not owe their emergence primarily to conquest. The first such example is that of the Angevin empire.

The Angevins derive their name from the House of Anjou. The Counts of Anjou of the First Creation start with Fulk I (909-42). After five generations the male line failed and thereafter, the county passed to Geoffrey the Bearded of Gatinais, a son-in-law of Fulk III, the fourth count, in 1060. After another four generations we come to Count Henry, who in 1154 succeeded to the crown of England as King Henry II, in right of his mother Matilda, the daughter of King Henry I (1100-35), the last male scion of the Norman house that had conquered England in 1066. The transition was thus by the simple rules of inheritance. A few years later by marrying Eleanor, the divorced wife of King Louis VII—who was Duchess of Aquitaine in her own right—he acquired the vast lands associated with the duchy—Poitou, Toulouse, Saintonge and Limousin—almost equal to the kingdom of England itself. The duchy of Normandy, and the counties of Maine and Anjou were already held by him directly. The king of France, the nominal overlord for his and his wife's French possessions, was completely overshadowed by him. The vassal was more powerful than the lord.

In the subsequent wars with France almost all would be lost. Anjou itself was ceded to the French king who made it an appanage for his younger son Charles. The history of this, the third house of Anjou, was the most remarkable of all. By his marriage Charles also became Count of Provence. His father-in-law had four daughters, and since three of them were already married to kings, the latter decided to settle Provence on his youngest daughter and Charles was thus the indirect beneficiary. Then in 1262 Charles was offered the crown of Sicily by the Pope. Sicily (which included much territory on the mainland, including Naples) was at that time held by Manfred, an illegitimate son of the late Emperor Fredrick II of the House of Hohenstauffen, who had long been a thorn in the side of the papacy. The Pope was anxious to be rid of Manfred too, and as Charles was agreeable to the conditions laid down by the Holy Father, an understanding was reached between them. Charles drove out Manfred who was killed in battle. But Charles proved a hard master; Sicily revolted and Charles was left with only the mainland possessions, and was therefore known as King of Naples. The Sicilian rebels invited King Peter III of Aragon to accept the crown of Sicily—as he was married to the only daughter of the unfortunate Manfred—and ultimately the island passed to the House of Aragon.

Charles of Anjou, Provence and Naples, notwithstanding the loss of Sicily, was, however, destined for further adventures. He went on a crusade, in the course of which he acquired territories in Greece, with the titles of Prince of Achaea and Despot of Epirus. From the dispossessed and exiled King Baldwin he purchased, in 1277, the title of 'King of Jerusalem', but of the last he was never more than king in name.

His son, also Charles, was invited by the Hungarian nobles to accept the crowns of Hungary and Croatia in 1307. His grandmother had been a daughter of King Stephen V, one of the later kings of the Arpad house, which had run out of male heirs. His son Louis was likewise invited to become King of Poland by the Polish nobles because his mother had been a Polish princess of the House of Piast, which too, like the Arpads of Hungary, was on the verge of dying out. Four Angevins would be kings of 'the lands of the Crown of St. Stephen' (as Hungary and Croatia were formally referred to), two would be crowned kings of Poland, while seven would wear the crown of the kingdom of Naples. It was a remarkable achievement, especially when one considers that these crowns were won with very little bloodshed.

But while Poland's dalliance with the House of Anjou was brief (only 29 years), it formed the basis of a lasting relationship with France. A hundred years later another prince of the House of France would be elected[3] and called to the throne of Poland. In 1573, after the death of Sigismund II, the last of the Jagellons of Poland-Lithuania, Prince Henry of Valois, the brother of King Charles IX, was among the five candidates under consideration by the Polish Diet. Henry won, and among the losers was Archduke Ernest of Habsburg. Considering that Ernest was a younger son of the Emperor, Henry's success speaks volumes for his personality. His brother Charles was but a poor specimen of a king (or of a man, for that matter), and in no position to canvass support for him. However, Henry's reign was destined to be short; Poland did not appeal to him, and he was appalled by the severity of the winter and the poverty in the countryside. The Polish nobles had been given to understand that Henry would marry the late king's sister, Anna, but he found her unattractive. Hence in May 1574 he slipped away quietly to France on receiving the news of his brother's death. The following year (by now he had been crowned king of France), after his refusal to return to Poland, the Polish Diet deposed him formally and started making arrangements for another election.

However, the most outstanding example of an empire cobbled together by marriages and diplomacy rather than war is that of the house of Habsburg. Starting out in the eleventh century as counts of Habsburg, a small castle in the Aargau (now in Switzerland, but then included in the Duchy of Swabia), they soon acquired more territory in Alsace and along the upper Rhine. When their chief, Rudolf, was elected emperor[4] he recovered Austria with its dependencies of Styria and Carinthia from King Ottokar II of Bohemia, who had usurped them after the extinction of the Babenbergs who had held them earlier. Thereafter they would remain Habsburg possessions and the title 'Archduke of Austria' would become the hereditary title of all Habsburg princes.

The next leap forward was in 1477 when Archduke Maximilian, son of Emperor Fredrick III, was married to Mary, daughter and heiress of Charles the Bold, the late Duke of Burgundy, who had been killed in battle while fighting the Swiss a few months earlier. The late duke had ruled over a mosaic of territories, some held as fiefs of his cousins, the kings of France, others of the emperor. His court was celebrated for its brilliance, and buoyed by the revenues of the wool-trade of the Netherlands, he was probably the richest prince in Europe, and aspired to be elevated to regal rank, something which only the emperor could do. Now, suddenly, all that was Maximilian's, first in right of his wife, and after her death in 1482 (as a result of a riding accident), as regent for his son. The dukes of Burgundy were so rich that when the Emperor Fredrick set out to ask for the hand of Mary for Maximilian, he had to borrow money from the Fuggers (who were the emperor's principal bankers) to make a good show, dressing his entourage in cloth of gold. So poor were the revenues of the empire in comparison.

In 1486 he was elected king of the Romans, and after his father's death in 1493, succeeded him as emperor. In 1486 he had married his son Philip to Joanna, the daughter of Ferdinand and Isabella, and heiress to the crowns of Aragon and Castile. This marriage would, in due course, bring Spain and its overseas possessions into the Habsburg fold. Then in 1515 the twin marriages celebrated between his grandchildren Ferdinand and Maria, and the children of the rulers of Bohemia and Hungary, Louis and Anna, were to prove decisive for the family fortunes. An agreement was arrived at with Louis, who succeeded to his father's thrones in 1516, that in the event of his dying issueless, Ferdinand would succeed him to the thrones of Hungary and Bohemia. Through this shrewd political union, the lands of the Danube basin were linked together at the very time when the Turks were preparing for their thrust into the heart of Europe. Ten years later this indeed came about when Louis was killed in the disastrous battle of Mohacs against the Turks, even though the better part of Hungary was lost to the Turks.

Neither India nor the Orient has any parallel to the Habsburg or Angevin super-states which owed so much to fortuitous marriages. No wonder it was said of Austria:

Bella gerant alii,
Tu, felix Austria, nube![5]

Cultural factors, custom and tradition are part of the explanation. In India, among the native Hindu princes, the tradition of direct succession prevailed. The throne could pass to a brother, and it often did, but it was highly desirable that it should continue to pass from father to son. And since polygamy was normal in princely families (partly to ensure the birth of a male) the production of a son was highly desirable for the women, for their ranking in the *zenana* or harem depended upon it. A *rani* who failed to conceive was next to nothing, a daughter was something, but it was a son that was most desirable. Only sons could succeed to thrones, and daughters were a liability, because dowries had to be provided for their marriages, and caste laws severely restricted the choice of a husband.

But men are sometimes infertile or impotent, and kings and princes were no exceptions, even in so fecund a country as India. Then clever, dominating consorts found other ways of producing infants. Spurious infants would be procured from needy mothers from outside the palace and passed off as the queen's progeny. Sometimes the king, who was loath to confess his impotence, would connive at the fraud, more often he turned a blind eye to it. Sometimes it would be managed with the connivance of a smart eunuch. And then there were eunuchs *and* eunuchs. Many a supposed eunuch was in fact the true father of many a prince. Stories of such spurious heirs abound in the annals of princely India. During the British Raj the political agents posted at princely courts monitored not only the happenings in the *durbar* and capital, but also the gossip of the *zenana*. Since the *sanads* of succession to a princely throne could only be issued by the Paramount Power, investigations were routinely carried out to establish the genuineness and legitimacy of the heir-apparent.

Sir John Shore,[6] then governor-general, in a detailed minute of 13 January 1798, discussed the legitimacy of the supposed sons of Asaf ud-Daula, the Nawab-Wazir of Awadh. Those were still early days, the term 'Paramount Power' had not yet been coined; it was still the East India Company which exercised power in India rather than the British Crown, and it was but 34 years since it had been conferred the *diwani* of Bengal by the Emperor Shah Alam. But already in Bengal and the Ganges valley, the British had arrogated to themselves the role of king-makers. The occasion for recording the minute was the deposition by the Company of Wazir Ali from the *masnad* of Awadh on account of his hostile attitude, a bare four months after his accession. Wazir Ali was replaced by his uncle Saadat Ali, in supersession of the claims of his numerous brothers.

The governor-general first discusses the mother of the deposed Nawab:

> ... the mother of Vizier Ally was a Fraushnee, or wife of a Fraush, now living: her name was Rehmut and she exercised the employment of a Fraushnee, the lowest occupation of a menial servant, in Tehseen's house, where females, purchased by the Nabob, occasionally remained until the increase of their numbers made their removal into the zenana necessary. Rehmut usually accompanied them there. Her monthly wages were four rupees. She was not confined to the zenana, but quitted it daily, which is the custom of all others of the same description, and went to her husband's house.... She had three children, the first a son, who died: the Nabob took him from his mother, paying five hundred rupees for him, and gave him the name of Mahommed Ameen. The second was also a son, and is now a Fraush in the department of Tehseen Ally Khan. The third was Vizier Ally....
>
> Tehseen further declares that the women of the zenana used to advise the Nabob to take children and bring them up, as he had none of his own. He allows that the Nabob ever acknowledged Vizier Ally as his own son: but when he was angry with him, he used to allude to the lowness of his origin; and on these occasions he said, in presence of hundreds, that he was not his son.
>
> The particulars thus detailed were collected from inquiries put to Tehseen at different times, and in a mode which I thought calculated to extract the truth, he underwent frequent examinations, both from the resident and myself. The papers, No. 1 and 2, translated were sworn to by Tehseen in my presence, and in that of the Persian translator.
>
> The detail in No. 3, which does not include Vizier Ally, applies to fifteen children of the Nabob; thirteen of whom were born in the zenana, of women purchased, and brought into it in a state of pregnancy; and two were born outside the zenana, and introduced into it when infants....[7]

Deceptions of this nature are inconceivable in European history. Law and custom did not permit polygamy. Custom did indeed allow a prince to indulge himself with mistresses—and many of them were of as humble an origin as the alleged mother of Vizier Ally—

but the lives of royal queens were an open book. Adultery—even on the part of the queen—was by no means uncommon, and the paternity of many an European monarch could perhaps be questioned, but the induction of spurious infants into the palace was unthinkable. In France even the lying-in of her Majesty was a public event, with scores of courtiers and their wives witnessing the birth of the queen's offspring.

Among the Hindu princes of India, however, in the event of infertility or impotence, there was the other alternative of adoption. A boy could always be adopted, and custom offered considerable choice in the matter. Usually the adopted prince would be taken from among the close cousins, but there was no fixed rule. The choice was usually made after consultation with ministers and powerful nobles. If the ruler died without effecting an adoption, the principal widow was authorized to do so. Thus there were posthumous adoptions as well, the most famous case being that of Tukoji Rao Holkar by Rani Ahalya Bai, the widow of Malhar Rao Holkar. Thus, unless the state was destroyed and annexed, Indian princely dynasties could continue *ad infinitum*.

And of course, the marriages of princes and princesses were even more emphatically a public event. While mistresses might be bought and sold, the marriages of princes were a matter of state concern, the subject matter of negotiation and hard bargaining, with dowries clearly specified. In England the marriage of the king or his heir required the approval of the parliament, and after 1689 it was specified that the consort had to be a Protestant. Among the Habsburgs and most German princes, family law clearly laid down from which families the consort could be chosen. She had to be of appropriate rank, a mere countess or baroness would not do; she had to be from the higher nobility. Even as late as the twilight years of the Austro-Hungarian monarchy when Archduke Francis Ferdinand, the heir-presumptive insisted on marrying Sophie Chotek, a Bohemian countess (and definitely not of royal blood) Emperor Francis Joseph insisted that the marriage would be treated as morganatic. Very reluctantly, at the time of the marriage (in 1900) the emperor granted her the dignity of 'Princess of Hohenberg', with the style of 'Serene Highness'. Nine years later she was raised to the rank of 'Duchess of Hohenberg' with the style of 'Her Highness'. But it was made plain that her children would never succeed to the throne. This was in spite of the fact that her parents were by no means nonentities; her mother was a Kinsky, one of the first families of Bohemia, and through other female ancestors she could claim descent from the sovereign houses of Baden, Hohenzollern-Hechingen, and Liechtenstein. She was in fact descended from Elizabeth, a sister of the first Habsburg emperor, Rudolf I, King of the Romans (1273-91)—but all this was of no avail.

In India too, marriages, especially of the daughters of Rajput princes, were a serious matter. But in the case of kings or heirs to the throne, only the first marriage was considered important. The senior *rani* was invariably of a noble family and carefully chosen. Later alliance, however, were frequently whimsical, and the women could be from all walks of life. There might even be simple village girls who may have caught the king's eye in the course of a hunt, as happens in the well-known play *Shakuntala.* Moreover Hindu customary law recognized several kinds of marriages, and not all consorts were of equal rank.

The same could be said of the marriages of the Turkish or Mughal emperors—or of the rulers of the successor states that arose from the wreckage of the Tughluq and Mughal empires. The caste rules that were applicable to the Hindus did not apply to them, but again while the first consort was usually selected with care, later additions to the harem could be just anyone. Many a courtesan or professional dancer or singer ended as an empress. But unlike the Ottoman *padishahs* of Constantinople the Mughal emperors were family men, and had no hesitation in entering into regular *nikah* marriages. The former—until the reign of Suleiman (1520-66)—did not marry as a matter of policy. So until the sixteenth century all the Ottoman *padishahs* were the progeny of slave-girls.

One cannot help noticing the stark contrast in the relative status of women in Europe and India. We know the names of the consorts of all European monarchs without exception, and we know who their parents were. Since marriage was one way of adding to one's territory, princes vied with each other for the hand of an heiress like Eleanor of Aquitaine, Mary of Burgundy or Joanna of Aragon and Castile. And the ladies were not mere pawns in the marriage market; they usually had some say in the matter. In many European states and families in which the Salic law was applicable, women were debarred from succession to states and feudal fiefs, but this did not affect their social position significantly.

In many ways the legal position of Muslim women under the ordinary civil law—the Quranic *shariah*—was superior to that of their Hindu or Christian sisters in India and Europe, but practically speaking they were mere chattels of no consequence, except in the rare instances when they were able to prevail over the male-dominant patriarchies by sheer force of personality. The case of the two '*begums* of Awadh' (Sadr us-Nisa and her daughter-in-law, Amat ul-Zohra, the famous 'Bahu Begum') is exceptional. It is unlikely that they would have been able to enjoy their vast wealth for as long as they did, had it not been for the support of the governor-general. Then there is the case of Hazrat Mahal, one of the wives of the deposed Wajid Ali Shah, who became the rallying point for the rebellion in Lucknow in 1857. In Jhansi there was Rani Lakshmi Bai. But these were very exceptional women in extraordinary times.

It is virtually impossible to write proper biographies of the consorts of Indian rulers. Barring a few notable personalities very little is known about them. In some cases we do not know even the names of the mothers of some of the emperors. And of course, in the case of the most celebrated of the Slave kings, Qutb ud-Din Aibak, Iltutmish and Balban, even the fathers are unknown!

NOTES

1. The Germany of the Middle Ages was much larger than the Germany of today, and included Alsace, Lorraine, the Netherlands, Belgium, Bohemia, Silesia and Austria.

2. It is another matter that Louis XIV chose to identify the Rhine River rather than the Vosges mountains as the natural frontier. The spoken patois of Alsace was a dialect of German rather than French.
3. The crowns of Poland, Hungary and Bohemia (like that of the Holy Roman empire) were, in theory, elective.
4. It was a bad time for the empire. After the death of Fredrick II of Hohenstauffen in 1250 there was a succession of weak emperors. Rudolf's immediate predecessor was Richard, Earl of Cornwall, a younger brother of King Henry III of England. Though emperor from 1257 to 1272, his title was only nominal, and he made only four brief visits to Germany. An extremely wealthy man he had purchased the dignity and was seemingly content with that.
5. *Let others wage war,*
   You, Happy Austria, marry!
6. Later Lord Teignmouth.
7. *The Asiatic Annual Register for the Year 1799, State Papers,* London, Debrett, 1801, p. 7.

CHAPTER 9

Nationalism

It is a common misconception that the European states are nation states while India is not, and that is supposed to be a peculiar defect in our 'national' psyche. As a matter of fact nation states—and the very concept of nationalism—are a relatively new phenomenon, and one that has already begun to fade away in the more developed countries of the world.

In spite of the old legends perpetuated by school history books about King Alfred in England, Clovis in France, and Charlemagne or Otto in Germany, it is absurd to suggest that any of them were animated by anything resembling a 'national' spirit. In the beginning they started out as tribal chieftains, but the republicanism of the tribal spirit soon gave way to feudalism with its hereditary fiefs. And if Alfred is seen today as an English king, in his own day he was a king of Wessex, i.e. of the West Saxons. The West Saxons were also only a small off-shoot of the great Saxon tribe. On the continent, Otto the Great and his father Henry the Fowler were also Saxons, and dukes of Saxony before they became kings of Germany. The revival of the imperial dream, the desire to recreate the old Roman empire of the West, and the opportunities for acquiring territory by inheritance and marriage all militated against the development of nationalism as we understand it today. Even the great tribal duchies of Germany soon lost their tribal identities. Otto the Great (936-73), himself Duke of Saxony married his son Liutdolf to Ida, the daughter and heiress of Duke Hermann of Swabia. He gave the duchy of Lorraine to Conrad the Red whom he later made his son-in-law. His cousin Henry was married to the daughter of Duke Berthold of Bavaria, and after his father-in-law's death became Duke of Bavaria. After the suppression of the rebellion of Duke Eberhard of Franconia, Otto broke up the duchy and divided the bulk of its lands between the bishoprics of Wurzburg and Bamberg.

Thus William the Bastard, Duke of Normandy, a descendant of Rollo the Viking, a Norseman of Scandinavian origin, was able to stake his claim to the throne of the Saxons of England. He defeated the other claimant and became king of England, to be followed two generations later by a Count of Blois, and then another from Anjou. Another Angevin count would later on become king of Sicily–a kingdom originally founded by another 'Norman' adventurer, Tancred of Hauteville, about the same time that the Norman Bastard was conquering England. A son of this same Angevin king of Sicily, as we have seen in the preceding chapter, became a king of Hungary and *his* son, in turn, was invited to become the king of Poland.

Kings and princes were above nationality. In the nineteenth century almost every ruling dynasty in Europe–including that of imperial Russia–was of German or Frankish origin. The only exceptions were Serbia and Montenegro, and these Slav states fell on the other side of the cultural fault-line of Europe.

The nationalist uprisings in the Balkans would result in the birth or rebirth of other kingdoms and principalities from the disintegrating mass of 'Turkey in Europe'. Greece, Rumania and Bulgaria arose, rejuvenated, between the years 1832 and 1879. Albania, last of all, emerged as an independent principality in 1914. One would have expected–since these were supposedly nationalist uprisings–that these new states would select their own native princes or partisan leaders as their new rulers, but far from it. Serbia with its two rival houses of Milosch Obrenovitch and Kara George was the solitary exception. All the others tamely accepted German princes who were imposed on them by the European powers as their rulers. So much for Balkan nationalism!

The Serbian uprising began in 1804 when the European powers were preoccupied with the Napoleonic wars, and in 1817 Milosch Obrenovitch was recognized by the Sublime Porte as prince of an autonomous Serbia. The Serbs thus made it on their own, without the intervention of any foreign power. Had their revolt started a few years later, like the Greeks, they too would have had a foreign prince foisted on them.

The Greek revolt started in 1821, but it soon became a pan-European cause, with volunteers (including the poet Byron) flocking to assist in the liberation of what was seen as the cradle of Western civilization. For a time it seemed that the Turks might prevail, but the destruction of the Egyptian fleet at Navarino Bay by a combined British, French and Russian fleet decided the war in favour of the Greeks. After another few years of desultory fighting, the Turks were forced to the conference table. The Porte agreed to grant independence; Britain, France and Russia guaranteed it and provided the Greeks with a king in the person of Otto, a younger son of King Ludwig I of Bavaria. When the turbulent and democratic Greeks threw out the autocratic German in a revolution in 1863, they were offered another prince, this time, George, a younger son of King Christian IX of Denmark.

Rumania which was composed initially of the two provinces of Moldavia and Wallachia, started out with a native prince, Alexander John Cuza, in 1859. He was, however, forced to resign by a revolution in 1866 and replaced by Charles (or Carol as the Rumanians called him) of Hohenzollern-Sigmaringen, a minor branch of the Prussian royal house. The Hohenzollerns would remain rulers of Rumania till 1947. Likewise Bulgaria, which revolted in 1875, was granted autonomy in 1879, and Prince Alexander of Battenberg, a nephew of Czar Alexander II of Russia, became its first prince. But he proved too independent for Russia's liking, so in 1886 he was forced to abdicate and was replaced by Ferdinand of Saxe-Coburg-Gotha, the scion of one of the several Saxon duchies in central Germany. Though the parent duchy was no bigger than Sigmaringen, a prince of that house had been made king of the Belgians in 1831, while another was the prince-consort of Queen Victoria of the United Kingdom. Since 1853, with the extinction of the male line of the House of Braganza, the throne of Portugal had also passed to another prince of Saxe-Coburg-Gotha, the son of Queen Maria II and her consort Ferdinand of Saxe-Coburg.

Albania was the last Balkan state to become independent, as a spin-off of the First Balkan War. Its first prince was William of Wied, a brother of Queen Maria of Rumania. He arrived in Albania in March 1914, but that anarchic country had always resisted control of any kind. Within months civil war broke out, and then in August the outbreak of the world war made matters even worse for the young and inexperienced prince. In September he was forced to flee the country. After the war Albania became an Italian protectorate, and, after a brief period as a republic, the monarchy was revived, this time under a native chieftain who ruled as King Zog (1928-39), the only Muslim king in Europe. He was more or less an Italian puppet, and would ultimately be deposed by them.

European nationalism is therefore a fairly recent–and largely fictional–development. In no country can it be identified prior to the nineteenth century. The French Revolution is supposed to have started it all. The English like to trace the beginnings of their national spirit to the Tudors, and more specifically to Queen Elizabeth I. The Tudors were indeed the first native dynasty since 1066, after all the Normans and Frankish Angevins or Plantagenets that had preceded them, but it is questionable whether any truly national feeling can be attributed to a people who so readily accepted the Stuart succession in 1603, and after deposing King James II in 1688 accepted, rather invited a Dutch prince to accept the English crown. Of course, the Dutchman too was actually a German prince of the House of Nassau, and gloried in the title of Prince of Orange–the latter being a small town in the Rhone valley. Holland, incidentally, was a republic, and its proper name was the United Provinces of the Netherlands. Its ruler was called *Stadtholder* but the post had become more or less hereditary in the House of Nassau. Europe was full of such contradictions.

But this Dutch prince, who ruled England jointly as King William III with his wife Mary (who was a daughter of the deposed king) was incapable of fathering an heir (he was supposed to be gay), so after he and his wife had died the throne passed to another daughter of the deposed James, named Anne, who was married to a prince of the House of Holstein-Glucksburg. But neither of Anne's numerous children survived her—most died in infancy—and the throne of England now went to another German prince, George, Elector of Hanover, of the former ducal house of Brunswick-Luneberg, who was also a great grandson of King James I. This dour German had left his wife behind him in Germany, imprisoned on account of alleged adultery, and arrived with two German mistresses instead. He did not even speak English and had to converse with his ministers in dog-Latin! Yet the English tolerated him.

At best one can say the English shared all the usual prejudices attributable to an insular people, and its governing elite, which was represented in its Parliament, was extremely suspicious of any meddling in the established religion of the country, namely the Church of England. The word 'nationalism' was unknown at the time, and its nearest equivalent—patriotism—had an unsavoury connotation. In the words of Dr. Johnson, the quintessential Englishman and final arbiter of literary taste in the eighteenth century, it was 'the last refuge of a scoundrel'. Soldiers still died for their kings in the Age of Reason, rather than their country. It was only in the nineteenth and twentieth centuries that it became praiseworthy and even fashionable to die *pro patria.*

There are other ways of looking at the 'Glorious Revolution' of 1688. The exaggerated hype given to it appears to have been a cover for high treason—which is how the 'Jacobites' saw it. But Niall Ferguson gives an entirely different angle to it. From 1640 onwards the Dutch were the principal rivals of the English in the Indies. A superior financial system and a central bank enabled them to raise loans cheaply in the market and build-up a strong navy. In fact, during the Protectorate the Dutch ruled the seas and on one occasion a Dutch fleet had sailed up the Thames and bombarded and burnt the dockside warehouses! That had the great Whig peers worried. The latter had over the years become closely involved with the merchants and bankers of the city who financed the trading voyages to India, and the growing Dutch ascendancy was a threat to their fortunes. Thus the invitation extended to William was in fact a sort of business merger. The Anglo-Dutch wars ceased and a tacit division of interests was negotiated, by which the spice trade and the East Indies were recognized as falling in the Dutch sphere, while India and the growing textile trade was recognized as being England's particular interest. All that hype about the revolution being a confirmation of British liberties and of parliamentary monarchy is in fact bunkum. It was mere propaganda to gloss over an outrageous act of high treason. The apprehensions regarding the Catholicism of James and his queen were in fact highlighted to appeal to the prejudices of the lower classes. Thus the Glorious Revolution was anything but patriotic![1]

There is also the curious case of Scotland. I had always been puzzled by the ease with which Scotland adjusted to becoming England's junior partner in the Union of Great Britain. The stout resistance put up by Wallace and Bruce at earlier attempts by England to conquer its northern neighbour constitute some of the more inspiring passages in British history. After that it was perhaps poetic justice that the throne of England should pass peacefully to a king of Scotland in 1603—especially since his own mother had been executed by the English queen after being kept a prisoner for seventeen years.

The succession was unchallenged; James got the throne by the ordinary rules of inheritance after the death of the woman who had ordered his own mother's execution. But when the English Parliament deposed the Stuarts after the Civil War, Scotland remained with England, although the union was at that time purely personal, both countries being separate kingdoms, each with its own parliament. True, Charles's Scottish policy was a mess. His High Church policy had antagonized the Scottish Kirk as well, the Civil War had been preceded by a 'Bishops War' in Scotland, and the Presbyterian Church which was predominant in the Scottish Lowlands had more in common with English Puritanism. Hence Charles was dropped by the Scots without any pangs of patriotic conscience. But the second Stuart expulsion of 1688 was also tamely accepted by the Scots. There was only the minor affair of the rising of 'Bonnie

Dundee', the Marquis of Claverhouse, and with the latter being killed in the first engagement, the rising collapsed. The Irish, on the other hand, who had no reason to love James, rallied to his support, simply because he was supposed to be a closet Catholic, married to an admittedly Catholic princess, Mary of Modena. No matter that she happened to be Italian. They paid heavily for their loyalty.

Fifteen years later the Act of Union was passed. By this Scotland ceased to be a separate kingdom and the Scottish Parliament too was abolished. The act had to be passed by the Scottish parliament too, but the Scottish parliamentarians were easily bought by generous dollops of cash. Some of the Scottish peers sold their vote for as little as 50 or 100 pounds. However, the duke of Atholl, one of the biggest magnates of the Highlands, was not ready to sell his vote so cheap. He protested that the Scottish nobles would not be admitted to the parliament at Westminster on the same terms as their English compeers, and that the Scottish members were getting only 45 seats in the House of Commons. 'He thus raised his price, got a thousand pounds and that silenced him. When afterwards charged with having sold his country he cynically replied that he thanked God he had a country to sell.'[2] When the Irish Act of Union was passed in 1801 it was much the same story. There were certainly as many Mir Jafars in the peerage of the three kingdoms of the British Isles as there were among the Indian *omrahs*.

Was the act of inviting Babur to invade India and overthrow the government of Ibrahim Lodi all that different from that of inviting Prince William of Orange to accept the crown of England? Likewise, in the eighteenth century it was Yahya Khan, a *subedar* of Lahore, who invited Ahmad Shah Durrani to come and make himself master of the Punjab. Najib Khan Rohilla was an enthusiastic partisan of the Afghan Shah; he looked after his interests in his absence, and assisted him in whatever way he could when he happened to be in India. Ruling elites, whether Indian or European, have usually their personal or corporate interests closest to their hearts. Britain had a parliament through which the landed aristocracy and untitled gentry and burgesses of the towns could act as a corporate body. India had no such body which could lend dignity to their corporate demands and grievances. India did not even have a hereditary nobility, so great officers of the state, whether Daulat Khan Lodi or Najib Khan, could only act as individuals, according to their perceived interests.

How foreign the modern concept of nationality was to the nobility of eighteenth-century Europe is well illustrated by the life and career of Maurice, Comte de Saxe and Marshall of France. He was an illegitimate son of Augustus the Strong, King of Poland and Elector of Saxony. At the age of twelve he entered the imperial service under Prince Eugene of Savoy and fought against France in the War of the Spanish Succession. Then for a time he served under Czar Peter the Great of Russia, and then for a few years under his father in Poland. There followed another short spell of imperial service against the Turks. After failing to get himself accepted as the duke of Courland, even though he was elected to the duchy, he eventually entered the French service and fought on the French side in the War of the Austrian Succession. In 1743 he was made Marshall of France, but he wasn't naturalized as a French subject until three years later!

Even the great Prince Eugene, hereditary duke of Savoy, and commander of the imperial armies in the War of the Spanish Succession, had first sought service under King Louis XIV, even though Savoy was a fief of the empire. His own father was a colonel in the French service. The court of the Sun King was the most brilliant in Europe and at the end of the Thirty Years War France was the foremost military power in Europe. Therefore, as a landless and penniless prince[3] who had to make his own fortune, his predilection for the French service was understandable. But his application for a commission in the French army was turned down because of his ugliness (he had a hump on his back), and the Sun King liked his officers to be handsome. The emperor, who at that time was engaged in a war with the Turks, was less choosy, so it was in the imperial service that Eugene was destined to attain military fame. In the War of the Spanish Succession, together with the Duke of

Marlborough he inflicted one stinging defeat after another on the French, and well may Louis have regretted his early rebuff when the young Savoyard had sought his commission!

This indifference to nationality and national origins persisted well into the twentieth century among the higher aristocracy, particularly among the military officer class of the monarchies of Europe which was dominated by the nobility and untitled landed gentry. At the battle of Tannenberg (1914) in East Prussia, the First Russian Army was commanded by General Pavel von Rennenkampf, an ethnic German from the Baltic provinces of Russia, while on the German side, the First German Corps was commanded by General Hermann von Francois who was of French Huguenot descent.

But the most piquant case of all was that of the English Battenbergs and the Saxe-Coburg-Gothas. The Baltic Germans were, after all, native to the east, and these descendants of the old Livonian Brothers of the Sword and the Teutonic Knights[4] of yore had been living on their estates in Livonia, Courland, Lithuania and Latvia since the fourteenth century or earlier, and had been subjects of Russia, at least since the times of Catherine the Great. As for the Huguenots, many of them had left France after the revocation of the Edict of Nantes by King Louis XIV in 1685. Being Calvinists, many of them had migrated to Holland and Brandenburg-Prussia. But the case of the English Battenbergs was quite unique. At the outbreak of the First World War the head of the British Navy, the First Sea Lord as he was called, was actually a German prince. Prince Louis of Battenberg was a cousin of Grand Duke Louis IV of Hesse-Darmstadt, the product of a morganatic marriage between the latter's uncle and a certain Countess Julia von Hawke. The Grand Duke was married to a daughter of Queen Victoria, and since the Battenbergs were poor, and Louis had a passion for the sea, he joined the Royal Navy with the recommendation of the Grand Duchess. He did well in his chosen career, and the outbreak of the war found him as the First Sea Lord at the Admiralty.

The outbreak of the war was accompanied by a wave of anti-German xenophobia, and a whispering campaign started against the

First Sea Lord, the implicit suggestion being that Britain's navy was not in the most trustworthy hands. Prince Louis relinquished his German titles, adopted the anglicized name of Mountbatten in lieu of Battenberg, and was granted the earldom of Milford-Haven in the peerage of the United Kingdom. But that was not enough, and he ultimately resigned. At the same time King George V became conscious of his own German antecedents. He was no longer a German prince, the kingdom of Hanover having passed to an uncle of Victoria's on account of the Salic law when William IV died. But Victoria's consort had been Prince Albert of Saxe-Coburg-Gotha, and ever since the British royal house had been styled as the House of Saxe-Coburg-Gotha which had a decidedly Germanic ring. So the king also changed his name by statute and took up the name of Windsor (after Windsor Castle, the principal country residence of the royal family), the family being known henceforth as the house of Windsor.

However, European royalty still regarded itself as a supranational fraternity, immune to narrow nationalisms. Since army and naval officers bore the 'King's Commission' in monarchical countries, and the king was the commander-in-chief, foreign princes could still find employment and refuge in the armies and navies of their royal and imperial cousins. Thus the Prince Imperial, the heir of the deposed Emperor Napoleon III was granted a commission in the British army and was killed in the Zulu War. Another Battenberg, Prince Henry, a younger brother of the future First Sea Lord, married Princess Beatrice (another of Victoria's numerous daughters), was granted a commission in the British army, and died of malaria in the Ashanti War (1896). Again, when the Greek royal family was forced to leave Greece following a republican revolution in 1924, Prince Philip, the son of Prince Andrew of Greece and Princess Alice of Battenberg—the latter a daughter of the former First Sea Lord, now Earl of Milford-Haven—was able to find a berth in the Royal Navy, thanks to his uncle, his mother's brother, the future Lord Louis Mountbatten of Burma. Philip's parents had split under the strain of exile; the father took to alcohol while his mother entered a convent. Philip, however, was destined for greatness, after a fashion. He would, in due course, marry Princess Elizabeth, the future queen of the United Kingdom, and is known today as the Duke of Edinburgh.

An essential concomitant of nationalism is the conviction that one's nation or *patria* is special and superior to all other nations or countries in the world. In that sense even the Indians of medieval times could be described as fanatically nationalist. Alberuni, the famous savant from Khiva, has described the Indians of the eleventh century as believing that there was 'no other country on earth but theirs, no other race of man but theirs, and no created beings besides them have any knowledge or science whatsoever'.[5] One is reminded of John of Gaunt's famous description of England, rendered more poetically by Shakespeare in *Richard II*:

This royal throne of kings, this scepter'd isle,
This earth of majesty, this seat of Mars,
This other Eden, demi-paradise;
This fortress built by nature for herself
Against infection and the hand of war;
This happy breed of men, this little world.
This precious stone set in the silver sea....[6]

The idea of *Bharatvarsha* as some kind of ideal and specially blessed country has persisted down the ages up to the present times. Most people think of their country like that; for the Chinese and Japanese all foreigners are barbarians (so was it for the Greeks and the Romans), and it is only recently that the Europeans and White Americans have begun to accept that maybe other people—the 'lesser breeds'—may actually be as human as they are.

What differentiates Indian nationalism from other brands is that it is more accommodating and inclusive—the multiplicity of languages and dialects, the plurality of races and the infinite divisions of caste and creed notwithstanding. In due course everyone can become an Indian. On the other hand, Europeans are so insecure that until the nineteenth century the general belief was that a country should have only one recognized religion, and even different sects of Christianity were regarded as separate religions. It was taken for granted that while members of minority sects might be permitted freedom of worship, they could not possibly be treated entirely as equals of those who subscribed to the recognized state religion. It was a long trek from religious toleration to religious equality. Even today the king (or queen) of England has to be a member of the church of England; he or she has to be the head of the church. The Indian situation where there is no recognized head of the Hindu religion (nor has ever been), or of Indian Islam would be bewildering for Europeans. Indians might even question the existence of a Hindu religion, or an Indian Islam. We have so many shades of belief and disbelief, and we do not think of that as being in any way unusual.

Language was an equally sensitive matter. As late as the twentieth century the use of the Germanic Alsatian dialect and the Celtic Breton was a penal offence in France. The use of the Gaelic and its variants of Cornish, Welsh and Erse were likewise banned in Scotland, Ireland, England and Wales. And then there is the sad case of the Basques of Spain.

The word is modern but genocide was in fact a standard Western way of dealing with people who were 'not like us'. The Western Slavs or Wends and the ancient Prussians have all disappeared. The Pomeranians and Mecklenburgers, also Slavs, hemmed in by Germans and Scandinavians, have been thoroughly assimilated and Germanized. Of course, the Germanized Pomeranians have also disappeared from East Pomerania now, being displaced in the forced population movements that followed the end of the Second World War. The English too tried something like that in Ireland, starting in Tudor times. Oliver Cromwell and then William of Orange tried their hand at it but failed. Hitler tried it with the Jews, the Poles, Gypsies and assorted *untermenschen.* He used industrial methods of mass destruction and came quite close to achieving his ends, but fortunately the Thousand Years Reich lasted only twelve years.

There is no definite evidence of such genocidal exterminations in Indian history, though of course one may object there is precious little chance of finding such evidence for Indian history itself is so poorly recorded. The aboriginal tribals of the forest are still there, though development has largely by-passed them, and they have been marginalized even in their own forest homes. With the caste system in place it was no longer necessary to actively persecute or exterminate people. But whatever happened to the Bhars? One comes across these people in all the old accounts of Awadh and UP. Apparently they were a ruling tribe spread over a wide area, and many of the annals of old Rajput families start with a wandering Rajput prince who enters the service of a Bhar chief, and then supplants him, usually by treachery. But now there are no people with a name resembling that of the Bhars. But names change. For instance, it is now taboo to refer to the former untouchable castes by their old names. The Yadavas are numerous and powerful in western UP, but the old nineteenth-century books only use that word in connection with the Yadavas of Deogiri in the Deccan. The modern Yadavas of Haryana and western UP were formerly described as Ahirs, but now, for some reason the old name has become unmentionable. Upward mobility is usually accompanied by a change of tribal or caste names.

There is, however, no overt attempt to assimilate. Diversity is taken for granted; *vive la difference!* That appears to be the essence of the Indian spirit. The European psychology, however, abhors diversity. Apart from the differences of class (which it cherishes), it cannot rest easy until it has standardized everything. It demands a standardized religion with a uniform theology and dogma, a standardized official language, weights and measures and standardized packaging. The Eurocrats of the European Union churn out reams of statutory laws and regulations on what would appear to be the most ridiculous subjects. For instance, until recently, only carrots of a certain colour, shape and size could be sold in department stores!

Nationalism was never a particular virtue possessed only by the people of western Europe. All people, everywhere, love their 'homeland'—only its definition varies. But what was recognized as nationalism in nineteenth and twentieth-century Europe was a particularly malign and baneful sentiment, the product of a jingoistic xenophobia. It was artificially stimulated by the ruling elites of the European states by means of mass education and the established national churches because it was considered indispensable for hyping the conscript armies of the *levée en masse* to the appropriate level of excitement in battle. No sensible man willingly sacrifices himself in war. The mythology of nationalism, however, provides a justification of sorts.

NOTES

1. Niall Ferguson, *Empire: How Britain Made the Modern World*, Penguin, 2004, pp. 22-4.
2. J.M. Macdiarmid, *The Deer Forests and How They are Bleeding Scotland White*, published by the Home Rule Association, 1926.
3. The House of Savoy (unlike most German princely families) followed primogeniture, the duke of Savoy was also Count of Piedmont and King of Sardinia, but these territories were indivisible. But since nobility was a caste in Europe, younger cadets of the house were entitled to the honorific title of 'hereditary duke of Savoy'. This was just an empty dignity with no lands or estates attached to it.
4. The Order was secularized in 1525 when the Grand Master Albert of Brandenburg converted to Lutheranism and became Duke of Prussia under the Polish crown. The Order lingered on, and still retained considerable properties elsewhere in Germany, but it had ceased to exercise political authority. The Livonian Order had been absorbed by the Teutonic Order in 1237.
5. Edward Sachau (ed.), *Alberuni's India*, p. 5, New Delhi: Indialog Publications, p. 5.
6. Shakespeare, *King Richard II*, Act II, Scene 1.

CHAPTER 10

Subaltern Histories: British and Irish

I used to think that the Indian peasant was infinitely worse off than the European farmer. His holding was tiny and the rent extracted by the landlord excessive, leaving him nothing beyond bare subsistence. In the event of a drought or flood he was faced by the threat of famine and death. In such circumstances he had no option but to leave his village and seek employment in already overcrowded cities where the streets were by no means paved with gold. We have all seen them, whole families on the heartless streets of Delhi, Jaipur, Mumbai or Pune, trying to earn a few rupees by peddling cheap handicraft items or working on roads and construction projects. One tries not to notice them, but they are there—all the time. Scores of movies have been made on this theme; socialism was fashionable in the 1950s and 1960s; we were building a Brave New World.

Of course, there had been peasant risings in Europe—including England—from the Middle Ages onwards, but one thought that things had changed after the French Revolution, when the last vestiges of feudalism and serfdom were abolished. Of course, Eastern Europe was a different world, but even in Czarist Russia serfdom was abolished in 1861. Serfs could no longer be bought and sold like the Negro slaves in the slave states of the American South. They too would be liberated four years later after a bloody civil war. In India we had neither slavery nor serfdom, though we did have bonded labour, debt-slavery, an oppressive caste system and *begar*, or forced labour. All this coupled with the tiny holdings and with 50 per cent of the crop going to the landlord, the lot of the Indian peasant seemed much worse. He *looked* poor.

In the US, or so it seemed, farms were routinely of hundreds and often of thousands of acres. Until a few decades ago free land was still available to immigrants for the asking. We thought that there really couldn't be any peasants as *we* knew them. But we learnt from Steinbeck's novels that this was only part of the truth. In the South where the plantations had been broken up after the abolition of slavery, there were sharecroppers and small holders with tiny holdings, and not all of them were Blacks.

Literature is produced, for the most part, by well-to-do people—and it is mostly about reasonably well-to-do people too. There is the occasional Gorky, Mrs. Gaskell or George Gissing, but these are few and far between. Books are written to be read, and only reasonably well-to-do people can afford to buy them, and naturally they would like to read about characters with whom they can identify. All of Hardy's novels are set in the imaginary Wessex countryside but it is only Jude, the eponymous protagonist of *Jude the Obscure*, who is really and truly poor. Henchard in *The Mayor of Casterbridge* auctions his wife, but he does that in a public house. In *Far From the Madding Crowd* Gabriel Oak loses his flock, and soon thereafter his farm, but he soon gets employment elsewhere; he is never truly down and out.

These novels give one an impression of a peaceful and prosperous countryside. Farmer Boldwood and Bathsheba Everdene are both tenant-farmers. Their landlord is never named, he is a remote and distant entity, even his steward never makes an appearance. He is far from being the local tyrant. When we meet Lord Warburton, master of an estate of 3,000 acres in *A Portrait of a Lady* he comes across as the ideal landlord, a man of culture with a sophisticated lifestyle. The gentlemen in Jane Austen's novels, which are all set in country houses, are similar. Georgian England was no doubt different from Victorian, but neither here do we come across any peasants, evictions, or any suggestion that the lives of the poor are anything but happy. In fact, the poor are almost invisible.

But real life is not always as it is portrayed in novels. Rural England was not quite a Garden of Eden or the Forest of Arden. Below the gentry with their incomes of, perhaps 'five or six thousand a year' were the real peasants, living very often in dire poverty, with the threat of eviction ever dangling above them like the proverbial sword of Damocles. The village commons where the peasants once grazed their cattle had in most cases disappeared, being taken over by the landowning gentry. The gentleman's park—often extending over hundreds of acres—had replaced it. In England the enclosure movement which resulted in this massive land grab took place mostly in the sixteenth and seventeenth—centuries. By Jane Austen's times it was largely a distant memory.

In the Scottish Highlands the gentry started the land-grab after Culloden. Until this time land was still held on feudal tenure in the Highlands. The rents which the crofters paid for their tiny patches of land were a pittance. The Highland lairds counted their wealth, not so much by their rentals in terms of pounds, but more by the number of swords they could muster. After the last Jacobite rising had been crushed, once the hangings, attainders and consequent confiscations were over, the clan chiefs were made landlords after the English pattern. The Heritable Jurisdictions Act of 1746 abolished the traditional jurisdiction exercised by the chiefs which had been guaranteed by Article 20 of the Act of Union of 1707.[1] By this Act the clan chiefs were stripped of their traditional right to call their men to arms. So far the land had belonged to the clan, and the chiefs, by virtue of their position had been its custodians and managers. Now they became actual owners.

Change began to be felt as soon as the old generation of chiefs gave way to the new. Since they had ceased to be chiefs and were now mere landlords the new generation was often absentee, living in cities like London or Edinburgh where they picked up the expensive habits and vices of English and Lowland gentry, whose incomes were generally much higher. Despite their large estates they found that their expenses exceeded their income. Much of the land had been leased out in large lots to their kinsmen, known as 'tacksmen', at nominal rents, because they served as their military officers and it was their responsibility to call out the men from among their subtenants and cotters (who were landless labourers) when the chief went to war. But since private war had been outlawed and they no longer had jurisdiction to call out their men they looked for ways to increase their incomes. When old leases expired they were not renewed, or the rent was doubled and often trebled, the increase being passed on by the tacksmen to their sub-tenants. Thus, the emphasis shifted from swords to rent, and rack-renting became the rule. The patriarchal chief became a landlord, and he proved to be as bad or worse than that stock character of Indian movies, the wicked Indian zamindar.

Some of the more conscientious tacksmen were able to read the writing on the wall, and they emigrated on their own, taking with them their sub-tenants because they saw it as an obligation on their honour. These were the lucky ones for they were able to plan their departure and take whatever capital they had with them. John Macdonald of Glenalladale, a cadet of the great Macdonalds of Clanranald, bought land on the island of St. John in the Gulf of St. Lawrence and in 1772 took an expedition of 'opprest people', to settle it.[2]

In the last decades of the eighteenth century it was found that the Cheviot sheep was particularly suitable for the Highlands. This coincided with a boom in the price of wool. It had been the experience of England that sheep rearing was more profitable than cattle or arable farming, and required far fewer men. In England the transition to pasture had started some three centuries earlier in Tudor times, and had been the spur to the first wave of enclosures. In Scotland this transition started in the last decades of the eighteenth century. Many chiefs leased out their lands to Lowland or English entrepreneurs for raising sheep. But before they could do this their factors had to get the land vacated, which started the painful process of evictions. Ironically it was all done in the cause of 'improvement' because, from the landlord's point of view, once people had been replaced with sheep there was an immediate improvement in the landlord's income.

The most notorious of the 'improving' landlords was the Countess of Sutherland.[3] She cleared her sprawling estates of as many as 15,000 people, replacing them with 200,000 sheep and 40 shepherds. The methods employed were heartless. The factors supervising the process would immediately demolish the dwellings, usually setting the timbers on fire to forestall any attempt at reconstruction. Some of the displaced crofters were at first relocated on miserable small-holdings along the coast with the idea of persuading them to become fishermen and harvest kelp from the sea. Finding it impossible to make a living most of them were then persuaded to emigrate to Canada or the Carolinas. Since they were penniless, they were sometimes sold as indentured labourers to plantation owners in America. The Free Church of Scotland–controlled by the landlords–actually cooperated with the slavers in transporting the evicted tenants to America and the Caribbean.

Even before Culloden, in 1739, Macdonald of Sleat and Macleod of Dunvegan had sold some of their people as indentured servants for the Carolinas.[4] The Duke of Atholl had become notorious on account of some early evictions between 1737 and 1753 on account of game, so that when the American war broke out and men were required for the king's armies, there was no response to his call for volunteers to fill the ranks of the Atholl Highlanders, in spite of the offer of perpetual tenancies. He had to pressgang his own clansmen to go and fight in America. Once the fighting was over, instead of sending them home to their families the duke contracted them out for further service with the East India Company. They were marched to Portsmouth from where they were to embark for India. When the soldiers came to know of this they mutinied as their original term of service had long expired and there was no offer of a fresh bounty, which was customarily given at the time of enlistment. The men mutinied and protested they were being treated as slaves. Their disembarkation were therefore countermanded and they were marched north to Berwick in Scotland where the regiment was disbanded. But when they returned home the outraged Duke evicted every single one of them in an act or vengeance. It was common for hard-pressed German princes to supplement their modest revenues by hiring out their troops in foreign wars. The Duke was only trying to emulate the Duke of Hesse–the most notorious of the German military contractors—many of whose troops had served under Cornwallis in the American war.[5]

Between 1840 and 1880 over 40,000 people were cleared from the Isle of Skye alone. Many of the Hebridean islands were completely depopulated to make place for deer and sheep. Between 1815 and 1853, 3,463,292 people emigrated from Scotland, of whom 1,791,446 emigrated in the six years commencing with 1846 when the potato famine broke out. As usually happens on such occasions there was widespread misappropriation of funds allocated for the relief of the starving poor. The conditions on the 'coffin ships' which bore the emigrants across the Atlantic were horrific; the crowding was even worse than on the slave ships which used to operate only a few decades earlier. Between 1847 and 1853 at least 49 ships, each carrying between 600 and 1,000 emigrants were lost at sea, and 17,600 Scottish emigrants died on the ships or in the quarantine stations of Canada and America.[6]

So severe was the depopulation that at the time of the Crimean war when recruiting parties were sent to drum up recruits, and the landlords called out their tenantry, the response was pathetic. The aged Duke of Sutherland was told to his face at one such meeting:

> I am sorry for the response your Grace's proposals are meeting here, but there is a cause for it.... It is the opinion of this county that should the Czar of Russia take possession of Dunrobin Castle and Stafford House next term that we couldn't expect worse treatment at his hands than we have experienced in the hands of your family for the last fifty years.... How could you expect to find men where they are not, and the few of them which are to be found among the rubbish or ruins of the country have more sense than to be decoyed by chaff to the field of slaughter.[7]

Such was the case of Scotland. Ireland was different; it was a conquered country. But, then, from one point of view, England too was a conquered country. William, Duke of Normandy, defeated King Harald and conquered England in 1060. It was only a hundred years later that Richard de Clare, second Earl of Pembroke, nicknamed Strongbow, landed in Ireland with a large body of Frankish knights. They had come as mercenaries to assist King Diarmait Mac

Murchada of Leinster to recover his lost kingdom from the High King of Connaught who had dispossessed him. Strongbow was successful, Diarmait was reinstated and, as in a fairy tale, he gave him his daughter in marriage and nominated him as his heir and successor.

But then two years later Diarmait died and Strongbow ascended the throne but was immediately faced by a general uprising. He hurried to England and sought the assistance of his liege-lord King Henry II, offering him all his lands and castles in return. Henry landed in Ireland with a large army in October 1171 and soon established his authority over Ireland. Strongbow was left with Kildare while Henry appointed his second son John viceroy with the title of *Dominus Hiberniae*, or Lord of Ireland. When John unexpectedly succeeded his brother, the childless Richard, as King of England in 1199, Ireland was brought directly under the English crown. And from that date began the troubles of Ireland.

Thus the Anglo-Norman/Angevin presence in Ireland is of very nearly the same vintage as England's, yet Ireland was treated with exceptional brutality, even worse than a colony. During the Hundred Years War with France and the civil wars between the houses of Lancaster and York, Ireland was treated with benign neglect. English control was purely nominal and extended to little more than the neighbourhood of Dublin, the seat of the viceroy and the English garrison. So when peace was restored in England by the Tudors, Henry VIII had to virtually re-conquer the country all over again. In 1541, after having put down a rebellion by the Fitzgeralds, he had himself proclaimed King of Ireland, raising the status of the island from a mere lordship to a kingdom. But the religious conflicts which beset the Tudor monarchy were not conducive to stability. The Irish remained loyal to the Roman Church, and there were repeated rebellions during the reign of Elizabeth.

It was Elizabeth who instituted the policy of 'plantations' under which land grants were bestowed on English gentlemen. The grantees were expected to cultivate the grants by planting English colonists on the land, the dispossessed Irish being left to shift for themselves. Naturally many of them became bandits and violence remained an endemic feature of Irish country life. The planters were naturally Anglicans, marriages between them and the native Irish were banned, and a series of draconian penal laws discriminated against the Catholics. For instance they could not bear arms, nor could they own a horse worth more than five pounds. In effect it meant that any Protestant gentleman could stop a Catholic gentleman on the road and deprive him of his horse by offering him five pounds for it, leaving him to walk home.

Catholics were deprived of the vote, excluded from almost every profession, even from humble jobs such as that of a constable or gamekeeper. They could not join the army or navy, but had to pay towards the cost of the militia at twice the rate paid by the Protestants. They could not pursue any trade outside their native cities and an exorbitant charge imposed on them, but not on Protestant tradesmen, put many of them out of business altogether. No Catholic could buy land, hold a lease for more than thirty-one years, or take out a mortgage or an annuity. An amendment to the Navigation Acts excluded Ireland from the shipping monopoly she had shared with England. A law passed in 1696 prohibited all imports from the colonies unless they came in English ships via England.

A more oppressive regime is difficult to imagine. The Statutes of Kilkenny enacted in 1366 prohibited 'any alliance by marriage, gossipred, fostering of children, concubinage or by amour, or in any other manner' between the English and the Irish. The object was to humiliate and demoralize the people and establish an apartheid regime like that which existed until recently in South Africa, and in the Southern states of the USA in the last century. Of course, such draconian laws would have been impossible to enforce on a regular basis in any country except perhaps in modern times, but, however, fitfully they may have been enforced in the sixteenth or seventeenth centuries, they certainly caused tremendous ill-feeling between the two communities.

There is nothing comparable in the history of India, notwithstanding the centuries of dominium by Turkish, Afghan or Mughal dynasties. In Turkey the Ottoman sultans permitted freedom of worship to their Christian and Jewish subjects. The various nationalities or *millets* in that polyglot empire enjoyed their own personal laws, and were free to follow any occupation or profession. As a matter of fact, for many centuries, the foreign office was manned by Greek Christians. The Grand Dragoman was in truth the Foreign Minister of the Ottoman empire! Besides this, most senior administrative posts, including that of Grand Vizier, were held by slaves recruited from among the Christian population of the Balkans.

Bad as was the lot of the Irish in Tudor times, it would get much worse during the Protectorate of Oliver Cromwell. During the English Civil War, Ireland again revolted and thousands of Protestant settlers were massacred. But after the Royalist collapse in England, Cromwell turned his attention to Ireland. Between 1649 and 1653 the reconquest was completed. It was a brutal war of annihilation. Massacres were commonplace and the entire populations of the towns of Drogheda and Wexford were put to the sword. Crops were destroyed and famine ensued. Captives were shipped as slaves to the West Indies. The governor of Galway, Colonel Stubbers is said to have sold more than a thousand Galway people and exported them.[8] At the end of it all the population of Ireland is said to have declined by one-third.

Over 12,000 veterans of Cromwell's army were given land in Ireland in lieu of arrears of salary. After the revolution of 1688 which brought King William to the throne Ireland exploded once again. The rebels were crushingly defeated in the Battle of the Boyne. Then followed another wave of 'plantations' and evictions, and it was around this time that Ulster acquired a Protestant majority. The people who were planted by William still cherish his memory through the Orange Lodges.

The stories that one reads of the atrocities committed by the landlords–for the most part Protestant grantees planted by Cromwell or William–defy imagination. The life of an Irish tenant counted for nothing. A tenant who begged that his sons be excused from forced labour because one was too lazy and the other too wild, allowed himself to be persuaded by his landlord to send them nevertheless, as he would 'talk them out of it'. When the boys failed to return in the morning he discovered that they had been hanged. 'You'll have ease from them now', the landlord assured him.[9]

In India one commonly hears stories of the wicked landlord or governor who would insist that any bride married within his jurisdiction should spend her first night in his bed. This *droit de seigneur* was routine in Europe at least till the end of the eighteenth century. Most people accepted it, and amazingly, wanted it as an honour. According to John Dunton, some leases granted by the Earl of Cavan contained clauses asserting this right, and the usual penalty for refusal, where there was a penalty at all, was eviction or an increase in rent imposed on the girl's parents. Even in late Victorian times a child got by the landlord had a privileged place in the community, but by then the custom itself had fallen into disrepute among most landlords and tenants, and had become secretive, the girls being summoned to the great house as servants.[10]

Whether or not there was any such legal right at any time has been disputed—certainly there is no authentic evidence of any such statute—but it was the normal practice in the British Isles for tenants to seek the permission of their lord for getting married. Doubtless this was a vestige of the bad old days of serfdom, but the permission was not always readily forthcoming. During the recruitment drive on the Sutherland estates the tenants called a public meeting and drew up an address to the newspapers:

> We have no country to fight for, as our glens and straths are laid desolate, and we have no wives nor children to defend as we are forbidden to have them. We are not allowed to marry without the consent of the factor, the ground officer being always ready to report every case of marriage, and the result would be banishment from the country....[11]

On top of all this there happened the great famine of 1845-50. The potato crop was destroyed by blight which had probably come via the United States. The Conservative government of Sir Robert Peel, recognizing the seriousness of the situation, ordered the import of maize from the United States and the setting up of a Relief

Commission. These measures by themselves did little to ameliorate the situation; the first shipments of American corn arrived only in February 1846, by which time starvation deaths were being reported. Peel then repealed the Corn Laws, as a result of which his government fell. The succeeding government of Lord John Russell was, however, criminally negligent.

Believing in *laissez-faire*, that the market would provide the food required, it did not even take the elementary precaution of banning the export of foodstuffs. Since under the Poor Law only those holding less than a quarter acre were entitled to relief, and the landlords were responsible for paying the 'poor rates' which financed the relief, the latter started evicting their tenants wholesale. Thus they reduced their liability for the poor rate and simultaneously freed their land for future development of pasture. The evicted tenants could only turn to the Poor House for relief, but the funds available for soup-kitchens, etc., shrank. People started dying like flies.

Irish soldiers sent £ 14,000 from Calcutta for relief, the British Relief Association, a private charity raised £ 200,000; even the Pope sent a donation. The Sultan of Turkey, Abdul Majid, declared his intention of sending £ 10,000, but the Queen requested that he send only £ 1,000, because she herself had sent only £ 2,000 and it wouldn't look nice if the people were to know that the Sultan had donated more than the sovereign herself. The Sultan sent £ 1,000, but also sent three shiploads of food. The English courts tried to block the ships, but the food was landed secretly at Drogheda, after the ships had been refused entry at Belfast and Dublin.[12] Even a group of American Indians of the Choctaw Nation sent $ 710, a spontaneous gesture from a people who had experienced starvation and death in their own forced migration along the Trail of Tears, sixteen years earlier.

The stream of emigrants rose to a flood. It is estimated that about a million people emigrated during the famine years, mostly to the United States, followed by Canada, Australia and New Zealand. More than a million died, and the population of the island was reduced by 20 to 25 per cent. The record of the Russel government is so bad that it was accused of intending genocide. John Mitchel, a pamphleteer of the Young Ireland movement wrote one of the first widely circulated tracts on the famine, *The Last Conquest of Ireland (Perhaps)* in 1861 which established the widespread view that the treatment of the famine by the British was a deliberate murder of the Irish, and contained the famous phrase: 'The Almighty, indeed, sent the potato blight, but the English created the Famine.'

Charles Trevelyan, the civil servant most directly responsible for the government's handling of the famine described it as 'a direct stroke of an all-wise and all-merciful Providence', which laid bare 'the deep and inveterate root of social evil'. The famine, he affirmed, was 'the sharp but effectual remedy by which the cure is likely to be effected. God grant that the generation to which this opportunity has been offered may rightly perform its part.'[13] Certainly these words do not suggest that he was doing his best to relieve the sufferings of the starving Irish. Did he really think that he had 'rightly performed' his part? He appears to have left everything to an 'all-wise and all-merciful Providence'. And where indeed lay wisdom and mercy in mass starvation unless the object was a providential reduction of the population?

One is reminded of the Bengal Famine of 1943-4 in which as many as two to three million Indians may have died. Here again the victims were subject colonials, and the rulers English. So little concern was shown by Churchill, then the prime minister, when Amery, the Secretary of State for India, pleaded for the release of food stocks in view of the developing calamity, that he sent off a petulant telegram to Viceroy Lord Wavell asking, if food was so scarce, why Gandhi hadn't died yet?[14]

The English persecution of the Scottish Highlanders and the native Irish appears to have been coloured by their perception of the Celtic Gaels as an alien 'other'. Time and again, from the Tudors onwards we come across words like 'savage' and 'barbarian' used to describe them. And this in spite of the fact that they were the monks of the Celtic fringe who kept the lamp of Christianity burning while Europe was an area of darkness. Christianity was brought to Roman Britain by Roman soldiers as early as the first century but the Romano-Celtic Church was overwhelmed by the Anglo-Saxon invasions which started soon after the middle of the fifth century, surviving only in Wales. About the same time Ireland, which had been outside the Roman sphere, was converted by St. Patrick, while St. Columba converted the Scots from his base on the Hebridean island of Iona. A number of monasteries sprang up and beautiful manuscripts of the Gospels like the Book of Kells and the Lindisfarne Gospels were produced.

Ireland suffered most of all from the Viking raiders who came in their long boats from across the sea. But Irish monks had already set up monasteries in Europe and started evangelizing activities among the Franks and the Germans. Hiberno-Scottish missionaries (generally described as Scot or Scotus) established celebrated monasteries at Sackingen, Reichenau, St. Gall, Konstanz, Cologne, Regensberg, Vienna, Melk, and at Bobbio and Fiesole in Tuscany, besides many others. They were known as *Schottenkloster* in Germany and it is to the evangelizing mission of these abbeys that the Germans owe their conversion to Christianity.

But over the centuries the Gaelic element among the Scottish gentry had been diluted. Most of the Lowland gentry were of Anglo-Norman origins. Neither Robert Bruce nor the Stuart kings were Gaels. From 842 to 1286 Scotland had been ruled by the house of Alpin and its related branches of Dunkeld and Moray (to the second of which belonged the well-known usurper Macbeth). When the House of Dunkeld returned to power in 1058 Scotland was being harried by the Danes and Norsemen. The last of the Dunkelds, Alexander III was succeeded briefly by his grand-daughter Margaret whose father was King Erik of Norway. After her short reign of four years and another brief interregnum a certain John Balliol fought his way to the vacant throne, basing his claim on his descent from King David (1124-53) in the female line. The Balliols themselves were an Anglo-Norman family whose origins were in Picardy, and who had estates in northern England, acquired during the reign of King William Rufus (1087-1100). As for the house of Bruce it derives its name from the French *de Brus* or *de Bruis*, being the modern village of Brix in the Cherbourg peninsula. The first Robert de Brus is supposed to have accompanied Duke William the Bastard when he set out to claim the crown of England. He would be rewarded with fiefs in Dorset and Surrey. It was his son, Robert who would forge a connection with Scotland.

David, the youngest son of King Malcolm III, spent some time as an exile in England while his uncle Donald was king. During his exile his sister married Henry, the brother and future successor of King William Rufus. About the same time Henry arranged his marriage to the heiress of the Earl of Northumberland, and it was with English backing that David set out to claim the crown of Scotland. Robert Brus (or Bruce) was one of the Anglo-Norman barons who accompanied him. His son would later on marry Isobel, the daughter of King David and it was on the basis of this marriage that his great-grandson would one day claim the crown of Scotland.

The Stuarts might just possibly be of Celtic origin because their ancestors had been hereditary stewards of the Bishop of Dol in the Duchy of Brittany, but this seems unlikely since Alan, the first of the family to come to Britain, came as part of the army of the Conqueror in 1066. One of his descendants Walter Fitz Alan, like Robert Bruce, also accompanied David on his expedition to Scotland. He acquired more lands in Scotland and David appointed him his Lord High Steward. This dignity became hereditary in the family, and gradually it was corrupted to Stewart or Stuart.

In early medieval Europe there were only two classes, the rich and the poor, and riches were most easily acquired through the control or ownership of land which was a monopoly of the nobility and untitled gentry. Rich men preferred to marry the daughters of other rich men in the hope of increasing their wealth, so nobles seldom married the daughters of commoners. Thus the nobility became almost a closed caste, and since the dominant racial element among the nobility was either German or Scandinavian, it soon became a fairly homogeneous body in cultural terms. But the poor could only find their wives in their immediate vicinity. Besides, being serfs, their mobility was severely restricted. So while the common people of Scotland, Wales and Ireland retained their original identities, and continued to speak their native Celtic languages, the nobility and the untitled gentry, the 'lairds' and the chiefs soon assimilated into the dominant Anglo-Norman, Frankish or Germanic culture of the conquerors. They became alienated from their peasants who came to be regarded as savages speaking a barbarous tongue.

Across the Channel, just below Normandy is Brittany. Its historical evolution was similar to that of Scotland and Ireland. It managed to retain its original Celtic language and culture for a considerable time. Originally comprising three kingdoms it was unified in 845. In 913 it was crushed by the Normans, but in 937 the Breton king managed to bounce back with the help of King Alfred of Wessex. But conscious of his weakness he dropped his royal pretensions and adopted the more modest style and title of 'duke'. Eventually in 1488 the Bretons were defeated by King Charles VIII and forced to accept subordination to France. Anne, the last duke's daughter, was forced to marry Charles in 1514, and after his death, his successor and cousin Louis XII.

At first a personal union, in 1532 it was made perpetual by the Edict of Union between Brittany and France. Ever since the process of assimilation has been going on, though a movement for Breton autonomy exists even today. The French state, however, is intolerant of dual affiliations, and the Breton identity is in a sense an outlaw identity. Brittany's history and language are not taught in schools and its historical capital, Nantes, is included in the department of Loire-Inferieure.

Just south of Loire-Inferieure lies the Vendée, where the armies of the first French republic waged a savage war of extermination, a war so terrible that it has been called the French genocide. The revolution professed to champion the cause of liberty, equality and fraternity. In practice this translated itself into republicanism, anticlericalism and universal conscription. There were riots in Brittany and the Vendée when the king was arrested and imprisoned; when church property was confiscated and the power of appointing parish priests given to local bodies controlled by the bourgeoisie of the towns there were more serious disturbances, for the peasants were attached to their priests. When the king was executed and conscription introduced, revolt flared in the Vendée and Brittany.

It was a popular uprising led by priests and local nobles. After some initial successes by the rebels, the Committee of Public Safety, which controlled the revolution, sent a large army to effect the 'pacification' of the region with instructions to the commanding general, Louis-Marie Turreau to 'eliminate the brigands to the last man'.[15] Twelve columns, known as the *colonnes infernales* spread fire and death; thousands were massacred, a scorched earth policy laid waste the countryside, with crops and farms fired, and villages destroyed. The slaughter was indiscriminate, without regard to the combatants' status, age or gender. By the end of 1793 General Westermann reported to Paris thus:

> There is no more Vendée. It died with its wives and children by our free sabers. I have just buried it in the woods and the swamps of Savenay. According to the orders you gave me, I crushed the children under the hooves of the horses, massacred the women who, at least for these, will not give birth to any more brigands. I do not have a prisoner to reproach me. I have exterminated all. The roads are sown with corpses. At Savenay, brigands are arriving all the time claiming to surrender, and we are shooting them non-stop.... Mercy is not a revolutionary sentiment.[16]

There were mass drownings in the river Loire, and mass executions by grapeshot fired from cannons. The war was fought with appalling cruelty. While the main fighting was over by the end of 1799, yet the Vendée remained a sore point with spasmodic outbreaks in 1813, 1814, and 1815. The estimate of the numbers who died during the conflict vary from 1,17,000 to 4,50,000, and the modern French historian, Reynald Secher has argued that the war in La Vendée was the first modern genocide.[17]

Whether the Vendéean war can be described as genocide or not is not the question here. What is undeniable is that European wars could be appallingly brutal, by no means any less than the horrors visited by Chengiz Khan and Timur Leng. The bombing of Hiroshima, Nagasaki, Dresden, Tokyo, Dusseldorf and Cologne, the battle of Stalingrad, the siege of Leningrad–they far surpass the horrors inflicted by these notorious conquerors. The wars of Indo-China, the carpet-bombing of Vietnam, the terrible battles of the First World War, the list is endless. How the American West was won is hardly a very inspiring tale.... The colonization of Mexico and Peru by the Spanish was scarcely more humane. The Belgian record in the Congo is disgraceful, while in Namibia, once known as South-West Africa, the Germans are said to have exterminated nearly two-thirds of the Hereros and half the Namaqas. In Europe proper we have the example of the Vendée, of Ireland and Scotland. Many terrible things have happened in India, but none of our atrocities approach the horrors of modern European history.

NOTES

1. By the Act of Union the separate legal identities of Scotland and England were erased. So far the union between the two kingdoms had been a merely personal one, but this was now endangered by the impending death of Queen Anne without issue. Her last surviving son, William, Duke of Gloucester, had died in 1700, and since her father, the deposed James II and his son were not acceptable on account of their Catholicism, the Act of Union was considered essential for retaining Scotland.
2. John Prebble, *The Highland Clearances*, London: The Folio Society, 2003, p. 10.
3. Elizabeth Gordon, later Duchess. Her husband, Lord Stafford, an English nobleman, was created Duke of Sutherland in 1832.
4. Prebble, op. cit., p. 10.
5. Steve Blamires, *The Highland Clearances,* http://www.clannada.org/highland.php
6. Ibid.
7. Prebble, op. cit., p. 252.

8. James Hardiman, *History of Galway*, cited by David Thomson in *Woodbrook*, London: The Folio Society, 2007, p. 98.
9. David Thomson, *Woodbrook*, p. 104.
10. Ibid., p. 103.
11. Prebble, op. cit., p. 252.
12. Abdullah Aymaz, *Gratitude to the Ottomans*, http://www.fountainmagazine.com/articles; *Illustrated London News*, vol. XIV, no. 378, p. 434.
13. Charles E. Trevelyan, *The Irish Crisis*, Whitefish: Kissinger Publishing, 2007.
14. Pankaj Mishra, 'Exit Wounds', in *New Yorker*, 13 August 2007.
15. Donald Sutherland, *The French Revolution and Empire*, Oxford: Blackwell, 2003, p. 222.
16. Norman Davies, *Europe: A History*, London: Pimlico, 1997, p. 705; Simon Schama, *Citizens*, London: Penguin, p. 188.
17. Reynald Secher, *A French Genocide*, South Bend: University of Notre Dame, 2003.

CHAPTER 11

The Indian Peasant

The rural poor have always been oppressed, everywhere in the world. The social oppression and discrimination suffered by the landless, former 'untouchable' castes is well known, and in various forms survives to this day. But the cultivating class—at least till the later part of the eighteenth century—was probably better off than that of Britain and Europe. Certainly better off than the tenant farmers of Scotland and Ireland. Or so it would seem. The concept of private ownership of land did not exist in India. The state was considered the real owner, with the cultivators enjoying only occupancy rights. As long as the land revenue was paid, the cultivator's 'tenancy' was, more or less, assured. And the state encouraged cultivation because that was the simplest way of increasing its income. One would imagine that the state would be a better landlord than a private individual.

The climate was favourable and—unlike Europe—crops could be cultivated all year round. Two, and sometimes even three, crops could be obtained from the soil. There was no snowfall in the plains, and, but for a few weeks in the north when frost could be expected, the peasant's requirement of clothes was modest. Thus it was possible to live frugally in India. Rural dwellings were no doubt modest—for the most part of sun-baked bricks with thatched or tiled roofs—but they were much more comfortable than the miserable hovels one came across in Scotland or Ireland. The cottages and farm buildings in English villages were more picturesque perhaps, and of more solid construction, but because of the heavier rainfall which was spread more evenly, the landscape was much greener. Adobe construction was just not possible in the British Isles, or in most parts of continental Europe.

The revenue was usually collected in kind. If the crop failed, the state also suffered. But once the British became rulers they preferred to substitute cash for kind. A cash-based land revenue system is harder on the peasant because while the prices of agricultural produce tend to fluctuate the revenue demand is fixed, and at times it may become an impossible burden.

The revenue demand was supposed to be based on average yields in a good or normal year, and the new rulers expected the peasants to make good the short-fall in a bad year from their savings in good years. But savings were in most cases non-existent. Agriculture has always been a mug's game; when brothers divide their holdings and assets there is usually no cash to be shared, only debts to be apportioned. The disastrous effect of insisting on a cash revenue was seen during the famines of 1770 and 1783, the last notorious as the *chalisa.*[1]

Sleeman has described how the early revenue settlements in the Nerbudda (Narmada) valley in central India tended to be too high. The revenue officials would not heed the requests for remission or reduction till the villages were partially or wholly deserted:

> The farmers and cultivators all emigrated, by degrees into the neighbouring districts of Nagpoor and Rewa, where they had more consideration and lighter assessments.... The lands of Mundula became waste, and covered with rank grass filled with deer; tigers to feed upon them, and carried off all the poor peasantry who remained and attempted to cultivate small patches; malaria followed and completed the work.[2]

The flaw in India was that the agency appointed for the collection of the revenue was apt to abuse its powers. Under ideal circumstances the revenue was collected directly from the cutivators, or rather their representatives or *muqaddams*, by the officers of the state. But very often it was collected indirectly through intermediary contractors, known variously as zamindars or *taluqdars* as in Awadh. These *taluqdars* paid a quit rent to the government and managed 'their' *taluqas* (or estates) with their own fiscal officers, and police establishments. But as pointed out earlier, these *taluqdars* did not actually own their estates; they were middle-men with the right—more or less hereditary—to collect the revenue from the actual occupants of the soil. Consequently they enjoyed many perquisites by way of rent-free land, free labour, and so on. In Awadh some of these *taluqdars* came from old families which, once upon a time, may have enjoyed chiefly status with only a token acknowledgement of the superior authority of a distant *padishah* or *sultan*. More often they were *noveau riche* speculators who had recently purchased the *taluqdari* rights in the hope of turning a profit. Sometimes they were courtiers or officials who mercilessly abused their powers while posted as *nazims* or *aumils* to acquire estates by force and coercion, the former owners being forced to surrender their rights for a pittance.

This was how the famous Mehdona estate (later known as the Ayodhya Raj) was built up by Raja Bakhtawar Singh and his brother Darshan Singh. Bakhtawar Singh was originally a sepoy in one of the Company's battalions, who attracting the notice of Nawab Ghazi ud-Din Haider, resigned the Company's service and entered that of the king of Awadh. He and his brothers, who soon joined him, were also appointed to high offices at court and held charge of various districts as *nazims*. It was during these field postings that the Mehdona estate was put together. Raghubar Dayal became notorious for the atrocities he committed on the landholders of the districts in his charge. Sleeman recollects the terrible stories he was told about Dayal. On the pretext of collecting revenue arrears villages and townships were plundered; men, women and respectable shopkeepers and merchants would be seized with the intention of squeezing them for ransom:

> Report from Bahraetch states, that Goureeshunkur, the agent of Rughbur Singh [*sic*] had taken four persons from among whom he had in confinement on account of balances, had them suspended to trees, and cruelly flogged, and then had their hands wrapped up in thick cloth, steeped in oil, and set fire to till they burned like torches; and that he sat listening to their screams and cries for mercy with indifference.[3]

Sleeman records that he received reports of ploughs and bullocks being seized and (presumably) sold, and how the more industrious cultivators, the Kachhies, Kurmis, and Lodhis had deserted the district because of his atrocities. As a result, in Gonda-Bahraich the revenue collections first showed a slight initial spurt from Rs.11.65 lakh in 1845 (when the district was under Wajid Ali) to Rs.14.01 lakh in 1846 after the assumption of charge by Raghubar Dayal. But the following year the receipts declined to Rs.10.28 lakh. Then the monster was transferred and replaced by his uncle Incha Singh, but the collections fell still lower to Rs.6.05 lakh.[4] Of course, under the pretext of squeezing the landholders for arrears, Raghubar Dayal would have appropriated considerable sums from the ransoms obtained for his private coffers.

But Raghubar Dayal was exceptional in terms of brutality. For the most part the *taluqdars* fought among themselves to enlarge their estates by seizing coveted villages from others. For this purpose they patronized robbers and dacoits who had their dens in the forests, which were plentiful in those days, even in the garden that was Awadh. These robbers preyed on the common cultivators, and shopkeepers and merchants of the small market-towns in the interior. The lawlessness and disorder was perhaps comparable to that prevailing along the Highland Line and the border counties of northern England where cattle-lifting was an ancient and honoured tradition.

There is little reason to suppose that the common cultivators were markedly worse off than the tenant farmers of Britain and Europe. In Scotland and Ireland the tenant holdings were often as small as those in the India of today–say as little as 3 acre. In eighteenth-century India they would certainly have been bigger, because the population would have been one-fifth of what it is today. Moreover, the British Isles and western Europe have a much more evenly distributed rainfall, and agriculture is not so heavily dependent on irrigation works as it is in India which has a prolonged and very hot dry season. In England and Western Europe (with the possible exception of Spain), however, the holdings were bigger, and, by the eighteenth century, the peasants were probably better off as compared to India. Much of France was peasant owned–

even before the Revolution—and the most visible sign was the horse-drawn plough. In India, on the other hand, the horse was never used for drawing the plough; it was an expensive animal, and used exclusively for riding. Oxen were invariably used for ploughing and carriage. European-style horse-drawn carriages were introduced only in the nineteenth century.

It was, however, rare for the Indian peasant to be ejected from his holding. He was, for all purposes, an 'occupancy' tenant. If he was oppressed too severely by a tyrannical *taluqdar* or *aumil* he could, as a last resort, abandon his holding and move to a neighbouring estate, beyond the reach of his oppressor. There was plenty of old fallow or virgin land available for cultivation.

The typical Indian village was managed by the village community itself, rather than the landlord's factor and managers—there being no landlords in the English sense in the country. By the village community is meant primarily the 'proprietary' body, which, as in the Scottish Highlands, often claimed descent from a common ancestor. These proprietors, or more properly, landholders, were closer to the free yeomanry of England than the landowning squirearchy, and the economic relations of these cultivating farmers with the village artisans, namely the carpenter, blacksmith, leather-worker and others were regulated by custom, each farming family paying the artisans who served it with a fixed measure of grain at harvest-time.

But notwithstanding this relative autonomy and security of tenure, the lot of the Indian peasant was far from enviable. The French physician, Francois Bernier visited India in the later part of the reign of Shah Jahan and made some perceptive observations regarding the country. He specifically considered whether it would not be more advantageous if the king ceased to be the sole possessor of the land, and the right of private property were recognized in India as it was in Europe, and came to the conclusion that this absence of the right to private property was a positive disincentive to progress and injurious to the sovereign himself. Bernier had travelled widely in the Orient. Before arriving in India he had visited Palestine, Syria and

Egypt, and it was from the port of Mocha in the Yemen that he set off on his voyage to India. Therefore he was familiar with the Ottoman administration, and his observations regarding the Mughal Empire and its institutions deserve respect.

He observed that in the provinces the governors and their subordinate officials squeezed the peasantry mercilessly, and made up for their short and uncertain tenures by their unbridled rapacity. He observed that much of the empire of *Hindustan* constituted tracts that were

> little more than sand, or barren mountains, badly cultivated, and thinly peopled; and even a considerable portion of the good land remains untilled from want of labourers; many of whom perish in consequence of the bad treatment they experience from the Governors. These poor people, when incapable of discharging the demands of their rapacious lords, are not only often deprived of the means of subsistence, but are bereft of their children, who are carried away as slaves. Thus it happens that many of the peasantry, driven to depair by so execrable a tyranny, abandon the country, and seek a more tolerable mode of existence, either in the towns, or camps as bearers of burdens, carriers of water, or servants to horsemen. Sometimes they fly to the territories of a raja, because there they find less oppression, and are allowed a greater degree of comfort.[5]

A few pages later, he again reverts to the oppressions practised by the officers of the Great Mughal:

> The persons thus put in possession of the land, whether as *timariots*,[6] governors, or contractors, have an authority almost absolute over the peasantry, and nearly as much over the artisans and merchants of the towns and villages within their district; and nothing can be imagined as more cruel and oppressive than the manner in which it is exercised. There is no one before whom the injured peasant, artisan or tradesman can pour out his just complaints; no great lords, parliaments, or judges of local courts, exist as in France, to restrain the wickedness of those merciless oppressors, and the *kadis*, or judges, are not invested with sufficient power to redress the wrongs of these unhappy people. This sad abuse of the royal authority may not be felt in the same degree near capital cities such as *Dehly* and *Agra*, or in the vicinity of large towns and seaports, because in those places acts of great injustice cannot easily be concealed from the court.

This debasing state of slavery obstructs the progress of trade and influences the manners and mode of life of every individual. There can be little encouragement to engage in commercial pursuits, when the success with which they may be attended, instead of adding to the enjoyments of life, provokes the cupidity of a neighbouring tyrant possessing both power and inclination to deprive any man of the fruits of his industry. When wealth is acquired, as must sometimes be the case, the possessor, so far from living with increased comfort and assuming an air of independence, studies the means by which he may appear indigent: his dress, lodging, and furniture, continue to be mean, and he is careful, above all things, never to indulge in the pleasures of the table. In the meantime his gold and silver remain buried at a great depth in the ground....[7]

Under the Permanent Settlement of Bengal and the Taluqdari settlements of Awadh the position of the cultivator became even worse. Even though these settlements were intended to benefit the peasant he had even lost the security of tenure which was earlier taken for granted. He was now a mere tenant-at-will. It was some time, however, before the significance of the change was realized.

It would be fair to assume that the Indian peasant was certainly no better off than his European counterpart. It is now fashionable to argue that at least up to the beginning of the eighteenth-century India (and China) were richer than any European country, and that the Chinese economy was the largest in the world, followed closely by India. As someone has remarked, this was hardly surprising since these two were the largest (save for Russia) and most populous countries of the world. Therefore it was not surprising that their emperors should be the richest in the world, but in terms of per capita income it lagged behind most countries of the Western world.

NOTES

1. So called because it corresponded to the year 1840 in the *Vikrami Samvat*–the most widely prevalent era in the north. *Chalis* of course is 'forty'.
2. William Sleeman, *A Journey Through the Kingdom of Oude*, vol. 2, London, 1858 (New Delhi: AES, 1995), p. 44.

3. Ibid., vol. 1, pp. 92-3.
4. Ibid., p. 95.
5. Francois Bernier, *Travels in the Mogul Empire*, New Delhi: Low Price Publications, 1989, p. 205.
6. A timariot was the equivalent of a *jagirdar* in Iran and Turkey, a *timar* being a *jagir*.
7. Bernier, op. cit., p. 225.

CHAPTER 12

Historical Memory

One remarkable feature about Indian civilization is the absence of any real historical memory. There is virtually no tradition of writing history. Apart from the *Rajatarangini* which is a late mediaeval text there is no known historical work of any length. There is no Indian Livy to record the history of imperial Pataliputra or Kannauj. No Thucydides to write the history of the Kalinga war. Ashoka and Chandragupta, the Mauryas and Guptas, notwithstanding the vast extent of their empires and their far-flung conquests, just did not exist in the mindscape of thirteenth-century Indian gentlemen. The *Ramayana*, *Mahabharata*, and the *Bhagvat Purana* seem their only idea of history. Thus any notable structure of indeterminate age was liable to be assigned to the times of the *Mahabharata*. According to popular tradition, the Old Fort of Delhi is supposed to have been built by the Pandavas, and most of the old medieval temples in Himachal Pradesh and Uttarakhand (which are usually of post-Gupta vintage) are also assigned to that remote age, supposedly built in the course of their wanderings in the Himalayas. It is almost as if, in the popular consciousness, whatever happened in the thousands of years thereafter was irrelevant and did not matter.

Archaeological evidence does in fact suggest that the mound on which the Old Fort of Delhi is built may go as far back as the 'Mahabharata Age' and that it might indeed be the site of the ancient Indraprastha. But the present structure is of relatively recent date. The walls probably go back to Rajput times, while the arched gateways and decoration suggest that they are of the pre-Mughal Sultanate era. According to the historians its present structure probably belongs to the Suri period, which would place it in the second quarter of the sixteenth century. It is also curious that while nearly all Rajput clans claim descent from either Sri Rama Chandra of Ayodhya, or Lord Krishna of Dwarka–or the Sun and Moon, or the sacrificial fire at Mt. Abu–there is no known family or clan which traces its descent from the Pandavas and Kauravas.

The difficulties that the historian of ancient India has to face were described thus by Basham:

> Thus our knowledge of the political history of ancient India is often tantalizingly vague and uncertain, and that of the medieval period, which we may take as beginning in the 7th century AD, is often but little more precise. History must be pieced together from passing references in texts both religious and secular, from a few dramas and works of fiction purporting to describe historical events, from the records of foreign travelers, and from the many panegyrics or other references to reigning monarchs and their ancestors which have been found carved on rocks, pillars and temple walls, or incorporated as preambles to the title-deeds of land grants; the latter, fortunately for the historian, were usually engraved on copper plates. The early history of India resembles a jigsaw puzzle with many missing parts.... Few dates before the middle ages can be fixed with certainty, and the history of Hindu India, as far as we can reconstruct it, is almost completely lacking in the interesting anecdotes and vivid personalities which enliven the study of the past for professional and amateur historians alike.[1]

Folk memory is not entirely blank, however. In the Punjab there are many stories still current of Raja Salvahana of Sialkot and his family. Agroha in Hissar district is supposed to have been the seat of another raja by the name of Aggarsen, who is supposed to have been the progenitor of the Aggarwal *banias*. But these are princes known only to folklore. Bards may still sing their ballads at country fairs, but they are unknown to history. The historical narrative, so painfully put together by the scholars of the eighteenth and nineteenth centuries only speaks of princes and emperors like Harsha, Kanishka, Chandragupta, and so on. But none of these names were familiar to either the gentry or the peasantry of the eighteenth century. Temple has ventured to suggest that Salvahana might be identified with 'Syalapatideva' whose coins are still found in abundance all over the Punjab,[2] but then, this is only a guess. Raja Salvahana is also described as an Indo-Scythian, which would place him in time somewhere around the eighth or ninth century, that is, before the Hindushahi dynasty, to which Syalapatideva is usually assigned.

Alberuni's *India* is the first significant work of Muslim/Turkish scholarship dealing with India, but his book is 'an account of the Religion, Philosophy, Literature, Geography, Chronology, Astronomy, Customs, Laws and Astrology of India about AD 1030.' Unfortunately he does not deal with history, though, while discussing the principal chronological eras used by the Hindus to date events, he mentions rulers like Harsha and Vikramaditya, and dynasties or tribes like the Shakas, Valabhis and Guptas. He also talks about the Shahiya dynasty of Kabul, which, according to him, was of Tibetan origin. This dynasty lasted for sixty generations. When they decayed, power was usurped by their Brahmin minister, who founded the Hindushahi dynasty, which produced the much more probable number of seven kings. He has given their names, which are well-known as the last four had to fight Sultan Mahmud of Ghazni. The Hindushahis were destroyed by Sultan Mahmud who then added Punjab to his already considerable empire, which included Khurasan and eastern Iran. There is also a brief chapter on the subject of Vasudeva (or Krishna) and the Mahabharata war.

This is all that Alberuni has to say about the history of India. His particular interest was in astronomy and the measurement of time. He does, however, observe that the Hindus did not pay much attention to the historical order of things and events: 'They are very careless in relating the chronological succession of their kings, and when they are pressed for information and are at a loss, not knowing what to say, they invariably take to tale-telling.'[3]

There are indeed a group of religious texts known as the Puranas which consist of narratives of the history of the universe from creation to destruction, and include genealogies of kings and saints, along with discourses on geography, cosmology and philosophy. But the historical element is so confused with improbable mythology that it is impossible to separate the two. And all the Puranas are in verse. It is almost as if the ancient Indians just could not write in simple, plain prose. Alberuni (like many after him) found this Indian predilection profoundly irritating. 'If the Hindus happen to get some book which does not yet exist among them,' he lamented, 'they set to work to change it into *slokas* (that is, metrical verse) which are rather unintelligible.... And if the verses are not sufficiently affected, their authors meet with frowning faces, as having committed something like mere prose, and then they will be extremely unhappy.'[4] Writing in plain prose was like committing a literary solecism. One sighs in vain for a simple book like Livy's history of the Roman Republic, or the *Anabasis* of Xenophon or Arrian, or Megasthenes' *Indika*, all of which can be read and understood by a schoolboy with only an elementary knowledge of Latin or Greek (with the assistance perhaps of a dictionary). The same can be said of the Arab and Persian historians like Budaoni, Ferishta and Abul Fazl. They all wrote in simple, easily intelligible prose.

And what is even more amazing, notwithstanding their much vaunted learning, is that by the fifteenth century the Indians had forgotten their ancient scripts and were no longer able to read the epigraphs which the Emperor Ashoka had caused to be inscribed on stone pillars and sundry rock faces all over his empire. In the reign of Firoz Shah Tughluq two such pillars were found in a village near Ambala. The local governor had them conveyed to Delhi as curiosities for the gratification of his sovereign. It is said that the emperor summoned the most learned Brahmins and asked them to read what was inscribed on the pillars, but it was to no avail. No one was able to decipher the ancient scripts.

The script was no other than Brahmi and it ranged from the plain Brahmi of the Mauryan period to the highly ornate variant which was fashionable in the Gupta period. Part of the inscription was in another script which came to be known as Kharoshthi. All along Sanskrit had been the usual language used in such inscriptions, and the Nagari script which was in use in Tughluq times (and is still in use today in the Hindi belt) was but a further development of

Brahmi, which is the mother of all Indian scripts ranging from the Gurmukhi and Takri which is used in Punjab and Jammu, to the Tamil and Malayalam of the south. Kharoshthi appears to have evolved from Aramaic and it was used only in north-west India. It is astonishing that it was only in the late eighteenth and early nineteenth centuries that Brahmi and Kharoshthi were deciphered at last—and it took an Englishman, James Prinsep, to do it.

The Indian scholastic tradition was oral rather than literary. The important texts had been handed down from generation to generation by word of mouth, and the recipient of the knowledge committed them to memory. That was why, in spite of their undoubted antiquity, we have no truly ancient written texts of the Vedas or the *Ramayana* and *Mahabharata*. Few manuscripts go back beyond the medieval period. The palm-leaf manuscripts which one comes across in the east may seem very ancient, but pundits in Bengal and Orissa continued to use dried palm leaves as late as the nineteenth century. It was not that more convenient mediums like paper were not available. Paper came to India from China as early as the twelfth century[5] and its manufacture started in Kashmir in the fifteenth century. The priests simply did not feel the need for many books. They knew the most important texts by heart. Some were preserved in these palm-leaf manuscripts, which were used basically as a mnemonic aid.

Of the huge hoard of manuscripts in India's libraries, museums and temples, there are very few that go beyond the thirteenth or fourteenth centuries. The priestly class enjoyed a virtual monopoly of knowledge and was not interested in its spread among the masses. So books, whether in the form of palm-leaf or birchbark manuscripts, were jealously treasured. The leaf of the palmyra palm—which was the usual medium—was a very inconvenient medium. Its width was usually less than two inches and though it was about twelve inches long it could only accommodate about five or six lines of writing. Illustrations, if any, were truly miniature. Birch bark provided a larger field and we have regular European style bound books with pages of birchbark. But the bark was fragile—much more fragile than the palm leaf. But no one was particularly bothered; there was virtually no demand for books–and the Brahmins did their best to ensure that it remained so. Those magnificent illuminated manuscripts, interspersed with full or double page painted illustrations, which were produced in the ateliers of Akbar and Jahangir were exceptional, and catered to a very small niche segment. The book, in the standard form that we know today, came to India from West Asia. In India, prayer books and scriptures used by the priestly class continued for a long time to be inscribed on long strips of thick hand-made paper, often only three inches wide, but as much as twelve inches long–still being produced in the same format as the palm-leaf manuscripts of yore! This was stagnation with a vengeance.

The ancient Romans used papyrus which is as fragile as birch-bark, but they also used parchment and vellum prepared from sheep-skin. The supply of papyrus dried up in the Dark Ages, but parchment continued to be used for important documents and in the scriptoriums of the abbeys and monasteries which became the repositories for great collections of books. Again it were the Arabs who brought paper to Europe, and its first factory was established in Moorish Spain in the twelfth century. About a century later it was being manufactured in Italy. Gutenberg set up his printing press around the year 1450 and this combination of a readily available, and far cheaper, writing material and moveable type resulted in an explosion of books and printing.

Now India is much closer to China than Europe, but though paper was indeed introduced early enough, and the first printing press was set up in Goa as early as 1556–the year Akbar ascended the throne–it did not have the slightest impact in India, outside Goa. There was not the slightest ripple. The first printed books in Indian scripts appeared only in the eighteenth century. The Indian tradition confined learning and intellectual activity to a limited class of people, and this class was simply not interested in the mass production of books or the wider diffusion of knowledge. It is possible that even in the eighteenth century the literacy rate in most European countries may not have been significantly higher than in India, but literacy was certainly spread over a much wider range of the population. In Europe also, during the thirteenth and fourteenth centuries the situation was not very different from that obtaining in India, when learning and letters was largely the monopoly of the priestly class. But with the onset of the Renaissance and the easier availability of books it burst its old bounds and spread to the bourgeoisie and the gentry as well.

This bursting of the bounds occurred as late as the nineteenth century in India, during the 'Golden Calm' that followed the British occupation of Delhi in 1803. The *Nai Taleem*, or the 'New Learning' became the craze of the day, but it was European scientific education and knowledge of the English language that was sought. There was no rediscovery of ancient classics as happened in Europe. Thus modern India is delinked from its past and looks towards the West. The study of ancient Indian history remains a field reserved for specialists, archaeologists and scholars. By and large, the youth of India is not interested in what may or may not have happened a thousand years ago.

Thus while the affiliation of modern Western civilization with the Hellenic civilization that preceded it is real, that of the modern Indian civilization in its latest phase with the old Indic civilization is weak. Myths, superstitions, half-truths and often wishful fabrications abound. Thus a P.N. Oak can argue—and convincingly for some people—that the Taj Mahal was a Hindu palace. Another can question whether there ever was an Aryan invasion of India at all. It is usually taken for granted by the vast majority of the people of India that the Mughal, or more precisely, the Mussulman Raj was a period of persecution for Hindus and other non-Muslims, that Hindu temples were systematically destroyed, and all those who embraced Islam were converted at the point of the sword. And but for Maharana Pratap, Shivaji and the Sikhs, India would have been completely Muslim (or nearly so) today. That ancient India was more Buddhist and Jain, rather than Hindu (in the sense in which that word is understood nowadays) would be indignantly denied by most people.

The Partition of the country in 1947, and its natural consequences have been responsible to a large extent for the disconnect of the present generation from its immediate past. Until 1947 Urdu, written in the Perso-Arabic script, was the *lingua franca* of north India, and it was the official language in most of the northern provinces, as well as in Hyderabad-Deccan. The finest poetry was written in that language. But suddenly after the Partition Urdu came to be identified with the seceding state of Pakistan, and Devanagari, one of the final evolutionary forms of the ancient Brahmi, suddenly became the flavour of the day. Hindi in the Devanagari script became the national language, and even though it never quite displaced English, it was enough to ensure the gradual withering away of Urdu.

Now we have the absurd situation that the average educated Indian of today is unable to read the inscriptions, cut in magnificent calligraphy on the gateways of Mughal monuments, which are the pride of the nation, even though they are only a few hundred years old. Even many Muslims who have received anglicized education are unable to read them. On the other hand, when the same people visit the ruins of the Roman Forum they have no difficulty in reading the inscription on the Arch of Titus, or that of Vespasian, even though it is in Latin. They may not understand it fully, but they can at least make out the name of the emperor who caused it to be erected. Tragically similar is the case of the modern Turk who is familiar only with the phonetic alphabet which was imposed on the newly born republic by Kemal Ataturk. But then the modern Turk can hardly be regarded as a very well-adjusted person, torn as he is, between two worlds, that of Islam of which he has been a part for so many centuries, and a secularism which is as sterile as the atheism of former Communist Russia. He aspires to be recognized as an European, and has been seeking the membership of the European Union, but as far as Europe is concerned, he remains a Muslim, first and last. A European, as far as they are concerned, has to be a Christian.

This disconnect with the past and tradition is the unfortunate lot of the Indian, particularly the educated Indian. A similar situation obtains in most of the former colonies. It is an irony of fate that Turkey, which, once upon a time, was the bogeyman of Europe, should find itself in a similar position. But our position is even stranger. We are, to all appearances, uninterested in our past. We prefer the snugness of our mythology to the reality of history.

Gribble, the author of *The History of the Deccan* (1896) has remarked on this indifference to history in his introductory preface. He describes an encounter with a young Hyderabadi noble who had just finished his studies in the Nizam's College:

> I asked him who was the first of the Bahmanee Sultans of Gulbarga, and he said that he did not know there had been any. He was equally ignorant of the fate of the last King of Golconda, although the remains of the old fortress are within an hour's drive of the city where he lived.

Gribble thought that his ignorance stemmed from a defect in the syllabus which over-emphasized the history of the metropole—the history of the empires based on Delhi. Struck by the young man's appalling ignorance of his immediate surroundings, he felt there was a need for writing regional histories. That is the justification he has given for his own work. It is a fine work, it needs no justification, and no doubt there was a need for it, but I am sure if he had quizzed the young man about the history of the Delhi empires, he would have been equally appalled.

NOTES

1. A.L. Basham, *The Wonder That was India*, New Delhi: Picador India, 2004, p. 45.
2. R.C. Temple, *The Legends of the Punjab*, vol. 1, Bombay, 1884, p. 1. Coins of Syalapatideva (or Spalapatideva, the more usual reading) are indeed common. They are of the 'Bull and Horseman' variety.
3. Alberuni, op. cit., p. 336.
4. Ibid., p. 96.
5. Sita Rameshan, 'History of Paper in India upto 1948', *Indian Journal of History of Science*, 24(2), 1989, pp. 105-6.

CHAPTER 13

The Wonder That was India

This was the title of a book, published in 1954 by Sidgwick and Jackson of London. It is a sympathetic account of ancient and medieval India, but since it was written after the Raj had been wound up, it is coloured to some extent by nostalgia. Its author, the late A.L. Basham of the School of Oriental and African Studies, was the son of a journalist who had served in the old Indian Army, and this family association would probably have further coloured Basham's picture of this country–though entirely to the latter's advantage. Later writers, particularly those inclining to the Indian Right, like Francois Gautier, may think that he was insufficiently sympathetic, and detect in his work a 'strong Western bias' smacking of condescension. However, that may be, and even if we concede that India is still great,[1] the more interesting subject is the contrast presented by its present poverty and the reputed wealth of yesterday.

Notwithstanding the fact that things have started looking up for the Indian economy, and it is no longer the basket case that it once was (which was not that very long ago), it is still way behind the countries of the West as far as the quality of life and per capita incomes are concerned. However, it is usually taken for granted (at least by Indians) that until the arrival of the Europeans, and the subsequent conquest of the subcontinent, India was *the* richest country in the world. China may perhaps have been its equal, may be it was a *little* richer (after all the Chinese did not have a caste system), but India was certainly superior and richer than the 'little' countries of Europe.

Much of this is self-delusion. There is no doubt that the wealth of the 'Great Moguls' was immense, that they could easily mobilize an army of a hundred thousand when the occasion demanded–at least in their heyday, when Sir Thomas Row, ambassador from the Court of St. James, presented his credentials to Jahangir. In the Middle Kingdom the resources of the Son of Heaven were, likewise, seemingly unlimited, at least as long as the Mandate of Heaven was not withdrawn. But outside the imperial palaces and beyond the charmed circle of the *omrahs* it was an entirely different world.

The wealth which impressed travellers like Terry, Bernier, Tavernier and others was that of the emperor and his court, and the high *omrahs* or grandees of the empire. The revenue collected by a state was largely dependent on its population, and in 1600 France, which was the most populous state in western Europe, had a population only a little over one-seventh of India. France's population in 1600 is estimated at 18.5 million, while that of India was 160 million! The total population of Western Europe at that time was below 74 million.[2] Coryate, Row and Terry were bound to be impressed, even though the empire of Jahangir did not yet include the southern peninsula. Vijayanagar, so fabulously wealthy, had been destroyed, but Golconda and Bijapur were still independent of the *padishah* at Delhi.

Besides the key element of population there were several other factors. In India the land belonged to the ruler who collected a rent, otherwise known as 'land revenue', from the cultivators. In Europe, on the other hand, the land belonged to the nobility and gentry who did not pay any such tax. The king too owned land, like any other noble, and usually he would be the largest landowner in the kingdom. But the European nobility was hereditary, while the *omrahs* of the Mughal empire were mere officials, whose entire property, moveable and immoveable, was liable to seizure by the emperor when they died, under the principle of escheat. The Indian nobleman was, for all practical purposes, a slave of the emperor. In Europe too, estates were sometimes escheated, but that was only when they happened to be entailed, and there were no natural heirs capable of inheriting according to the terms of the original grant or entail, but such occasions were rare. The monarch did collect a fee or fine when letters of succession were issued to the heir, but the gain to the monarch was nominal in comparison to the gains of the Mughal emperor as a result of escheat proceedings.

In his *Contours of the World Economy*, Angus Maddison has extrapolated other parameters such as world GDP, per capita GDP, and rates of growth for all countries of the world for this period of over 2,000 years. How he arrived at these figures is difficult to imagine, and no doubt there must be a considerable margin of error also, but it is, nonetheless, a brilliant *tour de force*. And for us, who are puzzled by the seventeenth- and eighteenth-century descriptions of the wonderland of India, these figures are particularly revealing.

The populations of both India and China have always been well above that of all the countries of western Europe. Up to 1700 it was nearly double. In the nineteenth century the rate of growth of population rose in Europe, while that of India (and China too) declined, but even so the gap was substantial. One would therefore expect that the GDP would naturally be higher. In fact, it remained so till 1820, but fifty years later there was a dramatic change. Western Europe had overtaken both India and China by 1870, its GDP being almost double that of China, and only a little less in the case of India. Of course, by this time the Industrial Revolution was in full swing in Europe, while the Indian and Chinese economies—once the leading industrial economies of the world—had lapsed into agrarian societies. The invention of the steam engine, the development of naval and military power, colonialism and protectionism had destroyed the industries of the Orient.

But when we come to per capita GDP, even as early as 1500, India and China were behind Western Europe; the figures for the former being \$550 and \$600, respectively, while the estimate for western Europe is shown as \$771. Maddison does not give figures for 1300 or 1400; he does, however, have figures for the year 1000. These show India and China as being ahead of Europe, but only just. The figure for these two countries is \$450, while that for western Europe is \$427. In the year 1000, Otto III of the Saxon House was Holy Roman Emperor in Germany. In India Sultan Mahmud of Ghazni was about to begin his plundering raids on the

Rajput states of north India, while in China the Northern Sung dynasty had just about embarked on its imperial career. For what it is worth, in the year 1 the figures for western Europe *and* West Asia are shown to be higher than those for India or China. In the first century of the Common Era the Roman empire was at its zenith, and while one may be skeptical about the statistics at this remote distance in time, the conclusion is hardly surprising.

In China the Han dynasty was in its last throes:

> ...in China the celebrations were over; retrenchment was the order of the day. Han troops would never again tramp across the high Pamirs into central Asia, nor take for granted Vietnam, whose first of many 'wars of independence' was about to erupt. In Chang'an the great public spectacles of Han Wudi's reign—military parades, tribute receptions and athletic meetings like those of Qin—had been either scaled down or abolished. Imperial hunting grounds were being neglected; stables stood empty as the emperor's equestrian establishment was halved. Hundreds of musicians and dancers had been dismissed as surplus to ritual requirement. The textile workshops in Shandong that had supplied the court with robes and furnishings had been shut down completely.[3]

Ominous portents were seen, the usual comets, meteors, earthquakes, floods and droughts—with a plague of flies as an unusual innovation. The dynasty was running out of available heirs and the Mandate of Heaven seemed to have run its course.

In India, the last of the imperial Mauryas had been murdered by his general, Pushyamitra Shunga, in 180 BCE. Then followed two centuries of chaos, with several incursions from the north-west; small kingdoms and tribal 'republics' rose and fell with bewildering rapidity, and it was only with the arrival of the Kushans at the commencement of the second century that order was restored in the north-west. It was therefore no surprise that India too should have fallen behind Mediterranean Europe and a West Asia which had only recently been brought under the control of Rome, after three centuries of secure domination under Seleucid Greek dynasties.

By 1500, according to Maddison, western Europe had overtaken China in per capita real income, technological and scientific capacity.[4] In his table of per capita GDP, Maddison has shown India to be a little behind China ($550 against China's $600) in 1500, so we may safely conclude that the west Europeans by-passed both India and China about the same time, that is some time in the preceding fifteenth century.

Nonetheless, even in 1620, the wealth of the 'Great Mogul' was mind-boggling. 'The Mogul,' wrote Terry, 'is master of an unknown treasure, having silver, as tis written of Solomon ... like stones in the streets; and certainly in far greater abundance than ever Soloman had.... Now he that can command what treasure he will, may likewise command what men he please.... Hence it is that the armies there consist of incredible multitudes.'[5] Elsewhere he declares that 'the Mogul' is 'the greatest and richest master of precious stones that inhabits the whole earth'. India was then the only known source of diamonds, and the kings of the Deccan in whose territories they were found were tributary to the emperor 'and they pay him as tribute many diamonds yearly'.[6]

Terry was no less impressed by the wealth of the nobles. He noticed that the *omrahs* were graded by the number of horses they were supposed to command, and they were paid accordingly:

> The Mogul in his far extended monarchy, allows yearly pay for one million of horse, and for every horse and man about eighteen pounds sterling per annum, which is exactly paid every year, raised by land, and other commodities which that empire affords, and are appointed for that purpose. Now some of the Mogul's most beloved nobles have the pay of six thousand horse; and there are others (at least twenty in the empire) that have the pay of five thousand horse; exceeding large pensions above the revenue of any other subjects in the whole world, they amounting unto more than one hundred thousand pounds yearly unto a particular man. Now others have the pay of four thousand horse; others of three, or two ... and so downward.[7]

Terry also observes that it did not mean that an *omrah* of 5,000 or 6,000 horses was actually expected to have so many horsemen ready for service. One who had the pay of 5,000 or 6,000 'must always have one thousand in readiness, or more, according to the king's need of them, and so in proportion all the rest'. As a result the king always had one hundred thousand cavalry, ready for service, wherever he was.

These nobles lived like princes, spending lavishly with an open hand. They maintained polygamous households with large retinues of slaves and servants, with huge wardrobes of splendid garments in silk and cotton. Because of the custom of escheat and the uncertainty of being able to pass any of their wealth to their children, there was a natural tendency to spend as much as possible by way of conspicuous consumption, and to die in debt! But it must be noted that besides these rootless *omrahs* who were (at least up to the reign of Jahangir) mostly of foreign origin or descent, there were many native–usually–Rajput princes who did have secure hereditary principalities of their own.

Bernier, who visited India a few decades later (in the years 1655 to 1669) during the reign of Aurangzeb, has left behind very interesting descriptions of India. He was not particularly impressed by Indian cities. While talking of Delhi and Agra he says, 'Those cities resemble any place rather than *Paris*; they might more fitly be compared to a camp, if the lodgings and accommodations were not a little superior to those found in the tents of armies.'[8] Apart from the palace-fort which was the royal residence, and the mansions of the greater *omrahs*, the bankers and merchants, most dwellings were mean and unimpressive, often built of mud with thatched roofs. There were very few people of independent means in the city; most people were dependent on the Court for sustenance, and the majority soldiers of various descriptions, drawing salaries from the imperial treasury every two months. An unusual delay in the disbursement of their salaries could cause acute distress, and the soldiers would start deserting. Bernier remarks, how towards the end of the war of succession between the sons of Shah Jahan (to which he was a witness) there was 'a growing disposition in the troopers to sell their horses, which they would have done if the war had been prolonged'.[9]

Bernier spent much more time in India than Terry or Rowe, so he had fewer illusions about the wealth of India. He did remark how India was a sink-hole for the world's gold and silver. Everyone paid for their imports from India with bullion as there were few goods which they could offer in return. India did import various articles, like 'copper, cloves, nutmegs, cinnamon, elephants, and other things' which were supplied by the Dutch from Japan, the Moluccas, Ceylon and Europe. Lead was imported from England, broadcloth from France, and more than 25,000 horses annually from Persia and Arabia, besides fresh and dry fruit from Central Asia and Persia, cowries from the Maldives, and so on. But these imports were rarely required to be paid for in bullion as the merchants usually found it advantageous to take back in exchange the productions of the country.[10]

While this should have been an enviable state of affairs, there were other factors which cancelled these natural advantages. Since no nobleman (save for a handful of native rajas) had any secure hold on land, and *jagirs* were held for short tenures, there was no incentive to invest in agriculture and make permanent improvements. Instead, the *jagirdars* were interested only in squeezing the maximum from the wretched cultivators, who, if pushed beyond endurance, abandoned their lands and took refuge in the territory of a native Raja–if there happened to be one in the neighbourhood. Otherwise they could abandon their village and seek employment in the towns and cities in some menial capacity–preferably under a nobleman or soldier with an assured income from the state. Should any person come into a substantial sum of money as the result of a successful business venture, he would do his best to conceal it. His mode of life would remain as simple as before, and he would often bury his money underground for future use. Thus large quantities of bullion in the shape of gold and silver coin would be withdrawn from circulation every year–and a substantial portion of it would be lost forever.

The arts cannot flourish in the midst of a population that is wretchedly poor, and where the few rich men are also obliged to simulate poverty. But for the patronage extended by the monarch and the greater nobles who kept a large number of artists and craftsmen in their service, the arts would have decayed entirely. The protection afforded by powerful patrons to rich merchants and tradesmen who were prepared to pay their workmen higher wages, tended also to preserve the arts. But, adds Bernier, it should not be inferred that the artisan or workman was held in great esteem in society, or that he could ever aspire to arrive at a state of financial independence. There was no space in medieval India for a Michelangelo or Leonardo da Vinci.

Nothing but sheer necessity or blows from a cudgel keeps him employed; he can never become rich, and he feels it no trifling matter if he have the means of satisfying the cravings of hunger, and of covering his body with the coarsest raiment. If money be gained, it does not in any measure go to his pocket, but only serves to increase the wealth of the merchant who, in his turn, is not a little perplexed how to guard against some act of outrage and extortion on the part of his superiors.[11]

The picture which he paints is grim indeed. Further, there were no colleges or academies comparable to the universities of Europe where ordinary people could acquire a sound education. The few scholars that existed were attached to religious establishments or to the households of the great nobles. So scholarship and scientific knowledge were limited to a select number of families and professional fraternities like the medieval guilds of Europe. There was very little innovation and nothing by way of invention. For instance, although the British imported saltpetre from India, English gunpowder was superior to Indian, because the English refined their saltpetre twice while the Indians were content with only one refining cycle. Their field guns and mortars were much too heavy, and their carriage far too clumsy. For master gunners they were content with hiring European or Turkish (i.e. *Rumi*) artillerymen as mercenaries, rather than take the trouble of training their own.

Bernier's observations on the mode of government of the Mughal empire, and of other Asiatic powers like Persia and Ottoman Turkey are contained in his 'Letter to Monseigneur Colbert' which was in response to a specific request from Jean-Baptiste Colbert who was the French minister of finance from 1665 to 1683, and in his time the most influential man in France. Colbert had just founded the Compagnie des Indes Orientales and he had desired to have a report on the commerce of India. There is probably an element of exaggeration in Bernier's criticism of India, and he may have hoped for some official recognition, which may be behind his frequent allusions to the beauties of the city of Paris and the superiority of the French mode of government. But apart from having gained an entrée to some of the more intellectual salons of Paris, he does not appear to have benefited financially—apart from what he might have earned from his book.

However, some of his observations are remarkably perceptive. In effect, he denies that the Great Mogul was particularly rich. Though he was in receipt of an immense revenue he could not be said to possess the vast surplus of wealth that most Europeans imagined he did. He conceded that his income probably exceeded 'the joint revenues of the *Grand Seignior* and of the King of Persia' but he was rich only in the sense that a treasurer is wealthy because he pays out with one hand large sums of money which he receives with the other.

Because of the absence of any right to private property, barring the tributary rajas who were native to the country, there was no territorial nobility in the territories of the Great Mogul, comparable to the European nobility. Therefore the *omrahs* or lords of the Mogol's court were not members of ancient families. They were often not even descendants of *omrahs*,

> because the King being heir of all their possessions, no family can long maintain its distinction, but, after the *omrah's* death, is soon extinguished, and the sons, or at least the grandsons, reduced generally, we might almost say, to beggary, and compelled to enlist as mere troopers in the cavalry of some *omrah*.... The *omrahs*, therefore, mostly consist of adventurers from different nations who entice one another to the court; and are generally persons of low descent, some having been originally slaves, and the majority being destitute of education. The *Mogol* raises them to dignities, or degrades them to obscurity, according to his own pleasure and caprice.[12]

He again reverts to the same subject and deplores that because of the precarious character of the the *omrah's* wealth, the imperial service could not appeal to people

possessing a high sense of propriety, affectionately attached to their Sovereign, ready to support by acts of valour, the reputation of their family, and as the occasion may arise, able and willing to maintain themselves, either at court or in the army, by means of their own patrimony; animated by the hope of better times, and satisfied with the approbation and smile of their Sovereign. Instead of men of this description, he is surrounded by slaves, ignorant and brutal; by parasites raised from the dregs of society; strangers to loyalty and patriotism; full of insufferable pride, and destitute of courage, of honour, and of decency.[13]

Clearly Bernier had a poor opinion of the Mughal grandees. And considering that this was written in the earlier part of the reign of Aurangzeb, it is clearly saying a lot. One wonders what he would have had to say about the nobles of the declining empire, of the *omrahs* of Jahandar, of Farrukhsiyar, Muhammad Shah and Shah Alam II.

It was virtually inconceivable that an *omrah* could ever contradict the emperor or argue a point with him. Terry observes that their 'necessary dependence' on the ruler bound them to 'such base subjection' that they would readily execute his most unreasonable and wilful commands:

The people here will do anything the King commands them to do; so that if he bid the father to lay hands of violence upon his son, or the son upon his father, they will do it, rather than the will of their King should be disobeyed: thus forgetting nature rather than subjection.

And this tie of theirs (I say) upon the King's favour, makes all his subjects most servile flatterers; for they will commend any of his actions, though they be nothing but cruelty; so any of his speeches, though nothing but folly.[14]

But this unquestioning compliance and blind obedience could only be relied upon while the emperor's star was in the ascendant.

As soon as it became evident that his fortune was on the wane the *omrahs*–like base rats–had no hesitation in deserting the sinking ship. This analysis of the character of the Indian (or rather, Mughal) nobility by Bernier and Terry explains the ease with which revolutions were effected and rulers overthrown. The nobles had no feeling of personal loyalty to the emperor. As soon as they perceived that his star was about to set they would desert his standards to offer their services to whom they perceived to be the new Man of Destiny. So wars of succession were usually short, because no principle was involved. The tenacity with which the Jacobite nobles of England and Scotland clung to their fallen monarch, and continued to attend his shadow court at St. Germain for three generations, in spite of poverty and exile would have been incomprehensible to a Mughal noble, or in Safavid Iran and Ottoman Turkey, for that matter. In the Orient, Might alone was Right.

One can, however, take comfort from one observation of Bernier's. He notes that when war threatened and the emperor needed funds urgently, provincial governments and other high dignities and posts at court would be virtually put to auction. He observes that Turkey and Iran were much worse in this respect when compared with India. At least up to the time of Aurangzeb.

The weaknesses of India and of other Asiatic empires were the usual weaknesses that arise from a despotic system of government. That power corrupts, and absolute power corrupts absolutely, is not merely a striking aphorism. In the West, even during the seventeenth and eighteenth centuries when 'absolutism' flourished, the kings were never as powerful as Asiatic sultans and *padishahs*. A permanent and hereditary nobility was a curb on royal arbitrariness. It was also a curb on wasteful expenditure, and good for the economy.

NOTES

1. Francois Gautier, *Rewriting Indian History*, Foreword, p. 3.
2. Angus Maddison, *Contours of the World Economy, 1-2030*, Table A.1, New York: Oxford University Press, 2007, p. 376.

3. John Keay, *China: A History*, Harper Press, 2008, p. 156.
4. Maddison, op. cit., p. 157.
5. Edward Terry, *A Voyage to East India, Etc.*, London: Wilkie, Cater & Hayes, 1777, p. 149.
6. Ibid., pp. 373-4.
7. Ibid., pp. 390-1.
8. Farncois Bernier, *Travels in the Mogul Empire*, New Delhi: Low Price Publications, 1997, p. 220.
9. Ibid., pp. 220-1.
10. Ibid., pp. 203-4.
11. Ibid., pp. 228-9.
12. Ibid., pp. 211-12.
13. Ibid., p. 230.
14. Terry, op. cit., pp. 392-3.

CHAPTER 14

Conclusion

This chapter sums up our observations and arrives at some conclusions which can explain, partially at least, the strikingly different characters of the historical narratives of East and West. It can be reduced to two vital essentials: the first relating to the position of women in the two civilizations, and the other to the ownership of land. *Zar, zoru, zameen*—gold (i.e. money), woman and land—these are at the bottom of most crimes, according to an old Persian saying. In a man's world the desire for these three highly coveted objects is the catalyst for most other actions as well.

Apart from that, the criminal activities of the rulers of the world constitute a major chunk of history. The lust for gold and money is universal; Indians and Chinese have the same regard for it as the Europeans, whether French, Scots, or German. Women and land give rise to the same passions everywhere, but the political space accorded to them varies in the two civilizations, and it is this variation which accounts for the different characters of the historical narrative. All other points of difference, such as the relatively smooth succession in European states, and the more confused and uncertain successions in India and in much of the Orient, the differing character of wars, the manner in which states have grown and evolved, the relatively greater respect for law and the evolution of democracy and representative government in one, contrasted with their absence in the other—all these ultimately stem from these two vital determinants.

And, interestingly, while this study started out as a comparative study of the history of the Indian world with that of western Europe, the observations and findings are generally applicable to most other states of Asia as well, namely the three Islamic variants of West Asia—Arab, Turkish and Persian—as well as China.

While all these civilizations are quite different, with unique characteristics, they have one common factor which is usually overlooked in ordinary discourse. *All* of the five—the Indian, Arab, Turkish, Persian and Chinese civilizations—have been ruled or dominated, for considerable periods of their history, by Turkish or Mongol dynasties having roots in the steppes of Central Asia. In China, of the last five imperial dynasties, only the Song and the Ming were indisputably native or Han Chinese. The Manchu and Yuan were both Mongol while the Tang who came from the borderlands of northern Shanxi were of mixed ethnicity: marcher lords, sinicized perhaps, but not quite Chinese. Thus, for nearly half of the last 1,500 years of its history, the Middle Kingdom was ruled by foreigners (or near-foreigners). And during much of the remaining half also, in the outer regions of China, in what are now Manchuria, Inner Mongolia, Xinjiang, Qinghai, Tibet and Yunan, the rulers were various non-Han 'barbarians' like the Jin (from whom the word 'China' is derived), Khitan, Xia, Liao, Nanzhao, Tanguts, Jurchen and others. The control over Tibet, even in the best of times, was very loose.

The Manchus retained their foreign character and resisted sinicization. Special laws were passed to ensure this, and, just as under the Yuan emperors, there were restrictions on dress and inter-marriage. The Han Chinese were required to shave the front of their head and plait the rest of the hair into a queue as a demonstration of their loyalty and love for their rulers—that being the standard hairstyle of the Manchus. This was understandably regarded as degrading by the native Chinese, and there were frequent rebellions in the early years which were ruthlessly suppressed. Ferocious massacres occurred in which hundreds of thousands perished.

Most of the Yuan emperors never learned the Chinese language, still less the script, and an army of translators was kept busy translating documents from Mongol to Chinese and vice versa. Nineteenth-century European writers commonly distinguish between the 'Tartars' (meaning Manchus) and the Han Chinese. Thus even though the 'Chinese' Tartars were not Muslim, they shared many of the characteristics of their Muslim cousins.

The first and most striking characteristic was the absence of any clear rules of succession. The inhabitants of the steppes were semi-nomadic pastoralists, and democratic in spirit. The chiefship was never formally hereditary. The chief had to be accepted by the tribe, and he made himself acceptable either by making his potential rivals little chiefs of their sub-clans—that is, by effectively buying their support—or by cowing them down or crushing them with an awe-inspiring demonstration of strength and ruthlessness. Naturally, the latter was the preferred option. When they founded kingdoms and empires by conquering the settled agricultural plains the same confusion regarding succession persisted. The succession was, as far as possible, limited to the descendants of the founder, but primogeniture could never be taken for granted. The successor had to prove himself worthy of the throne, and a fratricidal struggle was the usual recourse. Sometimes a successful *coup* did the trick, the other princes being murdered, blinded or imprisoned. On other occasions fraternal rivalries led to an all-out war. The Ottomans routinely killed the remaining brothers; later on they would be kept under restraint—in the 'cage' or *kafis* in the Topkapi *sarai*, or, in the case of the Indian Mughals, in the *salatin khana* of the Red Fort.

As pastoralist herders, the Turks had lived off their animals. When they conquered cultivated lands their first instinct was to turn farmland into pasture, but soon better sense prevailed, and the cultivating peasants became their human cattle. They exploited them to the hilt to extract the maximum 'revenue', but they stopped short of the intolerable lest their *riaiyah* should abandon their farms and run away. For industry and agriculture, they had a thinly disguised contempt, so wherever the Turk ruled, the land decayed. European travellers in the eighteenth and nineteenth centuries observed how the towns looked run down, and the villages poverty-stricken. Money—particularly coined metal—would be invariably scarce, at least among ordinary people.

Gribble, writing his pioneering *History of the Deccan* in the beginning of the nineteenth century observed how remarkable it was that when a native Hindu kingdom is established 'it at once acquires enormous wealth in gold and jewels'. This would attract the cupidity of the 'Mahomedans', but within a few years of his spoliation the Hindu prince would again be found to have accumulated a considerable hoard of gold. It was only when the kingdom had been annexed and the state brought under direct rule that it ceased to produce gold and precious stones. He concludes that under Turkish (he uses the term 'Mahomedan') rule there was 'little or no natural production, and no development of the country's resources. Under Hindoo princes, on the contrary, as long as they were left undisturbed, attention was paid to agricultural and irrigation works, and especially to mining industries.' The Turco-Mongol state was, thus, basically a predatory state. It did very little or nothing to encourage prosperity and development; it was as if the land was suffering from a permanent blight.[1]

It can be safely asserted that women are a suppressed minority nearly all over the world. It is a man's world, and patriarchy rules, but for the stray exceptions in Kerala and Meghalaya. But there was one vital difference between the women of western Europe and those of India and the rest of the Orient. In India, West Asia and China women were invisible in politics. Sometimes—as in the case of the famous Empress-Dowager Cixi of the Qing dynasty—they could attain temporary ascendancy as regents, but such opportunities were exceptional. In general, they counted for very little. In India, for instance, even their names are usually excluded from the genealogies! We sometimes do not even know the names of the mothers and consorts of kings.

But in Europe, in spite of many civil disabilities, women mattered politically. They could inherit property—including kingdoms and feudal fiefs—though only in default of male heirs. In the Orient, the ordinary Islamic *shariah* allowed women a share in parental property, even when brothers were present, but there was no question of women ruling states in their own right. There is indeed the unusual case of Sultan Raziyya, but her reign was brief, and she was soon overthrown. There is also the even more curious case of the central Indian state of Bhopal where four ladies ruled in the nineteenth and early twentieth centuries. In normal circumstances this would have been inconceivable, but India in the nineteenth century was passing through unusual times. The state of Bhopal had risen from the wreckage of the Mughal empire, its founder, Dost Muhammad Khan being a rebel who had made himself ruler by seizing imperial territory. But by 1819 when the first matriarch of this family became ruler as regent on behalf of her infant daughter, following the assassination of her husband, the *Pax Britannica* prevailed in India. None of her male relatives protested, for now it was the Political Agent of the British governor-general who decided the succession in 'Native States' rather than the *fainéant* emperor, Akbar II, himself a pensioner of the 'Company Bahadur'. The Agent was happy enough with her decision and saw no reason to interfere. She would thereafter be followed by Nawabs Sikander Begum (1860-8), Sultan Shah Jahan Begum (1868-1901) and Kaikhusrau Jahan Begum (1901-26). This Muslim matriarchy was an aberration which was possible only under the protective umbrella of the British Raj. What makes the case even more piquant is that Dost Muhammad Khan was of Afghan origin, and in popular imagination the Pakhtoon Afghans are probably among the most misogynistic people in the world.

But in western Europe women regularly inherited property—at least in the absence of brothers. In some states, however—particularly those that were ruled by families that traced their origins from the Salian Franks—they drew the line at kingdoms and feudal fiefs. The application of this so-called Salic law was, however, not very consistent. Sometimes we find that the succession is strictly agnatic; elsewhere succession is allowed through the female line as well, but excludes the females themselves, for example a grandfather without sons might be succeeded by his grandson, a son of his daughter, the daughter in question being still alive, or an uncle might be succeeded by his nephew, a sister's son, even within the lifetime of the sister. In India a formal adoption would have been necessary by the grandfather or uncle.

This Salic law was never invoked in England or Scotland, nor in Castile, Aragon and Navarre. Neither did it apply in Norman Sicily and Naples, where Constance, the daughter of King Roger II (who was of Norman descent) would pass the Sicilian crown to her son the future Emperor Fredrick II of Hohenstauffen. Sometimes, the application of the law was according to the state, sometimes based on the supposed tribal origins of the family. The English claim to the French crown was denied on account of the Salic law, and though the Capetians and their agnates, the Valois, and Bourbons consistently followed it as far as the succession to the French crown was concerned, it was never applied to the duchies of Aquitaine and Bourbonnais, nor to the counties of Champagne and Provence. Likewise in the Netherlands, we have women ruling in their own right in the counties of Flanders, Holland and Artois, and in the duchies of Hainault and Brabant. In 1890 the Salic law was invoked to separate Luxemburg from the modern kingdom of the Netherlands on the ground that it was applicable to the German holdings of the House of Nassau, and since the Duchy of Luxemburg was a part of Germany, it was separated from the kingdom and given to a male agnate of the House of Orange-Nassau (known as Nassau-Weilburg) while Wilhelmina, the daughter of King William III, was allowed to succeed in the kingdom. A few decades later when the Nassau-Weilburgs ran out of male heirs the law was amended to permit the succession of females in default.

Hanover was separated from the English crown on account of the Salic law in 1835, when Victoria became Queen of England. The succession of Queen Isabella II in 1833 in Spain was contested by her uncle Don Carlos on the basis of the Salic law. After the death of the uncle, his son, also Don Carlos, persisted in the struggle, and the 'Carlist' cause would be further taken up by *his* nephew—again another Don Carlos. All through the nineteenth and early twentieth century, Spain would be riven by civil strife—even though all the original kingdoms of medieval Iberia—Aragon, Castile, Navarre and Portugal—had known queens as their rulers, and the Salic law should not have been applicable. But the Bourbons who were the reigning dynasty in Spain in 1833 followed it in France, and King Philip V, the first of the Spanish Bourbons, had early in the eighteenth century decreed that the Salic law would prevail in the royal house of Spain also—mainly to ensure that the Spanish crown should never, under any circumstances, ever revert to the Habsburgs. But to ensure that the crown should pass to his daughter he promulgated the 'Pragmatic Sanction' of 1830.

This reminds one of the much more famous Pragmatic Sanction of 1713 which was devised by another doting parent, the Emperor Charles VI, to ensure the undivided succession of his daughter Maria Theresa to all the hereditary holdings of the Austrian Habsburgs. She would have been otherwise debarred from the succession on account of the same wretched Salic law. Notwithstanding his efforts in securing the guarantees of the German princes and other European powers, the succession of the Archduchess would be challenged by Fredrick II of Prussia leading to the War of the Austrian Succession and its sequel, the Seven Years War (1756-63).

The Salic law did not apply in the Scandinavian monarchies, but it did apply in Schleswig-Holstein (which was included in the German kingdom), hence it again featured in the Schleswig-Holstein dispute and was responsible for the two brief wars in 1848 and 1863.

Notwithstanding the prevalence of the Salic law in the royal house of France and most German families, the fact was that women could, and often did, succeed to kingdoms and lesser feudal fiefs like baronies, counties and duchies. The hands of these heiresses were keenly sought after in marriage by other princes, and thus carefully planned marriages were an easy way of building and consolidating states and family holdings. By marrying Eleanor, Duchess of Aquitaine in 1152, Henry II of England added the vast lands of the duchy to the English crown, and it was only after three centuries of intermittent war that France was able to recover its lands. Brittany was an independent state with a Celtic rather than Frankish population. Its rulers had once styled themselves as kings; later because of declining fortunes they would adopt the more modest style of dukes. With the marriage of its last independent ruler, the Duchess Anne, with King Charles VIII of France in 1491, and then with his successor Louis XII in 1499, France was at last able to incorporate Brittany into its territory. The county of Champagne was incorporated into the French kingdom in 1314, after the death of its last countess, Joan, the daughter of Count Henry III 'the Fat'. Joan (or Jeanne) had married King Philip IV, and the product of that union would succeed to the French throne as Louis X. Joan was also the queen-regnant of the little kingdom of Navarre, so as a result of the marriage the crowns of France and Navarre would be united for almost half a century. The death of Charles IV (1322-8) without issue ended the union of the two. Two and a half centuries later, however, with the accession of King Henry III of the House of Bourbon to the French crown, upon the extinction of the male line of the Valois, the two crowns would again be reunited. In due course the personal union would be made permanent by a law passed by the Estates of the two kingdoms.

The county of Provence became linked with France in 1266 when Charles I, of the Capetian House of Anjou married Beatrice, the daughter and heiress of Count Raymond Berenger of the House of Barcelona. Thereafter the county would remain an appanage of younger branches of the royal house until the death without issue of Count Charles III of Maine and Provence, when it reverted to the crown. The great county of Toulouse became an integral part of the kingdom of France with the marriage of Joan, the daughter of Count Raymond VII of the House of Rouergue in 1237 to Alfonso of Poitiers, a younger son of King Louis VIII of France. The marriage was without issue. After Joan's death, which happened five days after her husband's, Toulouse reverted to the French crown in 1271.

The story of the growth of the great duchy of Burgundy under a branch of the House of Valois (1363-1482), and of the House of Habsburg has been narrated elsewhere. They provide the most spectacular example of how great states, even empires, could be knitted together by carefully arranged marriages. However we look in vain for similar examples in the history of India or of the other countries of the Orient. Daughters, of course, were frequently given in marriage to other princes. Rajput rajas even gave their daughters to Mughal emperors, and Chinese emperors gave their daughters to *Khaqans* of the bordering states of Chin, Khitan, Xi and others, who also had imperial pretensions, as demonstrations of kinship. But these were princesses born in polygamous households; very often–particularly in the case of the Son of Heaven–the father would not be able to even name all his children, and the women were virtually traded as chattels. No territory went with these women, and they had no say in choosing their husbands. They were mere pawns of diplomacy and politics. In spite of the superior legal position of women with respect to property in Islam, and the exalted position accorded to sisters, daughters and mothers in Hinduism, in actual fact they counted for very little in royal families. Their position was far inferior to that of European princesses.

All said and done the insistence by the Christian Church on monogamy was largely responsible for the superior position of European women. Interestingly, even before the advent of Christ monogamy was customary in the Roman empire. But divorce, remarriage and adoption were also commonplace and easy in Roman days. There may have been female slaves in plenty in wealthy families, but the choice of heirs was restricted to legitimate sons. Thus the scope for succession disputes was limited.

With respect to the ownership of land the position is no different. One would imagine that it would be preferable to have the king or emperor as the sole owner of the land, rather than have it parcelled out among a large number of great nobles who would do their best to squeeze the maximum income from the cultivating tenants. The lot of the tenant farmer has rarely been a happy one, and we have seen how, in Scotland and Ireland it was probably even worse than that of the much abused Indian peasant. On the *latifundia* of the East-Elbian Junkers, and the estates of the Castilian aristocracy the peasants were mere labourers. Russian serfs at least had their own little holdings.

Landlords are supposed to be parasitical intermediaries who rarely do anything to actually improve the productivity of the farm. Their removal would, *ipso facto* improve the lot of the peasantry and the agricultural poor. So goes the argument. But it rarely happened that way. In the palmy days of the Mughal empire there were no landlords—or so it is supposed. But the emperor as the sole owner of the land could not be expected to forego his share of the profits of cultivation, and the land revenue, or the rent which was demanded by the ruler, constituted the principal income of the state. There were some *subas*—like Kabul—whose revenues were insufficient for defraying the cost of administration. But territory could not be abandoned simply because it was unprofitable, and the land revenue could not be waived because in these poor and thinly populated regions it was an assertion of sovereign control by the ruler. Since Kabul was otherwise an important frontier province bordering Iran, the revenues of certain districts of the neighbouring Punjab were permanently assigned to it, for meeting the costs of the provincial administration.

There was an elaborate bureaucracy to collect the land revenue, and ultimately this bureaucracy became as oppressive and exploitative as any landlord. In fact, because the field officers were subject to frequent transfers, particularly at the relatively senior levels of *faujdar*, *aumil*, *diwan* and *subedar*, the officers pressurized the collectors to collect over and above the legitimate demand by levying various illegal cesses and imposts which could then be skimmed off by the officers and divided among themselves. Not all *subas* and *sarkars* were equal, some were richer than others, while others were notorious for the difficulties posed in collection. Thus, for instance, no one wanted to be posted to the drought-prone, bandit-infested Deccan, but occasionally one had to go to such places. An emperor's favours were unpredictable; the fall from grace could be sudden, and it was a prudent *omrah* who salted away as much as possible for the proverbial rainy day. Bribes might have to be given to powerful and influential courtiers, and showy *nazars* were *de rigeur* for occasions like the *Nauroz*, the anniversary of the emperor's coronation–and whenever he was received in audience by the emperor or any other superior.

Since European nobles were owners of the land, they did not have to pay any land revenue. They did rack-rent their tenants, but since they were proprietors in perpetuity they took care to ensure that their serfs and tenants were not so hard-pressed that they abandoned the land–unless of course their interest lay in driving them away, as during the enclosure movement in England and the Highland Clearances when arable farms were being replaced by sheep pastures. The woods of 'Merry England' were the haunts of many a Robin Hood who mobilized these runaway or dispossessed serfs and lived by highway robbery. In the rest of Europe it was no different.

Since the king could not dispossess the nobles and gentry of their lands except for very exceptional reasons, the latter developed a corporate interest and were able to present a united front at critical moments and extort concessions and assurances from the monarch. These would be recorded in charters of which several copies would be made, to ensure that neither party resiled from the agreement. Thus the custom of calling a Grand Council of all the notables of the realm at periodic intervals was gradually established, and this Grand Council eventually developed into parliament composed of different houses or 'Estates', with each estate representing different interests. In England the parliament comprised only two houses, the French Estates General comprised three, while in certain kingdoms there were as many as four–the nobility, the church (represented by the bishops), the burgesses of the towns, and the knights and untitled gentry, the last three being clubbed together in England as the 'Commons'. The bishops, of course, sat with the Lords.

Of course, these bodies were not equally strong in each country and the rules of procedure varied greatly, but they ensured that absolute monarchy after the pattern of Oriental Despotism was impossible for any sustained length of time. There was a time when 'absolutism' did become fashionable in Europe, and taking France as a model, other monarchs successfully subverted their constitutions and established absolute rule—but only for a time. The financial crisis in late eighteenth-century France brought on by the extraordinary expenditures of the wars of the mid-century—the American War being only the final straw—had bankrupted France and forced the king to call the Estates General when all other expedients had failed.

The *omrahs* of the Great Mogul, on the other hand, had no lands which they could call their own, and they were entirely dependent on the emperor. He had made them, and he could break them. They drew their incomes from assignments of land revenue, but the *jagirs* from which they drew the revenues were not under their direct control, and every few years the *jagirs* would be changed. The imperial bureaucracy collected the revenue and deposited it with the *diwan*, who would disburse the requisite sums to the agent of the officer, who might be posted 500 miles away.

Most of these great *omrahs* had been nobodies before their elevation. They may, indeed, have risen by merit, but had they not been noticed by the emperor, their master, they would have languished in the middle rungs of the *mansabdari* heirarchy. The Indian system encouraged sycophancy and no one wanted to give frank advice to the ruler. In the later period the sycophants flourished.

The position of the native Indian princes—mainly the Rajput rajas—was a little different. These princes had substantial principalities of their own, but they were divided by internal rivalries and jealousies, and incapable of joint action. Moreover they had been incorporated in the *mansabdari* system; they were no longer mere tributaries, they were also *omrahs* of the empire, and competed with the other nobles for lucrative postings as *faujdars* of districts and governors of provinces—usually much larger than their own hereditary principalities. For minor princes like those of Kotah, Bundi, Kishengarh, Sirohi and Datia the imperial service was too valuable to be put at risk. Moreover the succession to their own principalities was not quite as assured as that to an English earldom or a German margraviate. Polygamy was normal in Rajput families, and though male primogeniture was the norm, exceptions were not unknown. Younger and junior consorts would sometimes succeed in securing the succession for their own sons, bypassing the older heir-apparent, or the ageing prince might be persuaded to carve out an independent appanage for a favourite, though younger, son. And the final say in such matters was that of the Great Mogul, for the succession could not be taken for granted until the *sanads* of succession had been issued by the appropriate office in the imperial capital. The disappointed aspirant always had the option of taking up arms to fight for his fancied rights.

Montesquieu had classified governments into three types: republican, monarchical, and despotic. In the despotic type the king (or despot) is governed by his own will and caprice, and the law is subordinate to his will. Indian and Oriental governments were all of the despotic variety, though in China, very often, the Son of Heaven might be only a pawn in the hands of the all-powerful imperial bureaucracy. In both republican and monarchical forms some kind of separation of powers was essential, but since the executive has a natural tendency to encroach upon the legislative and judicial functions, no separation could be effective unless the legislature and judiciary were strong. In oriental despotisms as everything was dependant upon the emperor there could be no effective opposition to his will. In Europe, on the other hand, the nobility, with its secure base in the land was in a position to stand up to the monarch's autocratic tendencies. Students of English history are familiar with the Magna Carta, or the Great Charter, which was extorted from King John in 1215 and is regarded as the bedrock of English liberties—at least of English *free men* (as distinguished from serfs). By this charter the king was forced to acknowledge that he too was bound by law. This sowed the seeds of what in due course would become the powerful writ of *habeas corpus*. After King John's death modified charters would be granted by his successor, and a Great Council, consisting initially only of earls and barons, was constituted. The composition of the Great Council would later be broadened to include two knights from each county, two burgesses from each borough, and two citizens from each city, as in what came to be called the Model Parliament of 1295. This parliament assumed the power of legislation and of approving taxation.

Similar bodies developed in Scotland, France, Spain and Poland between the twelfth and fourteenth centuries. Since Spain originally consisted of several independent kingdoms, there were several parliaments or *cortes*, in Leon, Catalonia, Castile, Aragon, Valencia and Navarre. In France the *parlement* of Paris had jurisdiction over the whole of France, but over a period of time the kings granted separate *parlements* for the provinces of Languedoc, Toulouse, Bordeaux, and Grenoble. Naturally the powers of these bodies varied from country to country according to local conditions and historical developments. In Spain, for instance, the *cortes* were soon overshadowed by the absolutist tendencies of the Habsburgs. In France another body, the Estates General, would overshadow the *parlements*, and would, in turn, be rendered non-functional under the absolutism of Louis XIV and his masterful minister, Cardinal Richilieu—at least for a hundred and fifty years.

In the Polish Commonwealth the *sejm* or the Polish Parliament evolved to the other extreme. The Polish monarchy—like several other monarchies in eastern and central Europe—was elective; the king being elected by the *sejm*. By the fifteenth century the Polish *sejm* had been organized into two chambers, an upper chamber called the Senate and a lower house known as the Chamber of Envoys. At each election solemn assurances were obtained from the king-elect whose powers became more and more circumscribed—as in the case of the Venetian 'Doge'. At first the resolutions were passed by majority vote, but in the later part of the seventeenth century the principle of the *liberum veto* was adopted by which a single deputy could veto the adoption of any resolution. This gradually reduced the Polish constitution to an unworkable anarchy, since any deputy could hold up proceedings. Foreign interference increased and the Polish-Lithuanian Commonwealth, once the most powerful state in Eastern Europe, was reduced to a state of pathetic helplessness. Attempts were made at reforming the constitution in the eighteenth century but it was now too late. Foreign interference did not cease; Poland's neighbours were now much stronger, and Poland a virtual vassal-state of Russia's. The 'Silent *sejm*' of 1721 had met under the shadow of Russian bayonets–Russian troops were actually present to ensure that the *sejm* passed the desired resolution. The Marshall of the *sejm* read out the proposed resolution, and it was passed unanimously with no other deputy being permitted to speak.

In 1764 the Empress Catherine had managed to impose one of her former lovers, Stanislas Poniatowski, on the Polish throne, and his attempts at reforming the constitution were frustrated by a *sejm* called at the behest of the Russian ambassador Prince Nicholas Repnin. The *liberum veto* was restored; but a group of nationalist nobles who met at Bar formed a confederation to resist foreign interference, and war broke out. In 1772 the first partition took place, followed by two others in the 1790s, ending with the complete division of the Commonwealth between the three great powers of the East–Austria, Russia and Prussia–described by the demoralized Poles as the Alliance of the Three Black Eagles (as opposed to the White Eagle of Poland).[2]

Poland is perhaps an extreme example of an aristocracy gone berserk. In general, however, Western democracy may be said to have its origins in the existence of a powerful, landed nobility, confident that its sons would inherit its estates. At first the Great Council consisted of only the senior nobles, later it would be broadened to include the minor nobility as well, or if they were too numerous, their representatives. Later the knightly class and the burgesses of the towns were also included. These again represented their respective counties and boroughs (towns with a charter, i.e. municipalities); there may be say twenty 'knights of the shire' but each shire or county sent only two members which would be elected by their peers. Later on in the nineteenth century the franchise would be further broadened to include progressively lower levels of the rate paying middle-classes and tenant-farmers, until finally universal suffrage became the general rule. But in most countries it would be a long time before women got the vote.

Until late medieval times this landed nobility was obliged to render military service to its feudal superiors–kings, in the case of tenants-in-chief, and dukes or earls in the case of barons or untitled gentry, who would usually be sub-tenants of the higher nobility.[3] But feudal levies, which were obliged to serve for only a limited number of days in a year, proved inadequate for sustained warfare, and in the later Middle Ages monarchs came to rely more and more on mercenary corps of professional soldiers. Eventually the feudal levy was abandoned completely in favour of a fixed commutation which partially financed the professional standing army. But the great landowners retained considerable capacity for mischief; the nobleman could always call out his tenantry, and the latter were in no position to refuse. The weaponry for war was not very expensive, and stacks of arms, mainly swords, pikes and matchlocks were available in the armouries of the castles and mansions of noblemen. It was this capability that was the most effective guard against royal tyranny.

In India, on the other hand, apart from the territory still held by native rajas, feudalism did not exist. All armies were professional, and paid in cash. As already pointed out there were no landed noblemen with heritable estates, and even though the money for the soldiers came from the land, the Mughal emperors and their Turkish/Pathan precursors took every precaution to ensure that no *malik* or *amir* ever acquired a long-term, semi-proprietorial interest in any large tract of land. Grants in perpetuity were sometimes made, but these were usually petty estates when compared to the extensive holdings of British and European nobility. Thus in India, particularly, and the Orient in general, there could be no effective opposition to royal tyranny. Only when the king happened to be extraordinarily incompetent or blood-thirsty would a caucus of nobles get together to depose him.

Assassinations and blindings are galore in the histories of India, Iran and Afghanistan. In England, on the other hand, if we ignore the dynastic struggles of Lancaster and York, there were only two such occasions in over 900 years. The more excitable French had a series of revolutions (and counter-revolutions) in the eighteenth and nineteenth centuries. But for these two countries, there is no other instance of kings and dynasties being overthrown by internal revolution in Western Europe. So deeply ingrained was the concept of 'legitimacy'.

It is all very well to say that the State and Religion should have nothing to do with each other. European states (as well as the USA) are presented as outstanding models of secularism and 'laicism'. We are all familiar with the sad history of Europe when religious dissenters were persecuted, tortured, and driven into exile. *Autos da fe*, or burning at the stake are associated chiefly with the Spanish Inquisition, but they also happened in Italy, France, England, Bohemia, and Germany as well. But even worse barbarities were committed when France abandoned the Roman Church in favour of the worship of Reason and the Supreme Being. The atrocities committed by the atheistic 'socialist' governments of Russia and Maoist China in the last century are notorious. One is forced to conclude that, however, bad the record of organized churches may have been, that of militant atheism (or secularism) is far worse. The existence of an organized and largely independent church has acted as a restraint to the unbridled tyranny of the executive.

Neither Islam nor Hinduism are organized religions comparable to the various Christian sects. There is no 'Pope' of Sunni or Shiite Islam—and there never was, except perhaps in the early Caliphate. But thereafter they were sultans first, and caliphs after that. No one took their religious pretensions seriously, and in the last Ottoman Caliphate, the Sultan-Caliph relied on the advice of the Sheikh ul-Islam, an official appointed by himself, in all religious matters. Individual dervishes like Saadi, Hafiz, Rumi, Jami, Ghazali and others like them would sometimes acquire a reputation for sanctity and attract large followings. Some of them founded semi-mystical cults, based on shrines or *khanqahs* which arose usually around their tombs. They existed outside official Islam, and were generally left alone, but occasionally someone like Mansur al-Hallaj or Sarmad would fall foul of the secular authorities and jealous *ulema*–like the 'Scribes and the Pharisees' of the Gospels in the case of Jesus—would accuse them of heresy and frighten the local ruler sufficiently to have them executed. But such incidents were rare.

The only religion other than Christianity which is organized hierarchically is the Lamaist Buddhism of Tibet and Mongolia. In the Dalai Lama we have a true theocratic ruler, similar to the Pope in the Papal States. The present Dalai Lama is the fourteenth of his line and the first was installed towards the end of the fourteenth century. The early history of Tibet is quite turbulent with emperors ruling from the seventh to the eleventh century. At the height of its power the Tibetan empire stretched as far as, and included, Mongolia. On several occasions it came into conflict with the Chinese and it was not always China that was the victor. If tribute was sent to the Son of Heaven, the latter often sent Chinese princesses as brides for the Tibetan rulers. But after the establishment of the Lamaist theocracy Tibet ceased to be an aggressive power.

Notwithstanding the atrocities that have been committed in the name of God and religion, on the whole, the existence of an organized Church has a moderating influence on politics and statecraft. Basham too has remarked on this:

> In Europe, however, the well-organized and centralized Roman Church often acted as a pacifying element in the situation; in India Hinduism, which had no all-embracing super-national organization, rather encouraged inter state anarchy by incorporating many martial traditions into the sacred Law.[4]

After the decay of the Caliphate Islam too lost whatever moral influence it may have had as an institution. And there never had been a priestly hierarchy in Islam comparable to Christianity, ranging from parish priests to bishops. Mosques were built by pious individuals, kings and communities which appointed their own *imams* and *maulvis.* In the early period there was no prescribed qualification for them—anyone who appeared to have knowledge of the scriptures could be appointed. Later on seminaries were established, and their graduates would be preferred. The *khanqahs* of Sufi establishments were entirely independent.

Anarchy prevailed in the world of Islam. Its pretensions to being a *dar ul-Islam* were mere propaganda. The Caliph tried to combine the role of a secular ruler with that of a religious authority. In the end he was just another ruler; the religious side shrivelled and died. The Roman Church, on the other hand, was an effective bulwark against the pretensions of the Holy Roman Emperor and the other kings of Europe. While the Pope was, in fact, endowed with territory and a powerful Italian prince, he never tried to compete with the emperor as a territorial ruler. The first Holy Roman Emperor was created by a Pope; subsequent emperors would also be crowned in Rome, at least for some time. By remaining separate there would always be a certain tension in the relations between the Pope and the emperor, and it was this tension that ensured a certain balance of power between the two centres. However, much one may regret the tragic failure of the brilliant Emperor Fredrick II, the *stupor mundi* of his times, and the viciousness, worldliness and stupidity of many of the Popes—it is also because of this balance that neither the Pope nor the emperor could be a tyrant for too long.

The Renaissance which partly inspired the Reformation, also, introduced an element of rationality in religion (relatively speaking). There were enough religious reform movements in Islam and Hinduism, but unlike Europe there was no cultural or intellectual Renaissance. Education remained limited to a tiny class, the vast mass of the people remained illiterate, and even though the printing press was brought to India within a hundred years of Gutenberg by the Portuguese, no Indian ruler or entrepreneur showed any interest in using it. Even in Ottoman Turkey the first printing press to use Arabic fonts was set up only in the eighteenth century, by a Hungarian Muslim—even though there were already presses printing books in Hebrew, Greek, Armenian and Latin.[5] The subject *riayahs* were in this respect far more advanced than their rulers.

For the Orientals, whether Muslims, Hindus (or Sikhs, for that matter), the Koran, *Ramayana* or the *Gita* were much more than mere books. There were various doubts which inhibited their mass production. Could one, for instance, guarantee that the ingredients of the printer's ink were not objectionable? Were all the workers who handled the printed sheets, vegetarians? Would the printed books be properly warehoused until their delivery? There was also the vested interest of the vast numbers of scribes and copyists against the introduction of such labour-saving innovations. In Europe the desire to read the sacred Bible was a spur to literacy and learning; in India there was actually a priestly prohibition against the handling of sacred books by the ordinary people. There was no such prohibition in the case of the Koran but in the absence of any intellectual ferment there was no incentive to produce large volumes of books. Robinson argues persuasively that print technology was adopted by Indian Muslims in response to the challenge posed by colonialism and Christian evangelizing activity. The Indian *ulema* used the new technology of printing to compensate for the loss of political power.[6]

Colonialism and imperialism brought India and Europe, the East and the West, into close contact. It was certainly closer than what the Indians would have desired, but even the forced intimacy between the alien rulers and the natives has had not altogether unhappy results. The formerly stagnant civilizations of the orient are once again in ferment, and things are on the move. Women have come out of the *zenana*, the idea of representative government—however, corrupt and venal it may be at present—has taken root and the printing press, the mass-media and, in recent years, the telecommunications explosion are together shaping a brave new world.

NOTES

1. J.D.B. Gribble, *History of the Deccan*, vol. 1, London: Luzac & Co., 1806, pp. 26-7.
2. The arms of the three Eastern powers include a black eagle, the Russian and Austrian being double-headed. The Polish eagle is white, and like the Prussian has only one head.
3. Barons also frequently held fiefs directly from the Crown. In the early days most of the nobles were known as barons, with only

a small handful of earls and dukes. Grades like that of marquess and viscount were created later.

4. A.L. Basham, *The Wonder That was India*, London: Picador, 2004, p. 129.
5. Ezel Kural Shaw, *History of the Ottoman Empire and Modern Turkey*, vol. 1, Cambridge: Cambridge University Press, 1976, pp. 236-7.
6. Ulrike Starke, *An Empire of Books*, New Delhi: Permanent Black, p. 30.

Bibliography

BOOKS

Alam, Muzaffar, *The Crisis of Empire in Mughal North India: Awadh and the Punjab, 1707-1748*, New Delhi: Oxford University Press, 1986.

Alam, Muzaffar and Sanjay Subrahmanyam, *The Mughal State, 1526-1750*, New Delhi: Oxford University Press, 1998.

Basham, A.L., *The Wonder That was India*, London: Picador, 2004.

Bernier, Francois, *Travels in the Mogul Empire*, New Delhi: Low Price Publications, 1997.

Cannadine, David, *The Decline & Fall of the British Aristocracy*, London: Papermac, 1996.

Castro, Amerigo, *The Spaniards: An Introduction to their History*, Berkeley/Los Angeles/London: University of California Press, 1971.

Chaussinad-Nogaret, Guy and William Doyle, *The French Nobility in the 18th Century*, Cambridge: Cambridge University Press, 1986.

Davies, Norman, *Europe: A History*, New York: Oxford University Press, 1996.

Ferguson, Niall, *Empire: How Britain made the Modern World*, Australia: Penguin, 2004.

Firminger, W.K., *Historical Introduction to the Bengal Portion of the Fifth Report*, Calcutta: R. Cambray & Co., 1917.

Gautier, Francois, *Rewriting Indian History*, New Delhi: Indian Research Press, 2003.

Habib, Irfan, *The Agrarian System of Mughal India 1556-1707*, New Delhi: Oxford University Press, 1999.

Grible, J.D.B., *History of the Deccan*, vol. 1, London: Luzac & Co., 1896. Reprinted by Rupa & Co., New Delhi, 2002.

Hodgkin, Thomas, *The Barbarian Invasions of the Roman Empire*, London: The Folio Society, 2000.

Huntington, Samuel P., *The Clash of Civilizations & the Remaking of World Order*, New Delhi: Penguin, 1997.

Irwin, H.C., *The Garden of India or Chapters on Oudh*, London: W.H. Allen & Co., 1880. Reprinted by Asian Educational Services, New Delhi/Madras, 2001.

Khaldun, Ibn, *The Muqaddimah* (translated and abridged by Rosenthal & Dawood), Princeton, USA: Bollingen Series, Princeton University Press, 1989.

Kulke, Hermann (ed.), *The State in India 1000-1700*, New Delhi: Oxford University Press, 1995.

Logan, William, *Malabar Manual*, vol. 1, Madras: Government Press, 1951.

Maddison, Angus, *Contours of the World Economy*, New York: Oxford University Press, 2007.

Malcolm, John, *A Memoir of Central India*, vol. 1, London: Parbury, Allen & Co., 1832.

Marshall, P.J. (ed.), *The Eighteenth Century in Indian History*, New Delhi: Oxford University Press, 2003.

Mayer, Arno J., *The Persistence of the Old Regime*, New Delhi: Pantheon, 1981.

Mingay, G.E., *English Landed Society in the Eighteenth Century*, London: Routledge & Kegan Paul PLC, 1963.

Morby, John E., *The Wordsworth Handbook of Kings & Queens*, Ware, Herts: Wordsworth Editions, 1970.

Moreland, W.H., *The Agrarian System of Moslem India*, Cambridge: Cambridge University Press, 1929.

O'Leary, Brenden, *The Asiatic Mode of Production: Oriental Despotism, Historical Materialism and Indian History*, New Delhi: Oxford University Press, 1989.

Prebble, John, *The Highland Clearances*, London: The Folio Society, 2003.

Qureshi, Ishtiaq Husain, *The Administration of the Mughal Empire*, New Delhi: Low Price Publications, 1990.

Sachau, Edward, *Alberuni's India*, New Delhi: Indialog Publications, 2003.

Schama, Simon, *Citizens*, London: Penguin, 1989.

Secher, Reynald, *A French Genocide*, South Bend: University of Notre Dame Press, 2003.

Shaw, Ezel Kural, *History of the Ottoman Empire and Modern Turkey*, vol. 1, Cambridge: Cambridge University Press, 1976.

Snyder, Louis L., *Fifty Major Documents of the Nineteenth Century*, Princeton, N.J.: Van Nostrand, 1955.

Starke, Ulrike, *An Empire of Books*, New Delhi: Permanent Black, 2008.

Sutherland, David, *The French Revolution and Empire*, Oxford: Blackwell, 2003.

Tacitus, Cornelius, *The Agricola and the Germania*, London: Penguin, 1970.

Terry, Edward, *A Voyage to East India*, London: Wilkie, Cater & Hayes, 1977.

Thomson, David, *Woodbrook*, London: The Folio Society, 2007.

Toynbee, Arnold, *A Study of History* (Somervell Abridgement), vol. 1, New York: Dell, 1965.

Trevelyan, Charles E., *The Irish Crisis*, Whitefish: Kissinger Publishing, 2007.

Wink, André, *Land and Sovereignty in India: Agrarian Society and Politics under the Eighteenth-century Maratha Swarajya*, Cambridge: Cambridge University Press, 1986.

ARTICLES, JOURNALS, WEB-PAGES, AND ONLINE PUBLICATIONS

Athar Ali, M., 'The Eighteenth Century: An Interpretation', *The Historical Review*, V, 1978-9.

Aymaz, Abdullah, *Gratitude to the Ottomans*, http://www.fountainmagazine.com/articles.

The Asiatic Annual Register for the year 1799, J. Debrett, London, 1801.

Blamires, Steve, *The Highland Clearances: An Introduction*, http://www.clannada.org/highland.php, http://www.rfs.scotshome.com/An Introduction to the Highland Clearances.html

Hardiman, James, *History of Galway*, Galway: Connacht Tribune Press, 1926. http://www.galway.net/galwayguide/history/hardiman.

Macdiarmid, J.M., *The Deer Forests & How they are Bleeding Scotland White*, Edinburgh: Home Rule Association, 1926.

Mukhia, Harbans, 'Was there Feudalism in Indian History?', from *The State in India 1000-1700*, ed. Hermann Kulke, New Delhi: Oxford University Press, 1995.

Rahim, A., 'The Rise of a Hindu Aristocracy Under Bengal Nawabs', *Journal of the Asiatic Society of Pakistan*, VI, 1961.

Sharma, Ram Sharan, 'How Feudal was Indian Feudalism?', from *The State in India 1000-1700*, ed. Hermann Kulke, New Delhi: Oxford University Press, 1995.

Index